Fragmenting Globalization

Fragmenting Globalization

*The Politics of Preferential Trade
Liberalization in China and
the United States*

KA ZENG *and* XIAOJUN LI

University of Michigan Press
Ann Arbor

For questions or permissions, please contact um.press.perms@umich.edu

Published in the United States of America by the
University of Michigan Press
Printed and bound by CPI Group (UK) Ltd, Croydon, CR0 4YY

First published March 2021

A CIP catalog record for this book is available from the British Library.

Library of Congress Cataloging-in-Publication Data

Names: Zeng, Ka, 1973– author. | Li, Xiaojun, 1981– author.
Title: Fragmenting globalization : the politics of preferential trade liberalization in China
  and the United States / Ka Zeng and Xiaojun Li.
Description: Ann Arbor : University of Michigan Press, 2021. | Series: Michigan studies
  in international political economy | Includes bibliographical references and index. |
Identifiers: LCCN 2020044307 (print) | LCCN 2020044308 (ebook) |
  ISBN 9780472074709 (hardcover) | ISBN 9780472054701 (paperback) |
  ISBN 9780472128372 (ebook)
Subjects: LCSH: International trade—United States. | International trade—
  China. | Business logistics—United States. | Business logistics—China.
Classification: LCC HF1379 .Z46 2021 (print) | LCC HF1379 (ebook) |
  DDC 382/.30951—dc23
LC record available at https://lccn.loc.gov/2020044307
LC ebook record available at https://lccn.loc.gov/2020044308

The University of Michigan Press gratefully acknowledges the support of the University of
British Columbia Scholarly Publication Fund (awarded to Xiaojun Li).

For
Vera

For
My Family

ACKNOWLEDGMENTS

The authors gratefully acknowledge the kind assistance and generous support provided by many individuals and organizations during various stages of this book's completion. Ka Zeng is grateful for the research incentive grant provided by the Fulbright College of Arts and Sciences at the University of Arkansas, as well as the scholar grant offered by the Chiang Ching-Kuo Foundation for International Scholarly Exchange, which provided substantial release time for her to concentrate on the research for and writing of this book. Xiaojun Li wishes to thank the Social Sciences and Humanities Research Council of Canada and the University of British Columbia for the financial support that allowed him to conduct extensive fieldwork for the book in China. He would also like to express his gratitude to the University of British Columbia Faculty of Arts and the East-West Center for providing the research leave that allowed him to finish writing the book.

We would like to extend our special thanks to Yonglin Cheng, Hao Zhang, Zhenjiang Zhang, and the Guangdong Institute for International Strategies for their help and support during the fieldwork, as well as those managers and officials who shared their stories and insights that became a key part of the book. We would additionally like to thank Yongzheng Li and Yang Zheng for their excellent research assistance and Dania Sheldon for her efficient and professional editorial assistance. The University of British Columbia Library offered a generous grant that facilitated the publication of this book.

The book further benefited from the valuable comments and suggestions offered by our colleagues. Erick Duchesne, Soo Yeon Kim, and Stefano Ponte in particular provided constructive feedback on earlier drafts of chapter 4. The two anonymous reviewers for the book manuscript offered many critical insights that helped to visibly improve and enrich the final product. Last but not least, we are grateful to Elizabeth Demers, our editor at the University of Michigan Press, for her belief in this project and her encouragement and support throughout the process.

CONTENTS

Digital materials related to this title can be found on the Fulcrum platform via the following citable URL: https://doi.org/10.3998/mpub.10147077

FIGURES

TABLES AND APPENDIXES

Tables

Appendixes

ABBREVIATIONS AND ACRONYMS

3PL	third-party logistics provider
ACFTA	ASEAN-China Free Trade Area
AMCE	average marginal component effect
AQSIQ	Administration of Quality Supervision, Inspection and Quarantine
ASEAN	Association of Southeast Asian Nations
BIT	bilateral investment treaty
BTIA	Broad-based Trade and Investment Agreement
CAN	Andean Community
CARICOM	Caribbean Community
CCER	China Center for Economic Research
CCPIT	China Council for the Promotion of International Trade
CEO	chief executive officer
CETA	Comprehensive Economic and Trade Agreement
CFIS	Chinese Firm-level Industrial Survey
ChAFTA	China-Australia Free Trade Agreement
China-ROK FTA	China-South Korea Free Trade Agreement
CM	common market
COMESA	Common Market for Eastern and Southern Africa
CPTPP	Comprehensive and Progressive Agreement for Trans-Pacific Partnership
CRP	Center for Responsive Politics
CU	customs union
DESTA	Design of Trade Agreements (database)
DSB	Dispute Settlement Body (WTO)
DVA	domestic value added
ECCAS	Economic Community of Central African States

ECOWAS	Economic Community of West African States
ECSC	European Coal and Steel Community
EEC	European Economic Community
EFTA	European Free Trade Association
ESF	European Services Forum
EU	European Union
EUKOR	EU-South Korea FTA
EURATEX	European Apparel and Textile Organisation
EUSFTA	EU-Singapore FTA
FDI	foreign direct investment
FEC	Federal Election Commission
FTA	free trade agreement
FTA-EU	Foreign Trade Association
FVA	foreign value added
GATT	General Agreement on Tariffs and Trade
GCC	Gulf Cooperation Council
GDP	gross domestic product
GVC	global value chain
HO	Heckscher-Ohlin
ICIO	Inter-Country Input-Output (Tables)
ICT	information and communications technology
IIPTA	investment-inclusive PTA
IIT	intra-industry trade
IMF	International Monetary Fund
IPE	international political economy
IP	intellectual property
IPR	intellectual property rights
ISIC	International Standard Industrial Classification
ISDS	investor-state dispute settlement
MFN	most-favored-nation
MNC	multinational corporation
NAFTA	North American Free Trade Agreement
NBS	National Bureau of Statistics (China)
NDRC	National Development and Reform Commission (China)
NOS	National Organizations Survey
OBM	original brand manufacturer
ODM	original design manufacturer

OECD	Organisation for Economic Co-operation and Development
OEM	original equipment manufacturer
OLS	ordinary least squares
PA	preferential agreement
PAC	political action committee
PTA	preferential trade agreement
R&D	research and development
RCEP	Regional Comprehensive Economic Partnership
RMB	*renminbi* or *yuan* (Chinese currency)
ROO	rules of origin
RP	related party
RTA	regional trade agreement
RV	Ricardo-Viner
SADC	South African Development Community
SIA	Semiconductor Industry Association
SOE	state-owned enterprise
SPS	(Agreement on the Application of) Sanitary and Phytosanitary Measures
SwissCham	Swiss Chinese Chamber of Commerce
TBT	(Agreement on) Technical Barriers to Trade
TiVA	Trade in Value Added (database)
TPP	Trans-Pacific Partnership
TPSEP	Trans-Pacific Strategic Economic Partnership Agreement
TRIMs	(Agreement on) Trade-Related Investment Measures
TRIPS	Trade-Related Aspects of Intellectual Property Rights
TTIP	Transatlantic Trade and Investment Partnership
UPS	United Parcel Service
USMCA	United States-Mexico-Canada Agreement
USTR	U.S. Trade Representative
VAT	value added tax
WBES	World Bank Enterprise Survey
WIOD	World Input-Output Database
WTO	World Trade Organization
WTO+	WTO-plus (provisions)
WTO-X	WTO-minus (provisions)

CHAPTER 1

Introduction

The Rise of Global Value Chains and Preferential Trade Agreements in the Global Economy

The U.S.-China trade war that has captured news headlines since 2018 reflects the United States' deep frustration with structural impediments to trade in the Chinese economy, as well as the emerging strategic rivalry between the world's two largest economies. In spring 2019, amidst the escalating trade tensions between the two countries, Washington singled out the Chinese tech giant Huawei, the world's largest telecommunications supplier and second-largest phone manufacturer, for the threat it posed to U.S. national security. On May 15, President Donald Trump signed an executive order banning "any acquisition, importation, transfer, installation, dealing in, or use of any information and communications technology or service of Huawei" without special approval (White House 2019).

The ban cast a gloomy shadow over the Chinese tech giant's global market expansion. Ren Zhengfei, CEO of Huawei, estimated in June 2019 that up to $30 billion would be wiped off Huawei's expected revenues for 2019 (Collins 2019).[1] Sharing the same woes with Huawei, however, were some of the largest tech firms in the United States, as Huawei sources nearly a quarter of its components from American semiconductor manufacturers, led by Broadcom, Flex, and Qualcomm (Garrett 2019). In response, the U.S. Semiconductor Industry Association urged the U.S. government to approve exemptions, claiming that there were no "national security concerns" in selling semiconductors to Huawei for "non-sensitive" products such as phones, and that the ban would only benefit foreign rivals (Leonard and King 2019).

The story of the intertwined fates of Huawei and American businesses epitomizes an important development in the international economy in the past couple of decades—namely the growth of global value chains (GVCs), whereby raw materials, parts, components, and services cross national borders multiple times before being used to make final products that are sold on world markets.[2] The production of electronic consumer goods such as the smartphones and laptops made by Huawei is often invoked to illustrate this phenomenon. One common example is the iPhone, which is designed by Apple in California and assembled by the Taiwanese firm Foxconn in its plant in Shenzhen, China, using sophisticated inputs that include flash memory, dynamic random access memory (DRAM), and application processors supplied by South Korean or Japanese manufacturers such as Samsung and AKM Semiconductor. The finished products then receive aftersales servicing in the United States and Europe and are ultimately sold in these markets. The final value of the product increases during each stage of the production process (Economist 2011).

The rise of GVCs also occurs in less technologically sophisticated products. Barbie dolls, for example, are made in a fragmented production chain, with the doll being designed at Mattel's headquarters in California and manufactured in Taiwan using ethylene plastics made from oil from an oil-exporting country such as Saudi Arabia or Russia. Other parts of the doll (such as the nylon hair, the cotton clothing, and the mold for the doll) are made in Japan, China, and the United States, respectively, with assembly of all these parts taking place at factories in Indonesia and Malaysia and quality testing conducted in California (Tempest 1996).

GVCs are also becoming increasingly prevalent outside the manufacturing sector. The production of Nutella, a famous hazelnut and cocoa spread sold in 75 countries, exemplifies the growing complexity of the agrifood value chain. While the brand is owned by the food-processing company Ferrero, headquartered in Italy, the product is processed in nine factories spread across five continents, with ingredients supplied globally, including hazelnuts from Brazil, palm oil from Malaysia, cocoa from Nigeria, sugar from Brazil and Europe, and vanilla flavor from China.

The global fragmentation of production further extends to the services sector, as firms increasingly outsource and offshore business and other services (such as computing, legal, accounting, management consulting, and public relations services) previously supplied domestically (OECD 2012a). Computer services, for example, feature lengthy value chains, with knowledge and information management (such as training and research) occupying the upstream portion of the value chain, consultative and advice activities in the middle, and client-relationship management at the end (Sako 2009). These value chains additionally include horizontal support activities such as accounting, human resource management, information technology, and customer services, activities that are often outsourced and offshored to countries in the developing world.

As a result of such developments, international trade now links domestic and foreign suppliers in a series of complex interactions and is increasingly influenced by the international strategies of firms that undertake foreign direct investment (FDI), outsourcing, and other production-related activities in locations that offer the necessary raw and intermediate materials at the most competitive prices or with the best quality. The rising share of intermediate and capital products in global trade volumes means that traditional trade, with each country producing finished products that are exported to another country, has declined in relative significance.

The growing importance of GVCs has led economists and international statistics agencies to search for new approaches to measure trade, in particular value-added trade (e.g., Koopman, Wang, and Wei 2012). It has also spurred an expanding body of literature on global production sharing and its impact on national industrial upgrading, productivity gains, and economic growth (Banga 2014; IMF 2013; OECD 2013b; UNCTAD 2013). While these efforts are valuable in enriching our understanding of GVCs, the significant shifts in the structure and patterns of world trade also call for a critical reassessment of traditional models of the political economy of trade.

This book contributes to this endeavor by focusing on the implications of growing GVC integration for the politics of preferential trade liberalization. Parallel to the rise of GVCs is the proliferation of preferential trade agreements (PTAs), including free trade agreements (FTAs) and customs unions (CUs). The number of active PTAs has risen from a few dozen in the early 1990s to more than 445 in 2017, according to the World Trade Organization.[3] Many modern-day PTAs include provisions regarding competition, investment, and intellectual property rights (IPRs), going substantially further than the trade rules of the multilateral trading system under the WTO and its predecessor, the General Agreement on Tariffs and Trade (GATT). One of the more recent examples is the now-defunct Trans-Pacific Partnership (TPP), a proposed large-scale regional trade agreement (RTA)[4] aimed at deepening economic ties between the United States and 11 other Pacific Rim nations, introducing a comprehensive set of rules on issues such as regulatory coherence, state-owned enterprises, competitiveness, and supply chains, in addition to addressing more traditional issues such as tariff and investment liberalization.

Two features distinguish PTAs from traditional multilateral trade liberalization. First, PTAs, as the name implies, offer preferential tariffs to their member states beyond traditional most-favored-nation (MFN) tariffs, i.e., the normal nondiscriminatory tariffs that a country can charge on foreign imports. Second, on nontariff issues, PTAs contain provisions that are often much stronger than those embodied in multilateral agreements, such as ones addressing trade-related investment measures, trade-related intellectual property rights, services, and public procurement (Horn, Mavroidis, and Sapir 2010). These measures increase a firm's ability to more efficiently and reliably import and export goods. They also reduce the complexity and heterogeneity of national standards to alleviate the burden of compliance and increase the competitiveness of exporters, in particular small and medium ones.

The parallel growth of GVCs and PTAs has received increasing scholarly attention. Recent studies (e.g., Bruhn 2014; Eckhardt and Poletti 2018) have highlighted the importance of the development of institutional frameworks for reducing trade barriers and harmonizing disparate national policies, rules, and standards governing trade and investment for the expansion of GVCs. However, despite this rapidly growing literature, we still know relatively little about the effect of GVC integration on firm preferences and political strategies. Furthermore, while a growing number of studies in both economics and political science (e.g., Baccini et al. 2018; Madeira 2016; Weymouth and Broz 2013) have emphasized the importance of heterogeneity among export-oriented firms with regard to size and productivity as determinants of firm preferences and behavior, few studies have explicitly considered how variations among firms with regard to their position in GVCs may shape their trade preferences.[5] This book takes up this question and offers a systematic analysis of the role of the growing fragmentation of production in driving firms' stances toward preferential trade liberalization.

Overview of the Argument

Existing research on the domestic politics of trade (e.g., Milner 1989) generally holds that firms more deeply embedded in the global economy through export or FDI are more likely to support free trade, and by extension preferential trade liberalization. While engaging these insights, we further argue that the preferential tariff and nontariff benefits provided by PTAs are more crucial for firms embedded in GVCs due to the constraints of supply chain networks, the disruption of which will likely be more detrimental than to firms without GVC linkages that can more easily divert their trade in the absence of established buyer-supplier relationships. This suggests that GVC integration can create a new cleavage in the domestic politics of trade policy, one that pits firms and industries more heavily dependent on foreign value added in their intermediate or final exports against those less dependent on intermediate goods trade in their production activities.

Specifically, firms whose products are manufactured with foreign value added should have increased incentives to lobby for preferential trade liberalization with countries with which they have strong ties in order to maintain unimpeded access to the necessary production materials and intermediate inputs. In addition, compared to producers of intermediate or final products who only serve the domestic market, businesses whose products are incorporated into the production of goods in foreign countries should also be more likely to support preferential trade liberalization to increase their ability to effectively compete with suppliers from elsewhere in foreign markets. In other words, firms with substantial *backward* GVC linkages (i.e., having a high level of foreign content in the production or export of their products) or *forward* GVC linkages (i.e., having a high level of their products incorporated in foreign production or exports) should be more likely to support preferential trade liberalization and the formation of PTAs with countries with which they have GVC linkages, to better capture the gains from trade in an integrated global economy.

We test these theoretical propositions using the experiences of firms and industries in both China and the United States, the world's two largest economies. Since embarking on a course of reform and opening to the outside world in the early 1980s, China has emerged as the center of global supply chain activities as a result of its rapid economic growth. To promote GVC integration, the Chinese leadership has actively pursued preferential trade liberalization and is currently involved in the negotiation of more than 10 FTAs, including the ambitious Regional Comprehensive Economic Partnership (RCEP), with key regional and emerging economies.[6] At the same time, the United States, along with other developed countries, continues to occupy a dominant position at the upstream end of global supply chains and has a relatively large share of its intermediate goods being absorbed in other countries' exports through forward GVC participation (OECD 2013c). Most recently, Washington has been actively seeking to boost supply chain competitiveness and reshape the global trade architecture with ambitious mega-regional trade agreements such as the TPP and the Transatlantic Trade and Investment Partnership (TTIP). Given both countries' central positions in GVCs, detailed analyses of the firm preferences and institutional structures that underlie the rise of PTAs should yield valuable insights into the GVC-PTA nexus. If our research were to produce similar findings in two countries with vastly different political and institutional structures, this could also help to underscore the generalizability of our core argument.

We utilize multiple methods to empirically assess our main theoretical arguments. In particular, we leverage novel data, including qualitative interviews and an original firm survey, collected from our fieldwork in China to examine the effect of GVCs on firms' trade preferences. Given the relative paucity of data on firm preferences toward preferential trade liberalization, the original data we collected afford us the opportunity to analyze this important question in one of the world's major economies. We then complement analysis of the China case with statistical analysis and case studies of the patterns of corporate support and lobbying for regional trade liberalization in the United States, as well as cross-sectional, time-series analysis of the pattern of PTA formation by the 62 countries included in the Trade in Value Added (TiVA) database, a joint initiative of the Organisation for Economic Co-operation and Development (OECD) and the World Trade Organization. The findings from these analyses collectively lend substantial support to our main theoretical conjectures, suggesting that the growing fragmentation of global production, trade, and investment activities may be altering the contours of trade policy and shifting the domestic debate over trade liberalization away from the traditional divide between export-oriented and import-competing industries.

This book promises to contribute not only to recent works, primarily by economists, on the effect of global supply chains on optimal trade policy (e.g., Antràs and Staiger 2012; Blanchard 2007, 2010) but also to the strand of the international political economy (IPE) literature emphasizing the distributional consequences of cross-border trade and production activities (Baccini et al. 2015; Baccini et al. 2018; Blanchard et al. 2016). On the latter, our analyses highlight the evolving pattern of firm and industry demand for preferential trade liberalization, driven by the growing integration of trade, investment, and production activities in the global economy. Additionally, the triangulation of both micro- and macro-level evidence drawn from analyses of firm preferences for trade liberalization and the design of PTAs, industry lobbying over a large PTA (i.e., the TPP), and the cross-national pattern of PTA formation should also help advance our understanding of the complex domestic coalitional politics behind the negotiation of modern PTAs, the widely divergent political regimes of the countries under consideration notwithstanding.

It should be noted that our focus on firm preferences and lobbying behavior with respect to preferential trade liberalization does not necessarily imply that pushing for trade liberalization in the form of official treaties represents the best or main channel through which firms seek to influence government trade policy. In addition to advocating for PTAs, for example, firms in the United States can directly lobby the government over trade issues of concern or over congressional bills that specifically deal with trade.[7] Firms can also exert pressure on the government by leveraging the threat of exit. These alternative channels may have become even more important in the current era, as the Trump administration has displayed a penchant for disengaging from official international treaties in favor of unilateral action.

Notwithstanding these alternative avenues of trade policy influence, firms will likely continue to see preferential trade liberalization as one of the tools for advancing their interests in light of the proliferation of PTAs in recent decades and the current trend toward the negotiation of the so-called mega-regional trade agreements such as the TTP, TTIP, and RCEP by the major economies. A close look at the politics behind the negotiation of PTAs should therefore allow us to provide a detailed analysis of the role of GVCs in driving societal coalitions over free trade and better illuminate the GVC-PTA linkage.

The rest of this chapter is organized as follows. First, we briefly summarize the existing literature on the politics of trade liberalization and recent scholarship on GVC integration and preferential trade liberalization. Next, we introduce the theoretical framework and main argument of the book, followed by a preview of the empirical analyses and findings. Finally, we summarize the major contributions and implications of the book.

The Politics of Trade Liberalization: A Review of the Literature

How can countries achieve trade liberalization in spite of domestic protectionist interests? IPE scholars respond to this question variously, with some focusing on various segments of society that demand protection (e.g., Hiscox 2002; Rogowski 1989) or on how domestic political institutions mediate societal demand and influence the supply of trade policy (e.g., Frye and Mansfield 2003; Milner 1989; Milner and Kubota 2005). Two models have helped researchers understand the effects of domestic interest groups. The Heckscher-Ohlin (HO) model predicts that cleavages between different factors of production (e.g. labor versus capital) over trade policy will occur under conditions of factor mobility. The Ricardo-Viner (RV) model instead expects such cleavages to fall along sectoral lines because some production factors cannot be easily moved between sectors.

In theories that stress factor specificity, individual trade policy preferences are shaped by how trade affects personal income, which is directly tied to the industry of employment. According to the sectoral model, firms are more likely to support free trade if they are more deeply integrated into the international economy through FDI, exports, or intra-industry trade than if they are in import-competing sectors. This is because firms more dependent on export or foreign production should be more concerned about the potential effect of foreign retaliation on their foreign operations and trade flows. Firms may also be concerned that protection at home could increase the competition that they may face in third markets; raise the costs of imports from subsidiaries, subcontractors, or foreign firms; and disproportionately benefit domestically oriented firms at their expense (Milner 1989).

While the above theories generate important insights into the domestic politics of trade liberalization and protectionism, the increasingly rapid pace at which goods and production are crossing national borders, the growing integration of GVC linkages, and the proliferation of PTAs compel us to revisit the distributional consequences of trade and its underlying domestic coalitional politics. This has led to a new wave of scholarship that more closely analyzes the ways through which GVCs may affect trade politics. For example, Jensen et al. (2015) suggest that U.S. multinational corporations (MNCs) that engage in more vertical FDI or intra-firm trade should be less likely to file antidumping petitions in the face of persistent foreign currency undervaluations and growing import competition. Johns and Wellhausen (2016) focus on the implications of outsourcing for property rights protection, arguing that foreign investors should be less likely to face property rights violations in host countries where they have a network of partner firms. Blanchard and Matschke (2015) further analyze the relationship between offshoring activities by U.S. multinational corporations and the structure of U.S. trade preferences, finding that the United States is more likely to offer preferential market access to host countries of American MNCs.

It should be noted that these studies tend to focus on the implications of GVC participation through FDI or associated related party (RP) trade for the political behavior of firms or industries. Relatively few studies have examined how the reorganization of international trade within global production chains may be altering traditional patterns of industry support for trade liberalization that are separate from ownership concerns. Even those studies that do address the trade policy implications of GVCs tend to emphasize the distinction between intermediate and finished products without developing a general model for capturing the complexity and diversity of GVCs. For example, Baccini et al. (2018) examine how GVCs interact with intra-industry trade (IIT) to influence the political economy of trade. Gulotty and Li (2020) find that Chinese firms with a high level of dependence on intermediate goods from TPP members are more likely to suffer the consequences of global production diversion from PTAs. While these studies advance our understanding of the implications of intermediate versus final goods trade for trade liberalization, they nevertheless fall short of developing a more general framework for assessing how GVC linkages affect industry/firm trade preferences.

Economists have also sought to understand the implications of GVCs by taking advantage of new data sources to advance existing political economy models of trade policy. Here it is worth highlighting the work by Blanchard et al. (2016), who incorporated the idea of GVC linkages into standard political economy models of trade with specific factors (Grossman and Helpman 1994; Helpman 1997) and looked more specifically at how the adoption of a value-added approach to assessing trade activities may have altered governments' incentive to impose import restrictions. Notably, this approach represents a novel extension of earlier work done by Ornelas and Turner (2008, 2012) and Antràs and Staiger (2012, 5) that shows that bilateral bargaining among value-chain partners exerts an important effect on optimal trade policy by influencing the "mapping from tariffs to prices." It innovates by shifting the analytical focus from multinational ownership

to input trade; in this way, it explains the extensive cross-border input linkages whose scale, for most countries and sectors, is increasing in comparison with multinational production.[8]

Furthermore, this approach conceives of supply chain linkages as
"direct trade in factor services (value-added content) on the production
side" in a world in which goods are "made in the world" with both domestic and foreign primary factors. Such a conceptualization enables scholars
to capture the most salient features of GVCs while "remaining agnostic
about particular details of supply chain relationships" (Blanchard et al.
2016, 2). Specifically, these researchers show that an increase in either the
level of domestic content in foreign-produced final goods or the foreign
content of domestically produced final goods leads to a decrease in final
goods tariffs.

More recently, Meckling and Hughes (2017) have examined the trade
policy preferences of firms in the solar photovoltaics industry. They find
that with the globalization of production in this industry, vertically specialized firms are more likely to support free trade because of their connections
with global supply chains. These firms specialize in specific stages of the
production process—for example, as global manufacturers highly dependent on imported inputs, as upstream suppliers to a global supply chain,
and as downstream users of final products. These findings suggest that
while the rise of global value chains expands the firm coalitions in favor of
open trade, the often conflicting demands of solar firms over trade policy
may also potentially undermine efforts to forge a coherent business coalition supporting clean-energy technologies.

This book combines the insights of Blanchard et al. (2016) and Meckling and Hughes (2017) with the cumulative knowledge about the domestic
politics of trade from IPE scholarship to develop an argument about how
GVCs may influence the pattern of firm preferences and lobbying for preferential trade liberalization. To the best of our knowledge, only a handful of
studies have explicitly examined how GVCs may affect domestic support
for or opposition to PTAs. For example, Chase (2003) emphasizes the
importance of economies of scale and regional production sharing for business support for RTAs, using the North American Free Trade Agreement
(NAFTA) as the main case. Manger (2009) highlights how the interests of
developed-world MNCs in gaining access to attractive investments in
developing countries are driving the proliferation of North-South PTAs.
However, these studies are based on either a single case or a particular form

of GVCs (e.g., multinationals). In both cases, the analytical foci tend to be on the political implications of FDI by MNCs rather than those of GVCs per se. In the next section, we focus more specifically on GVCs as a theoretical construct and build on recent literature on their political economy implications to derive our theoretical propositions.

Theoretical Framework and Argument

GVCs have important implications for trade policy because as a result of the reduction in transportation and transaction costs, the production activities of multinational firms are increasingly divided across specialized firms or plants across national borders. In these integrated GVCs, firms that directly engage in manufacturing, supply inputs to manufacturers, or provide services such as marketing, sales, and research and development (R&D) are considered "upstream" businesses, whose products often undergo additional production processes before reaching the end-users. This is in contrast to "downstream" firms that utilize the products and services provided by "upstream" businesses, making them the closest to final consumers. As firms that primarily engage in exports increasingly rely on foreign content in their activities, and as those that primarily engage in imports also increasingly have supply chain linkages with foreign users, the rise of GVCs will likely alter the calculation of firms that otherwise would have favored protectionist policies, hence expanding the constellation of forces supporting trade liberalization.

However, despite the growing importance of GVCs, their sheer diversity has presented considerable challenges to both theoretical and empirical analyses of the political economy of trade liberalization. As Blanchard et al. (2016) have pointed out, GVCs are characterized by the diversity of their organizational forms. While some are sequential in nature ("snakes"), others are roundabout ("spiders") (Baldwin and Venebles 2015). Similarly, while some GVCs are organized inside the firm, others may extend outside the firm to involve arm's-length relationships (Antràs and Chor 2013). It is also possible for GVCs to involve either bilateral or multilateral relationships. Following the lead of Blanchard et al. (2016), we conceive of GVCs as trade in factor services (value-added content). Since GVCs blur the distinction between goods produced at home and those manufactured abroad, such an approach can effectively account for the wide heterogeneity among

GVCs and help generate more general predictions about the effect of GVC integration on firms' trade policy preferences.

Nevertheless, we also depart from the framework in Blanchard et al. (2016) by focusing on the effect of GVCs on business demand for preferential trade liberalization instead of government incentives to impose trade restrictions. Specifically, we build on earlier studies of the political economy of the endogenous competition driving the proliferation of PTAs (e.g., Chase 2003; Manger 2009) to develop an argument that emphasizes how the redistribution of the benefits from preferential trade filtered through GVCs may influence firms' incentives to pursue these agreements. Underlying such an argument is the recognition that even those PTAs driven primarily by noneconomic considerations may reflect certain economic calculations involving domestic actors. In the following analyses, we lay out in greater detail the mechanisms through which GVC participation may increase firm support for preferential trade liberalization.[9]

Preferential Tariffs and GVC Participation

Accentuating the importance of tariff reduction is an important way that GVC integration can alter firms' preferences. In long supply chains where goods cross borders numerous times, even low individual tariffs can add up to significant trade costs (Bruhn 2014). Because tariffs are applied not just to value-added parts but to gross imports, exporters may end up paying taxes on parts that others have produced, which amplifies the importance of reducing tariff and nontariff barriers for countries located in different positions along the supply chain. Furthermore, by raising the costs of imports, tariff barriers negatively impinge on the comparative advantage of firms embedded in GVCs because a firm's competitiveness in the international market is significantly affected by its ability to source inputs inexpensively (OECD 2013b, 150). In addition to jeopardizing the competitiveness of those firms highly dependent on intermediate goods trade, tariffs may also harm producers that are heavily involved in trade in final goods. While domestic producers of final goods tend to benefit from tariff protection in the absence of GVCs, they should also see their competitiveness being eroded by tariff barriers in the presence of such networks. In other words, in a world linked by GVCs, tariffs start to exert not only a "beggar-thy-neighbor" but also a "beggar thyself" effect (Miroudot 2011).

The above argument that tariff barriers add to the complexity and costs of international sourcing of inputs is also borne out by existing studies. For example, research by the International Monetary Fund (IMF) (2013) has pointed to a negative relationship between a country's overall trade restrictiveness and its value-added exports, suggesting that production fragmentation may have an important role to play in limiting the use of tariffs on parts and components, as well as the use of other protectionist measures. Similarly, Baldwin and Lopez-Gonzalez (2015) show empirically that applied tariffs, especially those on intermediate products in developing countries, have experienced a sharp drop since the 1990s. This hints at the possibility that developing countries may be making a unilateral effort to reduce tariff barriers in order to facilitate GVC integration. Overall, there is evidence from previous research to suggest a potentially complementary relationship between the reduction of tariff barriers and increases in value-added trade.

Since a key feature of PTAs is the elimination of tariff barriers, such agreements address the above concerns of GVC-embedded firms. Member countries in PTAs can grant each other preferential tariff treatment that discriminates against third parties. While such practices may violate the WTO's MFN principle, Article XXIV of the GATT/WTO makes an exception if a PTA liberalizes "substantially all trade" and aims to create rather than divert trade. Hence, PTAs can offer member countries the opportunity to eliminate tariff barriers in areas where multilateral trade liberalization has been difficult, such as agriculture, fisheries, and other sensitive areas (Horn, Mavroidis, and Sapir 2010).

Non-Tariff Barriers and GVC Participation

Additional major obstacles for GVC-embedded firms are nontariff barriers, some of which occur at the border. Indirect costs, especially the "ability to move goods continuously, safely and economically" (UNCTAD 2013), affect the extent of a firm's GVC participation and competitiveness as much as direct costs. As studies have shown (e.g., UNCTAD 2013), lengthy and cumbersome customs procedures at borders can significantly magnify firms' costs, whereas easy border procedures can in some instances prove even more beneficial for trade than tariff reductions. Increasingly numerous, complex, and heterogeneous safety and quality standards can also generate considerable costs for GVC-embedded firms, especially for those sending their components to several countries, as compliance with conflicting standards means they cannot simply duplicate production processes (OECD, WTO, and UNCTAD 2013). PTAs' trade facilitation provisions can provide important means of reducing the burden for businesses that need to move their goods across multiple borders.

The tight interconnection of investment and trade in GVCs means that in addition to nontariff barriers at borders, businesses may need to pay particular attention to the effects of behind-the-border policies in areas such as investment regulations, IPR protection, and contract enforcement. For instance, for knowledge-intensive firms that rely heavily on R&D, exporting knowledge-intensive products to countries with a weak regulatory framework often accentuates the need for strong IPR protection (Bruhn 2014; Dean 2013). Furthermore, given that much of value-added trade is generated by MNCs (UNCTAD 2013), strong regulations regarding FDI can foster a sound business environment and remove investment barriers for foreign firms seeking to more efficiently organize their supply chain networks.

Once again, PTAs can respond to the above needs as they often contain more encompassing provisions in these areas. In addition to addressing issues beyond trade, such as competition and investment, PTAs frequently include terms that are much stronger than those in multilateral agreements and cover matters such as services and public procurement, as well as trade-related intellectual property rights and investment measures (Horn, Mavroidis, and Sapir 2010). Further, compared to the relatively slow shift toward the negotiation of bilateral investment treaties (BITs) in recent years, a growing number of PTAs now include investment chapters with clearly spelled out provisions on market access and establishment, nondiscrimination, investment regulation and protection, investment promotion, and dispute settlement mechanisms (Maur and Shepherd 2011; Miroudot 2011).

For example, under the investment chapter of the China-Australia Free Trade Agreement (ChAFTA), which entered into force in December 2015, each country is required to extend to investors from the other country national treatment and MFN status. The chapter additionally contains an investor-state dispute settlement (ISDS) mechanism that lays out the procedures for submitting a claim to arbitration, the conditions and limitations on the consent of each party, the conduct of the arbitration, and the transparency of the arbitration proceedings. These obligations, which can be invoked by both Australian and Chinese investors, promote investor confidence by stabilizing expectations regarding the settlement of investment disputes.[10]

In addition, PTA provisions often go beyond those contained in the WTO's Agreement on Trade-Related Investment Measures (TRIMs), such as local content requirements and quantitative export restrictions, to cover issues such as the use of export taxes (Horn, Mavroidis, and Sapir 2010). Many recently signed PTAs also make reference to international intellectual property conventions that go beyond the regulations contained in the WTO's Trade-Related Intellectual Property Rights (TRIPs) Agreement. Compared to the WTO's Agreement on the Application of Sanitary and Phytosanitary Measures (SPS) and the Agreement on Technical Barriers to Trade (TBT), which lay out regulations relating to technical standards as well as standards in areas such as food safety and health, PTA provisions frequently include more and stronger stipulations about product and process standards. In sum, because PTAs decrease heterogeneity and complexity in national standards and provide for stronger enforcement on matters of special relevance to investors, businesses with GVC linkages may find them particularly appealing as ways to ease transnational business dealings and thereby remain competitive in global markets.

GVCs and Firm Preferences for PTAs

That preferential trade liberalization can alter the calculations of GVC-embedded firms can be made clearer through a closer examination of the incentives such firms face. The largest and most immediate benefit of PTAs is the reduction of tariffs beyond those afforded by multilateral trade liberalization. But taking advantage of these benefits often entails additional costs for the firm (Bernard et al. 2012; Cruz et al. 2018; Dai et al. 2018; Kawai and Wignaraja 2011; SwissCham 2016, 2018). To qualify for preferential tariffs, for example, firms need to satisfy the complex rules-of-origin (ROO) requirements stipulated in the relevant PTAs by calculating and certifying the domestic content of the goods they export. Other ROO-related issues, such as obtaining adequate documentation and dealing with administrative procedures, often mean time delays, which in turn add to the overall business costs for firms.

Firms without substantial GVC linkages may not find it worthwhile to incur these costs. On the one hand, the margins of preferences in PTAs are often small compared to what firms already enjoy through MFN tariffs. On the other hand, the fact that these firms do not rely on suppliers or clients in specific geographic locations shaped by the value chain means that it would be easier for them to divert trade to other MFN markets if not taking advantage of the PTAs makes their products less competitive in those markets. Thus it is not surprising that recent research finds that, globally, PTA usage is very low (Thomson Reuters and KPMG 2015).

There are a number of reasons why firms embedded in GVCs may be incentivized to make use of PTAs despite the additional administrative and business costs. First, in the case of backward GVC linkages, that is, when a firm uses foreign inputs for the production of either intermediate or final goods, preferential trade liberalization will reduce the costs of inputs and therefore of its products. Because these inputs (e.g., raw materials or high-value components) are frequently an integrated part of GVCs and cannot be easily substituted by sourcing from domestic or other foreign markets at a competitive price, the gains from lower tariffs will be substantial. Additionally, if these firms in turn sell their products back or to other partner countries, they can benefit from the lower import tariffs on their exports. This double saving has the potential to increase the firm's competitiveness in both domestic and international markets.

Second, in the case of forward GVC linkages, that is, when a firm's domestic value added ends up in the production and exports of foreign intermediate or final goods, preferential trade liberalization will lower import tariffs in the destination countries, in turn reducing the costs of its products and therefore increasing its competitiveness in markets of PTA members. The revenues from increased sales and tariff savings can accrue to either domestic producers or foreign clients, but since forward-linked firms are more likely to be at the lower end of the value chain, PTAs would enable these firms to offer a larger share or even all of the gains to their foreign buyers as a means to foster and maintain their GVC partnerships, especially if the latter is considering the relocation of their supply chain networks to countries with cheaper labor and production costs.

Third, in addition to amplifying the benefits of tariff reductions, the fragmentation of the production process also alters the payoffs of firms that primarily serve the domestic market. For import-competing firms, who are not embedded in GVCs of any kind, traditional trade theory (e.g., Milner 1988; Rodrik 1995) suggests that they would oppose PTAs (or any kind of trade liberalization more broadly). However, if these firms also source foreign inputs for products made for domestic consumption, the calculation will be different. Specifically, while the preferential tariffs mean that these firms would still need to compete with cheaper imports of like products from PTA partner countries, they would also allow them to source parts and components from these countries at a lower price. In the meantime, the nature of the PTAs makes it possible for them to still enjoy most of the benefits of the protectionist policies already in place. On balance, therefore, these firms should be more likely to support PTAs with countries that serve as their main sourcing destinations.

Fourth, as we discussed earlier, PTAs often go beyond tariffs and cover a range of behind-the-border issues—such as IPR protection, investment regulations, and contract enforcement—that are particularly attractive to firms located upstream in GVCs that export knowledge-intensive products or services to countries with a weak regulatory framework. Large MNCs with extensive value chains can also take advantage of PTAs to more efficiently organize their networks of suppliers. In addition, PTAs can facilitate tariff-jumping FDI (Blonigen et al. 2004), allowing firms to expand into markets previously or newly closed due to high tariffs or antidumping duties, by investing and relocating their production to partner countries that have PTAs with those countries. Last but not least, the potential of PTAs to attract FDI into the home country also creates opportunities for firms embedded in GVCs to climb up the value chain, moving from OEM (original equipment manufacturer) to ODM (original design manufacturer) and even to OBM (original brand manufacturer) as they form joint ventures with their technologically more advanced partners.

All of the above mechanisms suggest that *firms with strong GVC linkages, either backward or forward ones, should be more likely to support preferential trade liberalization.* While backward and forward GVC linkages affect trade preferences in different ways, we expect them to similarly lead to increased support for PTAs. We emphasize the trade policy implications of these different forms of GVC participation in various parts of the book, focusing mainly on the effect of backward GVC linkages in our case studies of the TPP negotiations in chapter 5 and trade negotiations between Europe and Asia in chapter 6, and on the effect of forward GVC linkages in the rest of the empirical analyses.

Testable Implications of the Argument

Our overall theoretical argument suggests that GVC-embedded firms should be more likely to support preferential trade liberalization. In this section, we propose a number of observable implications of the arguments that can be tested empirically, including the impact of GVC linkages on firm support for preferential trade liberalization with countries with which they have such ties and how GVC linkages between countries may contribute to the formation of PTAs at the national level.

GVC Linkages and Firm Support for PTAs

The argument that GVC linkages facilitate trade liberalization is consistent with the insights generated by previous studies (e.g., Meckling and Hughes 2017) that both upstream and downstream firms in GVCs tend to favor open trade. In the case of PTAs, however, we expect that GVC-embedded firms will not support all PTAs uniformly. Instead they are more likely to favor PTAs that reduce tariffs and nontariff measures of those countries that are part of their GVCs. An American firm is more likely to support the TPP, for example, if it imports intermediate products from Canada or exports final products to Japan, since both of these countries would be members of the agreement. This leads to the following proposition about the effect of GVC integration on firm preferences for PTAs:

> Proposition 1.1: *Firms should be more likely to support preferential trade liberalization with a country with which they have strong GVC linkages, either backward or forward ones.*

In contrast to firms embedded in GVCs with PTA members, there are reasons to expect that firms with significant supply chain linkages with countries that do not belong to an existing or potential PTA may be less likely to support the agreement. In the context of TPP negotiations, which is the focus of the empirical analysis in chapter 5, we expect these firms to have been against the proposed agreement due to concerns about the substantial adjustment costs they would incur in shifting their supply chain relationships from China to TPP countries.

To understand why this is the case, it is important to recognize the discrimination that PTAs may generate against nonmember countries. Unlike in multilateral trade liberalization, member countries in PTAs can offer each other lower tariffs without extending the same to third parties. This can result in a "trade diversion" effect whereby trade shifts from nonmember countries that are more productive to member countries that are less efficient (see, e.g., Fernández and Portes 1998; Haftel 2004; Mansfield 1998; Mattli 1999). Similarly, a PTA can divert investment by motivating a firm to move its investment and trade relations with excluded countries to member countries so it can have better access to the upstream manufacturing tasks and intermediate inputs it needs for production (Baccini and Dür 2015; Blanchard 2015). Given that PTAs can generate significant costs through investment and trade diversion, producers with supply chain linkages to excluded countries should be less likely to support these agreements and may even be motivated to oppose them. This may be especially the case when the firm has extensive GVC linkages with the excluded country, such as China in the case of the TPP.

Although the TPP ostensibly aimed to promote regional trade liberalization, many viewed it as part of a strategy the Obama administration had launched to counteract China's increasing influence and power (e.g., Song and Yuan 2012) and to pressure Beijing into cracking down on unfair Chinese trading practices (e.g., USTR 2016). Excluding China from the TPP not only may have negatively affected Chinese firms' production and sales but also may have disrupted supply chain linkages for American firms that rely on importing intermediate goods from China. The market size of the TPP countries[11] means that these businesses might still have supported the TPP if the adjustment costs of moving their trade to member countries would have been outweighed by the creation of competitive sourcing options. But despite its rising wages,[12] China continues to be "a hub, or even the hub, of global supply chains." Consequently, industries strongly linked with it through supply chains would incur substantial adjustment costs if they were to shift their supply chain relationships to TPP member countries. The prospect of such adjustment costs might have motivated these firms to not endorse or even oppose the creation of the TPP.

As we noted earlier, the initial intention behind the TPP was to curb China's growing military and economic power and boost America's influence in Asia. Does politics matter when it comes to firms' trade preferences? While there is evidence (e.g., DiGiuseppe and Kleinberg 2019; Zeng and Li 2019) that individuals are strongly motivated by geopolitical considerations when forming their opinions on issues related to trade and investment, firms, as commercial entities concerned with profits or losses, should primarily be motivated by economic interests rather than political ones. Thus, although firms may want to follow the lead of the government in order to earn political points, as we show in chapter 5, this does not preclude them from locating production in China or maintaining sourcing relationships with Chinese firms, suggesting that political interests would have been preceded by commercial ones when the firms evaluated the TPP's long-term implications.

The above discussion about trade diversion and trade adjustment leads to the following proposition about firms embedded in GVCs with countries excluded from a PTA:

> Proposition 1.2: *Firms should be less likely to support preferential trade liberalization that excludes countries with which they have strong GVC linkages.*

GVC Linkages and Firm Support for Deep vs. Shallow PTAs

Thus far we have focused on the implications of GVC linkages for firm support for PTAs without considering the depth of these agreements.[13] Yet all PTAs are not created equal; some are more likely to entail more rigorous trade liberalization and investment protection measures than others (Lawrence 1996). In light of the growing variation in the depth of PTAs, there is reason to believe that firms with strong GVC networks should be particularly likely to demand deep PTAs with rigorous terms, as their extensive cross-border commercial activities should accentuate the need for enhanced protection from the risks associated with such activities. Not only do firms with extensive GVC networks source raw materials, components, and other inputs from foreign downstream producers and/or supply their products to upstream producers in third countries, but they may also establish subsidiaries in multiple locations overseas to produce products for either local sales (i.e., through "horizontal FDI") or exports (i.e., through "vertical FDI"). GVC-embedded firms may therefore be exposed to trade and/or investment risks. The investment risks are even more severe for firms engaging in vertical FDI, which often face the need to move inputs, components, and finished goods between the buyers (the firm's headquarters) and the suppliers (the firm's foreign subsidiaries) (Hanson, Mataloni, and Slaughter 2005; Helpman 1984).

Deep PTAs respond to the concerns of firms with extensive GVC ties by providing stronger trade and investment protection. Not only do PTAs increasingly contain the so-called WTO-plus (WTO+) provisions, or "traditional" provisions dealing with tariff issues that are much stronger than those negotiated at the multilateral level; they also include "WTO-minus (WTO-X)" dimensions that address topics beyond directly trade-related issues and that previously were only negotiated outside the WTO. Examples of such provisions include trade-related investment measures, trade-related intellectual property rights, competition, services, public procurement, and the environment (Horn, Mavroidis, and Sapir 2010). PTAs that include such "WTO-X" dimensions also differ from BITs in that they tend to extend the coverage of foreign investment from the postestablishment phase of investment, as is the case with most BITs, to the preestablishment phase (Busse, Königer, and Nunnenkamp 2010; UNCTAD 2007).

For example, Canada, the United States, and more recently Japan have been active signatories of not only BITs but also the so-called investment-inclusive PTAs (IIPTAs), which include both investment and trade protections (Hicks and Johnson 2011). The United States, in particular, leads the way in designing comprehensive PTAs. NAFTA, for example, is particularly "encompassing" because it includes the four modalities that determine investment conditions, specifically establishment, acquisition, postestablishment operations, and resale, in addition to covering such disciplines as MFN status, national treatment, and dispute settlement. In Asia, Singapore and Australia have agreements with the most comprehensive investment provisions, while other agreements have less extensive coverage (Kotschwar 2009).

In addition, deep PTAs can constitute a vehicle for narrowing the significant gaps or differences that may exist in business laws and regulations across national borders, thus assisting in the further development of production-sharing activities. For instance, the presence of monopolies, cartels, and other forms of private anticompetitive practices may prevent MNCs from taking full advantage of cross-national cost differences that could be realized through fragmenting production. The proliferation of TBTs may also frustrate corporate efforts to capitalize on the benefits of production sharing. Deep PTAs address these issues by including competition disciplines. A study by Teh (2009), for example, shows that more than a quarter of PTAs contain provisions that would prevent major telecommunications suppliers from engaging in anticompetitive practices. About one-fifth of these agreements also have an IP chapter dealing with anticompetitive behavior by IPR holders. Another study by Piermartini and Budetta (2009) of 70 PTAs similarly finds that 58 of these agreements contain TBT provisions that spell out conformity assessment procedures, harmonization standards, or transparency requirements.

Given that deep PTAs are more likely to address the concerns of GVC-embedded firms about behind-the-border measures that may impede their transnational trade and investment activities, we should expect a higher level of support for deep PTAs from such firms than those with less extensive GVC linkages. This leads to the following proposition:

Proposition 1.3: *Firms with strong GVC linkages, either backward or forward ones, should be more likely to support deep PTAs that contain more rigorous provisions than shallow ones.*

GVC Linkages and PTA Formation

Up to this point, our argument is mainly applicable at the firm level. However, it is possible that our theoretical contention may have implications for the formation of PTAs as well. While it is countries that decide whether or not to enter into a PTA, firms and industries play an important role by organizing into lobbies for or against preferential trade liberalization. As previous studies (Antràs and Helpman 2004; Bernard et al. 2007) have pointed out, highly productive firms are more likely to source inputs abroad and become integrated into GVCs. Given that productivity is a major determinant of firms' decisions to lobby and the level of their activity (e.g., Kim 2017), it follows that firms with strong GVC linkages should be more likely to organize and lobby in favor of preferential trade liberalization with the country or countries with which they have such relationships.

In emphasizing the benefits accruing to the "winners" of trade, the above argument so far has downplayed potential opposition to preferential trade liberalization stemming from other domestic interests in the context of GVC integration. Yet firms not embedded in GVCs—i.e., domestic producers of intermediate products and less productive producers of finished products—should be expected to oppose trade liberalization of intermediates for fear of either direct foreign competition or the potential competitive advantage that preferential trade liberalization provides to their domestic competitors. Indeed, there is evidence that domestic producers of intermediate goods are particularly likely to oppose trade liberalization (Baccini 2016). However, since PTAs only bring down trade barriers in member countries while leaving intact the level of protectionism against the majority of other, nonmember countries, these firms should be less motivated to engage in lobbying against these agreements.

Aggregating the incentives of these domestic actors within an industry—firms embedded in GVCs with PTA members and nonmembers, domestic producers of intermediate products, and less productive producers of finished products—suggests that, on balance, increases in the level of intermediate goods imports in an industry should be associated with stronger support for PTAs from firms with substantial GVC linkages to member countries and weaker opposition from import-competing firms.

Furthermore, it is reasonable to expect that government policy may at least in part reflect firm demand for preferential trade liberalization. Previous studies (e.g., Grossman and Helpman 1995) have shown that firms may be able to influence economic policy through lobbying and financial contributions. Firm lobbying has also been found to play an important role in shaping the formation and content of PTAs (Manger 2009). In the area of trade policy more broadly, Milner (1989) has documented how, as a result of the demand for trade liberalization by firms with growing international economic ties, the United States and France remained relatively open in the 1970s despite a relative economic slowdown that threatened to provoke strong protectionist pressures, as in the 1930s.

Given firms' demand for preferential trade liberalization and their ability to influence government policy, it follows that PTAs should be more likely to be formed between a pair of countries that have a large proportion of industries that are heavily dependent on GVCs, and that this logic should extend to industries with either strong backward or forward GVC linkages with foreign countries. To the extent that such industries expect to derive substantial benefits from further trade liberalization, as the theoretical mechanisms posited above would lead us to expect, then we should expect them to more aggressively lobby their governments to sign PTAs with their trading partner(s).

Proposition 1.4: *PTAs are more likely to be formed between a pair of countries whose domestic industries have either strong backward or forward GVC linkages with each other.*

Preview of the Empirical Analyses and Findings

The book is organized as follows. Chapter 2 provides an overview of the two key concepts used in the book—GVCs and PTAs—showing how they have evolved over time and how researchers have attempted to measure them. In addition, we use the cases of China and the United States to illustrate how the two phenomena are potentially linked, by documenting both the roles of Chinese and American firms in global supply chains and recent efforts of the two countries to create their respective FTA networks. This part of the discussion helps set the stage for the empirical analyses that follow.

Chapters 3 to 6 test the above propositions empirically with a variety of cases and methods and proceed along two interrelated dimensions, moving from the micro-level (firm) to the macro-level (country), *and* from preferences (attitudes) to behaviors (lobbying), and then to policy outcomes (PTA formation). We choose to focus primarily on China and the United States in our empirical analyses because both provide suitable testing grounds for our theory. China has emerged as a center of global manufacturing and supply chain activities as a result of the country's rapid economic ascent over the past few decades, whereas the United States, as the biggest home country of MNCs, has a large number of businesses heavily enmeshed in the global economy through a dense network of interconnected supply chains. Global supply chains are thus particularly important for businesses in both countries as they seek to access international consumers and effectively compete in the global marketplace.

We begin our empirical inquiry by unpacking the micro-foundation of the theory. In chapter 3, we trace the experiences of Chinese firms with two recent free trade agreements, signed by China with South Korea and Australia, respectively, in the coastal provinces of Guangdong, Jiangsu, Shandong, and Zhejiang. We select these four provinces as the site of our fieldwork because together they account for the lion's share of China's trade since the reform started in 1978. The substantial supply chain linkages that firms in these four provinces have developed with foreign manufacturers thus make them ideal to establish the micro-foundations of our theoretical propositions.

Drawing on interviews with Chinese firms located either upstream or downstream in GVCs in a variety of industries and with government officials in the customs and trade bureaus, as well as state and local documentary materials, we show that firms embedded in GVCs are more likely to benefit from PTAs than those without such linkages and, as a result, have become a core constituency for supporting these agreements. These firms are also more likely to seek both informal and formal channels to push for their interests in existing FTA negotiations as well as future ones with countries such as Canada.

In chapter 4, we supplement findings from the fieldwork with an original firm-level survey of more than 500 Chinese executives, designed to test our proposition regarding firm preferences for preferential trade liberalization (*proposition 1.1*). In the survey, we asked a set of questions designed to tap the firm's position in GVCs, including their backward and forward GVC linkages, as well as their attitudes toward international trade generally and preferential trade liberalization specifically. We expect that after accounting for other factors that may affect a firm's trade policy position, including firm age, size, ownership, productivity, and product substitutability, those with strong backward or forward GVC linkages should be more likely to demonstrate a favorable attitude toward preferential trade liberalization.

In addition to the attitudinal questions, we also designed a conjoint experiment in the survey to explore firms' preferences for the design of PTAs, including the degree of tariff reduction, the time required for the PTA to enter into force, the presence and content of dispute settlement mechanisms, investor protection, IPR protection, and provisions for trade remedies. We use the experimental design to explore whether GVC-integrated firms are more likely to prefer deeper PTAs that address nontariff barriers and behind-the-border issues (*proposition 1.3*).

The results from both the survey questions and the conjoint experiment support our main theoretical propositions, showing that firms with strong backward or forward GVC linkages are indeed more likely to demonstrate a favorable attitude toward international trade in general, and preferential trade liberalization in particular. They are also more likely to have strong preferences for PTAs that include rigorous provisions regarding investment protection and IPR protection.

Moving from firm preferences to lobbying for preferential trade liberalization, we focus on the pattern of corporate lobbying for the TPP by the Fortune 500 companies in the United States in chapter 5. As the TPP would have represented the largest modern PTA if it had come to fruition, the recent intense lobbying by the corporate sector for the conclusion of the agreement and for the delegation of negotiation authority over international trade agreements to the executive branch, through the so-called trade promotion authority (TPA), provides us with an excellent opportunity for examining the potential impact of GVCs on firm lobbying for preferential trade liberalization.

In our analysis of the TPP lobbying pattern, we emphasize the political implications of growing foreign content in exports (i.e., backward GVC linkages) because this is how the business operations of the vast majority of the Fortune 500 companies in the United States are organized today. We have to leave out analysis of the effect of forward GVC linkages because, to the best of our knowledge, data specific to TPP countries are not yet available for this measure. Using a most likely case design, we first select two industries—one with low GVC linkages to TPP countries and high GVC linkages to China (as represented by the transportation and warehousing industry) and the other with high GVC linkages to TPP countries and low GVC linkage to China (as represented by the rubber manufacturing industry)—and examine the degree to which the preferences and behaviors of firms in these two industries are consistent with our theoretical expectations (*propositions 1.1 and 1.2*).

We further generalize the findings from these "most likely" cases in a multivariate analysis of the pattern of lobbying by Fortune 500 companies for the TPP in the United States. We construct TPP lobbying measures (such as donations, trade report submissions, and general support for the TPP) using lobbying reports and other public information. We then assess whether firms' lobbying activities are influenced by their GVC positions. Our empirical findings point to a positive and statistically significant relationship between a firm's GVC linkages with other TPP countries and its lobbying and election funding activities over the TPP. Moreover, the results show that firms with strong GVC linkages with China, a country that is excluded from TPP negotiations, are less supportive of the agreement.

While chapters 3, 4, and 5 mainly provide micro-level evidence of the impact of GVCs on firms' preferences and lobbying for preferential trade liberalization, chapter 6 shifts the analysis to the macro-level by exploring the impact of GVCs on the pattern of GVC formation cross-nationally (*proposition 1.4*). We first illustrate the logic underlying our cross-national study with a mini-case study of the role of GVC-embedded firms in driving PTA negotiations between the European Union and Asian countries. We then present the results of our statistical analysis of the impact of GVC linkages on PTA formation for the 62 countries included in the TiVA dataset. The findings lend substantial support to our main theoretical contentions, indicating that while a pair of countries whose domestic industries have extensive backward or forward GVC linkages are more likely to form PTAs, this effect is particularly pronounced when home-country industries have extensive forward linkages with their foreign counterparts.

Chapter 7 summarizes the main findings of this book and discusses their theoretical and empirical contributions, highlighting in particular the contributions of our findings to the research programs on PTAs and GVCs as well as to the study of trade politics in China and the United States. We further consider the policy implications of our analysis for ongoing PTA negotiations against the broad backdrop of the rise of protectionism in the global trading system, contemplating the potential for GVCs to cushion the impact of protectionist tariffs and sustain the momentum toward trade liberalization in the future. This chapter concludes by identifying a set of questions for future research.

Contributions and Implications

In highlighting the evolving pattern of societal cleavages over free trade, this book promises to contribute to the international political economy literature on societal demand for trade policy. As mentioned earlier, previous studies (e.g., Milner 1989; Schattschneider 1935) generally emphasize how firms engaged in exports or multinational production should be more likely to support free trade policies. In particular, export-oriented firms should be more likely to be in favor of free trade than import-competing ones due to fear of foreign retaliation or interruptions to intra-firm trade. Our study goes beyond this insight, suggesting that there are heterogeneous trade policy preferences even among export-oriented firms. Specifically, firms with more extensive supply chain linkages with overseas businesses (such as those that predominantly export intermediate products to foreign producers) should be more favorable toward free trade than those less embedded in GVCs (such as those that primarily sell final goods to foreign producers). Similarly, among firms that primarily import goods from abroad, those that also export their products to international markets should be more favorably disposed toward trade liberalization than those that primarily sell their products to the domestic market.

These expectations lead us in chapter 4 to examine the trade policy preferences of four types of firms with varying GVC involvement: (a) exporters with strong backward and forward linkages, or what we call *traders*, who engage in both imports and exports and who therefore are most heavily embedded in GVCs; (b) *exclusive exporters*; (c) *exclusive importers*; and (d) *domestic firms that engage in neither export nor import*. We expect—and found some evidence—that traders are most likely to support preferential trade liberalization, followed by the other three groups in descending order.

In other words, exporters who simultaneously engage in imports should be more favorably disposed toward preferential trade liberalization than exclusive exporters with no importing activities. Similarly, exclusive importers should be more likely to support preferential trade liberalization than purely domestic firms.

Taken together, our analysis shows that by nullifying the differences between homemade and foreign-made goods and by disconnecting the location of final goods production from the country where the value added in those goods originated, GVCs change businesses' stance on free trade. In other words, the rise of GVCs and multinational production has led to firms that both import and export a combination of intermediate and final goods and, as a result, participate in global production networks in ways that cannot be captured by the simple dichotomy that pits export-oriented against import-competing firms. By adopting a value-added approach, we were therefore able to develop a more general model of how production fragmentation across national borders affects industry trade preferences, beyond previous studies' emphasis on outsourcing, FDI, and other ownership concerns (e.g., Bradford et al. 2015; Johns and Wellhausen 2016; Osgood 2017, 2018). Our analysis further allowed us to extend the "new new trade theory" (Bernard et al. 2007; Helpman et al. 2004; Melitz 2003), which highlights how heterogeneity among exporters with respect to size and productivity influences their preferences, to show that another important dimension to look at is what products firms trade *and* what position they occupy in the fragmented global production process.

The literature is presently missing a consideration of how industries respond to countries excluded from a PTA, so our work addresses this omission. We emphasize that businesses may be more inclined to support trade liberalization if they are integrated with members of a possible trade agreement through GVCs. We also show that in industries closely linked to non-PTA members through GVCs, firms will be less likely to support the agreement and in some cases may even oppose it, potentially because they are concerned that the tariff-liberalization provisions in the proposed PTA will generate costly adjustments in supply chain relationships. Although our focus is on an excluded country (China) that is emerging as a global center of manufacturing activities, our findings nonetheless should illuminate how industry trade preferences may change in response to PTA exclusion as global supply chain integration grows.

Our findings also shed new light on the preferences that underpin PTA negotiations. While previous studies have emphasized the part played by multinational production, investment discrimination, or political institutions (e.g., Baccini and Dür 2015; Chase 2003; Manger 2009; Mansfield, Milner, and Rosendorff 2002), we make a case for how industry preferences for PTAs may be affected by GVCs. Through a case study of the TPP, we demonstrate how important GVCs can be in directing PTA negotiations.

In addition, our detailed analyses of the trade preferences of Chinese firms show that these firms increasingly resemble those in other major economies such as the United States, in that ownership is no longer a major determinant of the firms' preferences and behaviors. Fieldwork evidence presented in chapter 3 further suggests that Chinese firms have been able to take advantage of both formal and informal channels of influence to shape the government's FTA policy, as a result of the pluralization of the country's decision-making process. Such evidence hints at the reduced influence of the state over Chinese firms and the growing constraints that global economic integration places on the Chinese leadership. It also helps to explain why Beijing has been championing the cause of trade liberalization in the international arena amidst the global retreat from free trade (Leng et al. 2018; Yan 2018).

Last, our findings have substantial policy implications. In particular, they help us understand how the responses of both American and Chinese firms to the negotiations of modern trade agreements such as the TPP may be shaped by their position in GVCs. In unraveling the complex domestic coalitional politics behind PTA negotiations and identifying new winners and losers from the process of fragmentating globalization, the findings should also help us in devising the appropriate strategies for overcoming potential domestic opposition to trade liberalization and for sustaining and expanding the constellation of domestic forces in support of the free trade agenda. These findings are particularly important at a time when the rise of protectionist sentiments in major advanced industrialized countries is threatening to significantly restructure cross-border supply chains and exerting a negative impact on the sourcing of parts and components at both regional and global levels (Bown 2018).

CHAPTER 2

Conceptualization, Measurement, and Two Illustrative Cases

Given that the development of global value chains (GVCs) is a relatively recent phenomenon and that scholars and practitioners are just starting to conceptualize and quantify GVC integration, it is important that we introduce the reader to this key concept and its measurement. Further, since one of the primary purposes of the book is to show how GVCs may affect firm-level preferences for and the formation and depth of preferential trade agreements (PTAs), it is also necessary for us to provide an overview of contemporary PTAs and the variation in their depth of coverage.

This chapter serves to provide an introduction to these two key concepts used in the theoretical argument and empirical analyses of the book: global value chains and preferential trade agreements. We first document the expansion of GVCs in recent decades and describe measures of the concept that have been proposed so far. This is followed by a discussion of the rapid growth of PTAs during the same period and the variation in the depth of these agreements. We additionally provide a review of recent literature that addresses the nexus between GVCs and PTAs.

In addition to this broad overview, we use the cases of China and the United States to further illuminate these two concepts. We focus on China because the country has risen as a major center of global manufacturing activities with extensive supply chain linkages to the rest of the world in a short span of four decades. The story about the emergence of China as the hub of global supply chains and how this process has been associated with the signing of a flurry of free trade agreements (FTAs) between China and its trading partners can therefore shed valuable light on the potential role of GVC integration in spurring these agreements. At the same time, as the world's largest economy, the United States has a high level of involvement in

GVCs, in particular through forward GVC linkages and in sectors such as services. While not traditionally a leader of FTAs, Washington has more recently stepped up its support for regional trade liberalization, notably through the so-called mega-regional trade agreements such as the Trans-Pacific Partnership (TPP) and the Transatlantic Trade and Investment Partnership (TTIP). In the second half of this chapter, we therefore provide more detailed background information on the two countries' growing involvement in GVCs, the FTAs they have signed, and the ones under consideration. These discussions will help contextualize the empirical analyses in chapters 3, 4, and 5.

Global Value Chains and How We Measure Them

In today's highly globalized economy, international production (including design, manufacturing, marketing, and distribution), trade, and investment activities increasingly take place in multiple countries. This growing fragmentation of production across national borders has given rise to GVCs, which involve "the full range of activities that firms and workers do to bring a product/good or service from its conception to its end use and beyond" (Gereffi and Fernandez-Stark 2011, 7). Value chains are distinct from supply chains, as they go beyond the latter's emphasis on manufacturing- and distribution-related activities to also include activities such as design and branding that create value for a product, though not necessarily transforming it physically.[1] A GVC is also different from a value chain in that it spreads across multiple firms and locations instead of being confined to a single firm or geographical location.[2]

The rise of GVCs has been driven by multinational companies seeking to maximize efficiency and profitability by restructuring their global operations through outsourcing and offshoring activities. It has been given additional momentum by the significant reduction in trade, transportation, and communication costs, regulatory policy reforms that promoted trade and investment liberalization, and growing consumer demands in Asia as well as in many new emerging economies (OECD 2012a).

The adoption of the term "global value chains" in the 2000s followed an extensive body of literature on global commodity chains (GCCs), or "a network of labor and production processes whose end result is a finished commodity" (Hopkins and Wallerstein 1986, 159) that developed rapidly in the

1980s and 1990s. Originating in the world-system school, the GCC research program later evolved into a more coherent research paradigm with the publication of a collected volume entitled *Commodity Chains and Global Capitalism*, edited by Gereffi and Korzeniewicz (1994). Gereffi (1994) in particular used the example of the apparel commodity chain extending from raw materials such as cotton, wood, and synthetic fibers to final products such as garments, to illustrate the processes and transformations embedded in GCCs.

In the early 2000s, some scholars (e.g., Blair 2005; Gereffi et al. 2005; Humphrey and Schmitz 2000) began to use the term GVC to explicate the global chains framework. GVC was adopted both to avoid the narrow focus of the term "commodity" on undifferentiated products with low entry barriers and to better capture the determinants of the organization of global industries. Gereffi et al. (2005) further propose a theoretical framework for value-chain analysis in addition to outlining different types of GVC governance.

It should be noted, however, that despite the difference in terminology, both GCC and GVC studies have focused on a set of key concepts and questions, including: (a) the organization of a global commodity/value chain and the role of the most powerful players (or "lead firms") in it; (b) the distributional effect of the governance structure of the chain, that is, how the way the chain is governed affects the distribution of gains among the countries, firms, and workers in both developed and developing countries that are part of it; and (c) the factors that influence the possibility for chain participants to "upgrade" from low to high value-added activities.[3] Since the GVC concept was first introduced, it has been particularly valuable for capturing the increasing fragmentation of production across national borders, the "specialization of countries in tasks and business functions rather than specific products" at a time when many goods and services are "made in the world" instead of solely at home, and the role of networks, global buyers and global suppliers (OECD 2012a, 10).

The rising importance of GVCs has rendered traditional statistics increasingly inaccurate for capturing the reality of world trade. An often-cited case that illustrates the problems with conventional trade statistics has to do with the production of an Apple iPod. As some studies (e.g., Dedrick et al. 2010) have shown, of the $144 total factory-gate price of an iPod, less than 10 percent can be attributed to value added in China where it is assembled. The bulk of the components are imported from Japan, with a smaller portion coming from the United States and South Korea. Furthermore, the vast majority of the value added from the production of an iPod accrues to Apple, even though the company does not engage in manufacturing at all. Another example is General Motors (GM)—despite being a well-known American car manufacturer, only about 37 percent of the company's value added is actually "made in the USA"; 30 percent of GM's value added derives from South Korean inputs, with many other different countries supplying the various parts of a vehicle (Grossman and Rossi-Hansberg, 2006).

Driven by the need to develop a better understanding of the positioning of countries and industries in GVCs, international trade economists (e.g., Alfaro et al. 2017; Antràs et al. 2012; Antràs and Chor 2013; Fally 2012; Fally and Hillberry 2018; Miller and Temurshoev 2017; Wang et al. 2017a) have recently introduced a number of GVC measures that better reflect the complexity of the changing structure of global trade and production. In the following section, we provide a brief introduction to some of the earlier measures that have been developed to capture GVC linkages before turning to the most recent measures we employ in this study.

Earlier GVC Measures

Earlier measurement of GVCs breaks down a country's gross exports (EX) into two different components: domestic value added (DVA), or the domestic content embodied in exports that directly contributes to value creation in the economy and thus to gross domestic product (GDP), and foreign value added (FVA), or the foreign content such as raw materials and intermediate goods imported from other countries that is embodied in exports. Hummels et al. (2001) use FVA as an indicator of vertical specialization because it captures the extent to which a country is integrated into global production networks through the use of imported intermediates.

Since it is possible that instead of being absorbed by consumers in the importing partner country, parts of DVA embodied in exports may end up in third countries or return to the home country via the exports of the partner country. Koopman et al. (2010) further take into consideration the DVA embodied in third countries' exports (DVA3) to derive a new measure of GVC participation: the sum of the inputs a country sources from abroad through downstream participation and the amount of its own value added that ends up in third countries' exports via upstream participation as a share of its total exports. In other words:

$$GVC\ participation = (FVA + DVA3)/EX = (FVA/EX) + (DVA3/EX)$$

In the above formula, the first component captures downstream participation while the second term reflects upstream participation. Compared to the indicator for vertical specialization introduced by Hummels et al. (2001), this measure more fully captures GVC participation because it takes into account not only downstream but also upstream participation. A country is more deeply enmeshed in global production networks the higher this measure is.

Still another frequently used indicator, VAX, measures GVC participation as the share of value-added exports (VA) in total exports:

$$VAX = (VA/EX)$$

Developed by Johnson and Noguera (2012), this measure focuses on value-added exports, or DVA embodied in final foreign demand. Value-added exports is conceptually different from DVA in exports because it only takes into account the portion of domestic content that undergoes additional production stages across borders to reach its final destination.[4] The VAX ratio is thus a forward-linkage-based measure of value-added exports and helps to provide an indication of the intensity of production sharing. A higher VAX ratio may also reflect successful upgrading to higher value-added production activities.

While the VAX ratio has been touted as "state of the [art]" and an "appealing inverse measure of the importance of vertical specialization in [. . .] world production" (Antràs 2016, 6), it has also been criticized for not being well-behaved at the sector, bilateral, or bilateral sector level. As Wang et al. (2013) point out, as a forward-linkage-based measure of value-added exports, the VAX ratio is often not bound by one, because value-added exports may exceed exports. Furthermore, even if the VAX ratio is redefined to be a backward-linkage-based measure, it still may not be able to reveal countries' different positions in GVCs because two countries may have identical ratios of value-added exports to total exports for very different reasons.

For example, even though the United States and China may have an identical hypothetical ratio of value-added exports (VAX ratio) of 50 percent, this number may nevertheless obscure important differences in the positions of the two countries. While the VAX ratio of 50 percent in the

Chinese case suggests that value added from foreign countries (such as Japan, South Korea, or the United States) accounts for half of China's gross exports, the same ratio in the U.S. case indicates that half of the U.S. gross exports are value added in the country's intermediate goods that are absorbed by other countries in their production of goods that are exported back to the United States. Therefore, even if the VAX ratio is properly defined, the ambiguities inherent in its definition mean that it is still unable to capture some of the important features of global production sharing.

Toward a New Accounting Framework for Value-Added Trade

In order to address the above perceived weaknesses of the VAX ratio, Koopman et al. (2014) developed a framework for decomposing a country's total gross exports into nine value-added and double-counted components, which can in turn be grouped into four buckets. However, this method only allows for trade decomposition at the aggregate level instead of at the bilateral, sector, or bilateral sector level. To address this shortcoming, Wang et al. (2013) proposed a disaggregated accounting framework for generalizing Koopman et al.'s (2014) method to the bilateral and sector level. A key innovation of the method developed by Wang et al. (2013) is that it decomposes DVA into domestic value added that are exported indirectly through other sectors' gross exports and those embodied in a sector's gross exports that include value added from other sectors. The method additionally takes into proper account a country/sector's gross exports that are derived from the value added drawn from other countries/sectors, in addition to the contributions of a given country-sector to its own intermediate and final goods exports. In applying this accounting framework, the value added of a country-sector and double-counted components should be equal to its gross exports. This approach thus improves upon the work of Koopman et al. (2014) by clearly decomposing value added into producer (or forward-linkage) based and user (or backward-linkage) based components.

Applying this approach to a hypothetical world of three countries, we can have country A export intermediate goods to country B, which can be used in country B for the production of either final goods or another type of intermediate input. Intermediate inputs produced in country B may be either consumed domestically or exported to country A or a third country C. This leads to a total of nine different possible direct or indirect final destinations of absorption: intermediate trade flows from A to B, B to A and A to C, as well as final trade flows among the three countries in both directions.

Based on the decomposition of gross bilateral intermediate trade according to these final destinations of absorption, Wang et al. (2014) break down gross trade flows at any level of disaggregation into 16 value-added and double-counted components, which can in turn be grouped into four buckets. The first bucket contains a country's value-added exports that are consumed abroad (or DVA), similar to the concept of "value-added exports" proposed by Johnson and Noguera (2012). The second bucket includes the part of a country's DVA that is initially exported but eventually returns home (RDA). The third bucket consists of foreign value added that is used in the production of a country's exports and eventually absorbed by other countries (FVA). The last one is the "pure double counted terms" that occur as a result of intermediate goods crossing borders multiple times and can include double-counted value added that originates in either home or foreign countries (PDC). Figure 2.1 provides an illustration of these four major buckets (and their finer components) of a country's gross exports as well as the accounting relations between these components, as proposed by Wang et al. (2014).

It is important to note that the above approach highlights the distinction between backward- and forward-linkage-based GVC measures. While a forward-linkage-based measure of value-added exports includes a sector's value added that is indirectly exported via the exports of other sectors of the same exporting country, a backward-linkage-based measure of value-added exports includes the value added from all sectors of a given exporting country embodied in a given sector's gross exports (Wang et al. 2014). Thus a forward-linkage-based measure of value-added exports in the U.S. electronics sector would count that sector's value added embodied in U.S. exports of automobiles and chemicals but not the value added from these sectors embodied in U.S. electronics exports. Conversely, a backward-linkage-based measure of U.S. value added embodied in U.S. electronics exports would include value added in intermediate inputs from all other sectors/countries (such as glass from country A, rubber from country B, and transportation and design from the home country) used to produce gross electronics exports but would exclude the value-added contributions of the U.S. electronics sector to the gross exports of other sectors in the United States, such as automobiles. As such, it allows one to better distinguish domestic from foreign value added in a country's ratio of value-added exports to gross exports.

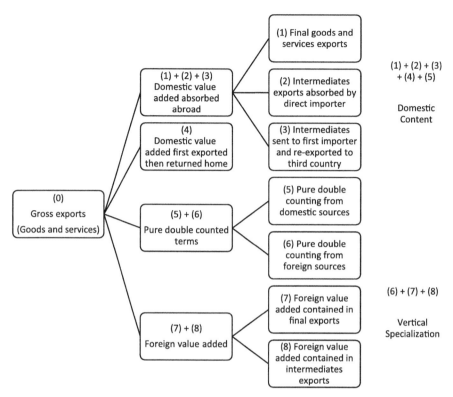

Fig. 2.1. Conceptual Framework of the Gross Trade Accounting Method Proposed by Wang et al. (2014)

Note: This figure is adapted from Wang et al. (2014).

Applying the above framework to U.S.-China bilateral trade in electrical and optical equipment would yield a different estimate of the size of the bilateral trade imbalance in this sector than conventional trade statistics. Bilateral trade flows in electrical and optical equipment between the two countries represent the largest among all product groups, with the sum of two-way flows reaching $212 billion in 2011. According to traditional trade statistics, bilateral trade in this sector is highly imbalanced, with Chinese exports to the United States (which stood at about $176.9 billion in 2011) amounting to about five times that of U.S. exports to China (or about $35.1 billion in the same year).

Decomposing bilateral trade flows according to the final destination of absorption would point to the substantially different value-added structures of U.S. and Chinese exports. Importantly, while the share of DVA in gross exports is much higher for the United States (81 percent in 2011) than for China (70 percent in 2011), the FVA share is higher for Chinese exports than for U.S. exports. This points to the greater importance of DVA for U.S. exports and of FVA for Chinese exports and the different positions the two countries occupy in global production chains. In particular, as the United States produces and exports parts and components, and as part of the value added in its exports returns home as embedded in imports from other countries, it is on the upstream of the GVC. In contrast, China is on the downstream of the chain, as few of its value added products return home as intermediate goods in other countries' exports. Due to these differences in the structure of value-added composition, the size of the U.S.-China trade imbalance in this sector becomes much smaller when measured in terms of DVA rather than in gross exports (Wang et al. 2014).

Two important databases based on this gross trade accounting framework have emerged for analyzing the composition of trade flows that better reflect the reality of global manufacturing, where products are "made in the world." The first one, which we briefly discussed in chapter 1, is the Trade in Value Added (TiVA) database and the second one is the World Input-Output Database (WIOD), compiled jointly by 11 research institutions with funding support from the European Commission (EC) between 2009 and 2012.[5] The most recent release of both databases as of this writing occurred in 2016, with the TiVA database covering 62 economies from 1995 to 2011, and the WIOD covering 43 countries from 2000 to 2014.

In addition to its broader coverage of both the number of countries and time periods, the TiVA database provides a vast range of indicators that disentangles the labor, capital, and intermediate input contributed domestically from foreign value added embodied in the goods as they cross national borders for further processing (OECD 2012b). It also includes more disaggregated elements of value-added trade needed for the calculation of backward and forward GVC linkages. For these reasons, we use the TiVA database for our empirical analyses in chapters 5 and 6.

Using the TiVA database, we can illustrate the rise of GVC trade over time. Figure 2.2 presents the share of re-exported intermediates in total imported intermediates in the four major sectors—agriculture, mining, manufacturing, and services—for the 62 countries and select regions. Re-exported intermediates are intermediate imports used either directly or indirectly in the production of goods and services for export in terms of total intermediate imports. In 2011, the most recent year in the 2016 release, an average of 45 percent of intermediate imports were re-exported to third markets.

However, figure 2.2 reveals wide variation in re-exported intermediates, across both countries and industries. Notably, there is an inverse correlation between country size and re-exported foreign intermediates, with larger and more diversified economies such as the United States and Japan having much lower shares (about 20 percent) than some of the smaller economies, such as Hungary, Singapore, and Luxemburg (over 70 percent).[6] Figure 2.2 additionally suggests that the re-export of intermediates increasingly characterizes not only the traditional sectors of agriculture, mining, and manufacturing but also the services sector, where the contributions of value-added trade may at first blush seem less readily apparent.

Another way to show the rise of GVCs is by looking at the share of a country's exports that are produced with domestic versus foreign value added. Figure 2.3 presents these measures. Looking first at panel (a) of figure 2.3, which displays the average share of domestic and foreign value added in the exports of the 62 economies in the TiVA dataset, we can see that the overall share of domestic value added still outweighs that of foreign value added in exports, but the latter has been increasing steadily over time, from 21.2 percent in 1995 to 27.2 percent in 2011. When we further examine the share of foreign and domestic value added in the gross exports of individual countries, as shown in panel (b) of figure 2.3, a pattern similar to figure 2.2 emerges, as countries vary widely in terms of their domestic value added. Not surprisingly, countries that re-export a higher share of their imported intermediates are also the ones that have more domestic value added in their gross exports.

Measuring GVC Linkages at the Firm Level

The above measures examine GVCs at the country or industry level. While the same approach can be applied at the firm level, it is almost impossible to obtain the input-output information necessary for calculating GVC linkages for individual firms on a large-scale, systematic basis. A couple of recent studies (e.g., Alfaro et al. 2017) attempt to get around this by combining information from input-output tables with data on the production activities of individual firms. The limitation with studies like this, however,

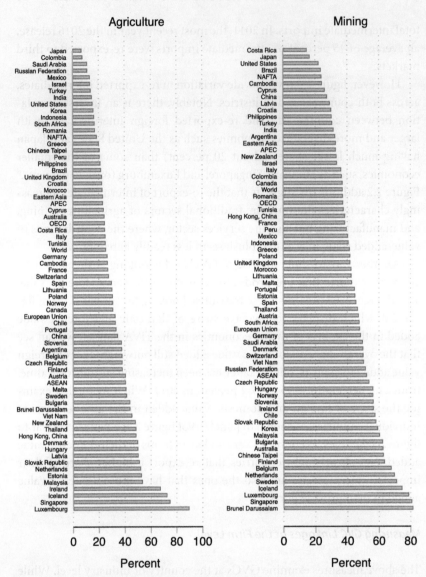

Agriculture

Japan
Colombia
Saudi Arabia
Russian Federation
Mexico
Israel
Turkey
India
United States
Korea
Indonesia
South Africa
Romania
NAFTA
Greece
Chinese Taipei
Peru
Philippines
Brazil
United Kingdom
Croatia
Morocco
Eastern Asia
APEC
Cyprus
Australia
OECD
Costa Rica
Italy
Tunisia
World
Germany
Cambodia
France
Switzerland
Spain
Lithuania
Poland
Norway
Canada
European Union
Chile
Portugal
China
Slovenia
Argentina
Belgium
Czech Republic
Finland
Austria
ASEAN
Malta
Sweden
Bulgaria
Brunei Darussalam
Viet Nam
New Zealand
Thailand
Hong Kong, China
Denmark
Hungary
Latvia
Slovak Republic
Netherlands
Estonia
Malaysia
Ireland
Iceland
Singapore
Luxembourg

0   20   40   60   80   100

Percent

Mining

Costa Rica
Japan
United States
Brazil
NAFTA
Cambodia
Cyprus
China
Latvia
Croatia
Philippines
Turkey
India
Argentina
Eastern Asia
APEC
New Zealand
Israel
Italy
Colombia
Canada
World
Romania
OECD
Tunisia
Hong Kong, China
France
Peru
Mexico
Indonesia
Greece
Poland
United Kingdom
Morocco
Lithuania
Malta
Portugal
Estonia
Spain
Thailand
Austria
South Africa
European Union
Germany
Saudi Arabia
Denmark
Switzerland
Viet Nam
Russian Federation
ASEAN
Czech Republic
Hungary
Norway
Slovenia
Ireland
Chile
Slovak Republic
Korea
Malaysia
Bulgaria
Australia
Chinese Taipei
Finland
Belgium
Netherlands
Sweden
Iceland
Luxembourg
Singapore
Brunei Darussalam

0   20   40   60   80

Percent

Fig. 2.2. Re-exported Intermediates as Percentage of Total Intermediate Imports by Major Industrial Sectors

Source: OECD, TiVA dataset, https://stats.oecd.org

Note: Data for 62 countries plus select regions in 2011.

Services

Manufacturing

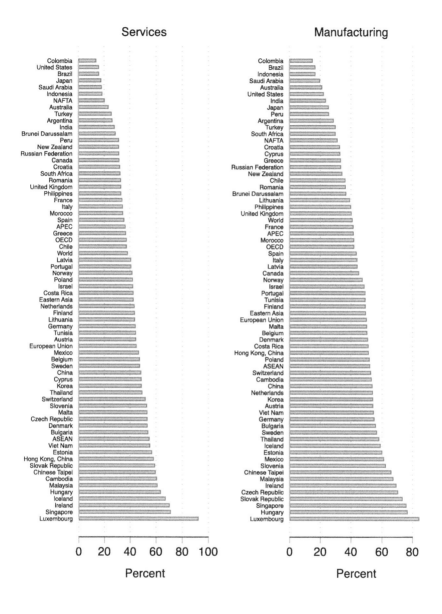

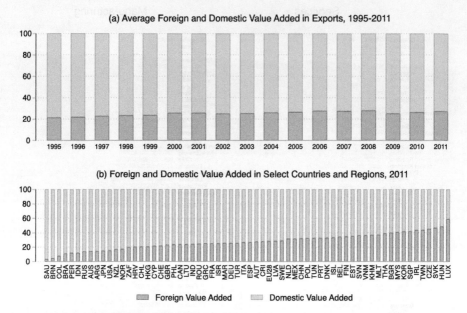

Fig. 2.3. Domestic and Foreign Value Added Embodied in Gross Exports
Source: OECD, TiVA dataset, https://stats.oecd.org

is that even though the unit of analysis is the firm, the data used to construct GVC linkages are still at the industry level. In other words, firms that
belong to the same industry will have the same GVC measure.

Alternatively, one can simply use industry-level GVC measures as a
proxy for firms within the same industry under the assumption of homoge-
neous production processes across firms within a given sector. This assumption, however, has become problematic with the emergence of new research
informed by heterogeneous trade theory (e.g., Melitz 2003). In the context
of global production networks, for instance, firms producing goods or services for export markets may use different production processes than firms
producing the same goods or services for domestic markets.

Developing more detailed firm-level GVC measures to reflect such heterogeneity is often challenging. A recent attempt is Ahmad et al.'s study
(2013), which constructs value-added measures using trade microdata
from Turkey. Specifically, they match trade and business activity information at the firm level by drawing from three data sources: a firm census from
Turkey's Annual Industry and Service Statistics database; import and export
flows from the Turkish trade register; and production data from the Annual

Industrial Products Statistics database of TurkStat. Such data are rarely available in most other countries.

Some recent efforts to address this problem seek to capture GVCs using new "bottom-up" business surveys instead of the "top-down" measures based on international input-output tables. Two such surveys are the Eurostat International Sourcing Survey and the 2010 National Organizations Survey (2010 NOS). The Eurostat International Sourcing Survey examines the relocation of the domestic production of goods and services to foreign countries for 13 European countries during the 2001–2006 period. The survey yields valuable information on both the geographical and industry distribution of the sourcing activities of European producers (Rikama et al. 2008). The 2010 National Organizations Survey, made available by the Inter-University Consortium for Political and Social Research, in turn provides quantitative data on the domestic and international sourcing activities of both private- and public-sector organizations in the United States. In particular, the 2010 NOS provides detailed data on the types of international locations and costs of 333 companies involved in international sourcing (Brown and Sturgeon 2014). Both surveys have been used to delineate the scope and operation of the sourcing activities of companies involved in GVCs in Europe and the United States.

As will be detailed in chapter 4, we adopt a similar approach by conducting a survey of business executives in China. In the absence of reliable firm-level input-output data, we asked firm executives a set of questions about the firm's import and export profile, the answers to which were then used to construct a proxy for its GVC linkages. While these measures do not capture the firm's precise GVC position, they should allow us to approximate to our best ability its level of GVC embeddedness.

Preferential Trade Agreements

In the previous section, we discussed the concept and measurement of GVCs in anticipation of the empirical analyses in the following chapters. In this section, we turn to the other phenomenon of interest: preferential trade agreements. We first provide an overview of the various forms of PTAs, their rapid proliferation in recent decades, and their effects on trade. We then review recent efforts to empirically measure the scope and depth of PTAs. The clarification of both of the two key concepts underlying this book—GVCs and PTAs—will facilitate the following discussions of how they may connect with each other.

The Proliferation of PTAs in the Global Trading System

PTAs are international agreements among a set of countries to promote economic integration by improving and stabilizing market access among member nations. This is typically achieved through the granting of preferential tariff treatment by member countries to each other, a practice that deviates from the most-favored-nation (MFN) principle at the heart of the World Trade Organization (WTO) and its predecessor, the General Agreement on Tariffs and Trade (GATT). Under the MFN principle, countries cannot discriminate between their trading partners by granting preferential tariff treatment to one partner country but not another. Instead they must extend any market access agreements negotiated with their trading partner(s) to all other WTO members. While the GATT/WTO enshrined the principles of MFN treatment, nondiscrimination, and national treatment in order to facilitate trade liberalization among member countries, Article XXIV of the GATT permitted bilateral and regional PTAs among its members on the condition that these arrangements did not result in increases in the level of trade protection against other members (Bhagwati 2008).

Even though we use the terms PTA, FTA, and RTA interchangeably throughout this book, it is important to note the differences between them. First, since members of most PTAs belong to a well-defined geographical area, regional PTAs are also called regional trade agreements (RTAs). Examples of RTAs include the Association of Southeast Asian Nations (ASEAN), the North American Free Trade Agreement (NAFTA) and its most recent successor, the United States-Mexico-Canada Agreement (USMCA), and the European Union (EU). Second, compared to PTAs that aim to lower but not completely eliminate tariff barriers, free trade agreements (FTAs) often have the introduction of zero tariffs as their ultimate objective. Furthermore, unlike PTAs, FTAs generally cover all or a larger portion of trade in goods and services. In other words, FTAs can be considered as the final goal of economic integration between two countries, with PTAs serving as a first step in that process. Still another important difference between FTAs and PTAs is that whereas FTA members generally maintain individually optimal external tariffs, this is not always the case with regard to PTAs as members in certain PTA arrangements, such as in a customs union (CU), can adopt common external tariffs (Saggie and Yildiz 2010; Saggi et al. 2013).

PTAs can be either bilateral or multilateral. Preferences extended to PTA member countries need not be extended to all trade among them, and the coverage also often depends on the type of PTA negotiated. Frankel et al. (1997) propose to classify PTAs into five categories, including free trade areas, CUs, preferential agreements (PAs), common markets, and economic unions.[7] In a free trade area, member countries agree to reduce or eliminate trade barriers on most, if not all, products traded among them. The ASEAN-China Free Trade Area (ACFTA) and the European Free Trade Association (EFTA) provide good examples of free trade areas. In CUs such as the Andean Community (CAN), the Caribbean Community (CARICOM), and the Gulf Cooperation Council, member countries further agree to maintain a common external trade policy, in addition to liberalizing trade with each other.

While free trade areas and customs unions are more common forms of PTAs, there are also preferential agreements (PAs), which grant member countries preferential access to particular segments of one another's markets;[8] common markets (CMs), in which member countries agree to maintain a liberal stance toward the movement of factors of production such as capital and labor among each other; and economic unions, whereby member countries go even further to also coordinate fiscal and monetary policies (Bhagwati 1993; de Melo and Panagariya 1993; Bhagwati and Panagariya 1996). These PTAs can therefore be distinguished from one another by the level of integration, with PAs being the least integrative and economic unions embodying the highest level of integration.

Examples of the three latter types of PTAs can be found in the history of economic cooperation among Western European countries in the post–World War II era. In 1957, the six original members of the European Coal and Steel Community (ECSC) signed the Treaty of Rome establishing the European Economic Community (EEC), thereby transforming the grouping into a CU. The deepening of economic ties among European countries subsequently led the EEC to evolve into a common market with the conclusion of a Single European Act in 1986. In 1992, 17 European countries further signed the Maastricht Treaty establishing the EU, an economic union that entails not only trade cooperation but also monetary union among member states.

During the past few decades, PTAs have proliferated rapidly, despite the progressive strengthening of the multilateral trading system. Since 1995, more than 400 PTAs covering trade in goods or services have been notified to the WTO, and almost all of the WTO members are member to at least one PTA.[9] While the European Union has the largest network of PTAs in the world, other world regions have also witnessed a rising number of PTAs. For example, NAFTA, signed in 1993, was aimed at promoting economic integration among the United States, Canada, and Mexico. In South America, Mercosur, consisting of Argentina, Brazil, Paraguay, Uruguay, Venezuela (suspended since December 1, 2016), and a few other associate members, was established in 1991 to promote the free movement of goods, people, and currency among member countries. As well, African countries have moved to establish a number of PTAs in recent decades, including the South African Development Community (SADC), the East African Community, the Common Market for Eastern and Southern Africa (COMESA), the Economic Community of West African States (ECOWAS), and the Economic Community of Central African States (ECCAS). Even Asia, a region that has tended to lag behind in the establishment of PTAs, has seen strong momentum toward preferential trade liberalization in recent years. As of July 2016, 260 PTAs involving at least one Asian country were in force, signed, or being negotiated.[10]

The issues covered by PTAs vary considerably. Most agreements cover trade in goods, trade in services, or both. Some go further to include disciplines on foreign investment, labor rights, and the environment, and even contain provisions in sectors not covered by the WTO (Horn et al. 2010). More recently, the major negotiating economies have shifted trade negotiation emphasis toward the so-called mega-regional trade agreements. This change is a result of the stalemate in the WTO's Doha Round trade negotiations, geopolitical and national security concerns (especially in the United States) about the rise of China, and the growing interest of multinational firms in global supply chains to protect foreign investments, further reduce the costs of shipping goods across national borders, and improve product regulations across different markets. Three prime examples of mega-PTAs—the Trans-Pacific Partnership (TPP),[11] the Transatlantic Trade and Investment Partnership (TTIP) negotiations between the United States and the European Union,[12] and the Regional Comprehensive Economic Partnership (RCEP) negotiations spearheaded by China[13]—have raised the potential for these agreements to serve as the primary means of dealing with trade and investment relations among member countries, and therefore important questions about the future of the multilateral trading system centered on the WTO (Bown 2017a).

The Trade Effects of PTAs

The growing prominence of PTAs in the global trading system has spurred considerable scholarly interest in the economic welfare implications of these agreements. In particular, as PTAs liberalize trade among members but discriminate against third parties, the recourse to regionalism at a time of the rapid expansion of global trade has prompted questions about whether these agreements are stumbling blocks or stepping stones to trade liberalization on a global scale (Frankel and Wei 1996; Limao 2006; Bhagwati 2008).

Following the pioneering work of Viner (1950), economists have framed their analysis of the economic effects of PTAs in terms of trade creation and trade diversion. Trade creation occurs when the reduction of trade barriers within an agreement leads member countries to shift imports from less efficient producers outside the bloc to more efficient producers within it. In contrast, there is trade diversion when trade is shifted from more efficient producers within the arrangement to less efficient producers outside of it as a result of preferential tariff liberalization (Viner 1950).

Viner's original framework has inspired a relatively large body of literature regarding the impact of PTAs on the open multilateral trading system.[14] However, empirical analysis of the trade effects of PTAs has yielded inconclusive evidence. As Clausing (2001, 678) put it, the challenges of empirically sorting out the economic effects of PTAs are so daunting that extant empirical work on this subject cannot answer "even the most basic issue regarding preferential trading agreements: whether trade creation outweighs trade diversion." For example, while some studies have produced strong evidence pointing to the trade-creation effects of PTAs (e.g., Baier and Bergstrand 2007; Clausing 2001; Magee 2008), others conclude instead that PTAs may either exert a trade-diversion effect or have no effect on member countries' trade volume (Krueger 1999).

The Depth of PTAs

Still another dimension of PTAs that has captured considerable scholarly attention is variation in the design, in particular the depth of these agreements. In the context of international institutions, "depth" refers to the extent to which an international agreement constrains state behavior or, as Downs et al. (1996) put it, "requires states to depart from what they would have done in its absence." Deep international trade agreements not only contain significant tariff liberalization measures but also include more rigorous provisions with regard to the liberalization of services trade or the protection and liberalization of foreign direct investment (Baccini et al. 2015; WTO 2011). They additionally contain provisions that address behind-the-border measures such as technical standards, food safety, animal and plant health measures, intellectual property rights (IPR) protection, and competition rules that discriminate against foreign producers.

By harmonizing international product standards or technical regulations, these policies may help reduce transaction costs and promote market integration. Strong discipline against IPR infringements may facilitate market access and technology transfer for exporters and foreign investors. Competition provisions may in turn promote exports and foreign investment by addressing cross-border anti-competitive practices (Maskus and Penubarti 1995; Piermartini and Budetta 2009). Together with the level of tariff concessions, these provisions concerning services, standards, investment, IPR, competition, and government procurement define the depth of a trade agreement (Baccini et al. 2015).

A number of studies have sought to measure the depth of coverage of PTAs. In a study of U.S. and EU PTAs, Horn et al. (2010) classify the subjects covered by these agreements into two categories: "WTO+" and "WTO-X provisions." "WTO+" provisions are those whose commitments exceed what the parties have accepted at the WTO, even though they generally fall under the WTO mandate. Examples of such provisions include customs regulations, export taxes, antidumping rules, countervailing measures, technical barriers to trade (TBTs), and sanitary and phytosanitary measures (SPS). In contrast, "WTO-X" provisions are those not currently covered under the WTO, such as investment, labor, and environmental standards (Hoffman et al. 2017).

Horn et al. further examine the extent to which the obligations contained in the agreements are legally enforceable, as well as the "depth" of legally binding commitments or the magnitude of the undertakings involved. The legal enforceability of PTA obligations is determined by the clarity of the language used in the text of the agreement, with the assumption that clear, specific, and unambiguous legal language should be more legally enforceable because it is more likely to be successfully invoked by a complainant in a dispute settlement proceeding. The depth of an agreement has subsequently been measured by the number of enforceable provisions covered by an agreement or the frequency with which a particular provision is implemented (Orefice and Rocha 2014; WTO 2011).

Building on the approach of Horn et al. (2010), the WTO conducted a study of 100 PTAs signed by 178 countries in 2011 that highlighted the potential overlap between existing PTAs and the WTO, documenting in detail the range of commitments as well as the depth and legal enforceability of the provisions embedded in these agreements. A number of other studies (e.g., Hofmann et al. 2017; Kleimann 2014; Villalta Puig and Dalke 2016) have also adopted similar approaches to analyze the legal enforceability and depth of PTA provisions.

In addition to these attempts by economists to analyze the content of PTAs, political scientists have also more recently engaged in similar endeavors, the most notable of which is the Design of Trade Agreements (DESTA) database, developed by Dür et al. (2014). The database, which covers 809 PTAs signed between 1945 and 2016 that include specific provisions regarding preferential liberalization of trade in goods and/or services, codes the depth of each agreement according to the provisions in 10 areas of cooperation: market access, services, investments, IPR, competition, public procurement, standards, trade remedies, nontrade issues, and dispute settlement.

Specifically, the DESTA database contains two measures of PTA depth. One is an additive index (*depth_index*) that encompasses seven PTA provisions, including not only whether the agreement aims to create a full trade area by requiring that member states reduce all tariffs to zero but also whether it contains any substantive provisions with regard to services trade, investments, standards, public procurement, competition, and IPR.[15] The other depth measure (*depth_rasch*) is derived by conducting latent trait analysis, a type of factor analysis for binary data, on a total of 48 variables that capture the depth of an agreement in areas such as services liberalization, IPR protection, and trade-related investment measures. Specifically, the analysis is performed using the Rasch model, which assumes that each item captures one underlying latent dimension but with different weights, to generate a value. This procedure is thus able to take account of the differential effects of each dimension in measuring countries' PTA commitments. According to Dür et al. (2014), these two measures are highly correlated, with a Pearson correlation coefficient (r) of 0.90. Furthermore, both measures point to a substantial increase in the depth of PTAs during the past two decades, despite considerable variation across agreements.

Figure 2.4 presents the growth in the number and depth of PTAs from 1948 to 2014, based on the DESTA database. As it shows, the number of PTAs signed each year increased steadily during the period under consideration, peaking at a total of 43 in both 1992 and 1995. Parallel to the growth in the number of PTAs is an increase in the depth of these agreements. The average of *depth_index* has risen from 1.00 in 1948 to 6.60 in 2014, while that of *depth_rasch* has increased from −1.34 to 1.55 during the same period.[16]

As we will discuss in more detail in chapter 6, we use the DESTA database for our empirical analysis on the formation and depth of PTAs due to its comprehensive coverage of the period for which the TiVA dataset is also available. Compared to other datasets on PTAs, such as the one provided by the World Bank, the aggregate PTA depth scores available from the DEPSA dataset also facilitate the ease of interpretation.

GVCs and Deep PTAs: Some Preliminary Evidence

The connection between GVCs and PTAs has more recently received some scholarly attention. With a couple of exceptions,[17] most research on this issue focuses on the role of deep PTAs in stimulating trade, particularly value-added trade, rather than vice versa. For example, an earlier study by Estevadeordal and Suominen (2005) examines the effect of rules of origin (ROOs) in PTAs on trade flows, including trade in intermediate goods, finding that PTAs with restrictive and selective ROOs in final goods boost input trade among PTA members, thus inducing trade diversion in intermediate products.

Using the DESTA database, Dür et al. (2014) employ the gravity model to estimate the effect of PTAs on trade flows. The findings suggest that PTAs, especially deep agreements that address behind-the-border trade barriers, exert a positive effect on trade flows. *World Trade Report 2011* (WTO 2011) similarly suggests that countries with deeper agreements tend to have higher trade volumes than those with shallow ones, as one additional provision in the PTA is associated with a 2 percent increase in trade in parts and components on average. More recently, Noguera (2012) and Johnson and Noguera (2014) have examined the impact of PTAs on bilat-

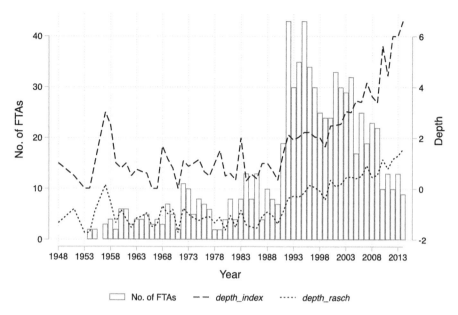

Fig. 2.4. Growth in the Number and Depth of Preferential Trade Agreements, 1948–2014
Source: DESTA database.

eral trade flows versus value-added trade flows, finding that PTAs have a stronger effect on the former than on the latter. Specifically, PTA signatories are likely to experience a 23 percent increase in total trade volume, compared to 15 percent in value-added trade during the first five years following the signing of the agreement. This is because while tariff liberalization should reduce the costs of moving goods multiple times across national borders, therefore facilitating trade in intermediate goods, the value-added trade measure only counts such multiple border crossings once instead of multiple times, thus making the effect of PTAs less pronounced for the value-added measure than for the gross measure. A study by Gonzalez (2012) yields similar results, showing that an FTA leads to a 25 percent increase in the value of intermediate imports once the endogenous formation of trade agreements is controlled for.

Drawing on recently available World Bank data on PTA provisions, Osnago, Rocha, and Ruta (2016) employ the gravity model to assess the impact of PTA depth on GVC integration, measured by both trade in parts and components and trade in value added.[18] The study finds that PTAs play an important role in boosting GVC participation, as each additional PTA provision is associated with a 1.5 percent increase in bilateral parts and components trade and a 0.4 percent increase in re-exported value added. The same study additionally considers the possibility that deep PTAs may be more effective in boosting trade in sectors with a higher level of GVC integration, and yields some evidence in support of the conjecture.

Orefice and Rocha (2014) use an augmented gravity equation to examine the impact of deep integration on production network trade. Deep integration is measured using a set of indices of the depth of the key issue areas covered in 96 PTAs between 1958 and 2010, while production network trade is measured using import values in parts and components as a proxy. The empirical results indicate that deeper agreements may lead to a 35 percentage points increase in production networks trade between the trading partners. Further, they find that this effect is particularly pronounced with respect to trade in automobile parts and information and technology products rather than textiles products.

Overall, existing research has mostly focused on the effect of deep PTAs in boosting value-chain integration. So far, few studies have specifically addressed the possibility that the causal arrow could run in the other direction, that is, rapid GVC growth may in turn stimulate the formation of PTAs, in particular deep PTAs with rigorous trade and investment liberalization provisions.[19] We address this gap in the literature through both systematic cross-national analyses of the effects of GVCs on PTA formation and an in-depth examination of the firm preferences that underlie the observed empirical patterns.

The Cases of China and the United States

In this section, we further draw on the examples of China and the United States to shed light on the two key analytical constructs of this study: GVCs and PTAs. Since our analysis of the effect of GVCs on firm trade preferences is based mainly on these two country cases, the background information presented in this section also helps to set the stage for the empirical analysis that follows.

China in Global Value Chains

China's participation in GVCs has gradually deepened as a result of the country's growing integration into the global economy. As China's export drive in the earlier years of the reform process primarily took the form of export processing, whereby Chinese firms imported raw materials, equipment, and intermediate products for further processing before exporting to other countries, it has increasingly become embedded in GVCs. The iPhone or iPad embossed with "Designed by Apple in California. Made in China" provides a good illustration of this phenomenon. While highly indicative of the growing fragmentation of production across national borders, this phrase may only factor in the beginning and end of a long and complex global production chain without also taking into account the hundreds of other imported components needed to manufacture these products.

With China's emergence as a "world factory" and a manufacturing hub for many multinational corporations, it has increasingly integrated into GVCs at a much faster pace compared to most other countries. This is illustrated in figure 2.5, which presents the average backward and forward GVC linkages of China between 1995 and 2011 in comparison to the rest of the countries included in the TiVA database. China's average backward GVC linkage with the rest of the TiVA countries—defined as the FVA embodied in exports as a percentage of China's total exports to these countries—increased from 0.25 percent in 1995 to 1.85 percent in 2011. At the same time, its forward GVC linkage with these countries—defined as DVA embodied in the partner countries' exports as a percentage of the source country exports—has increased from 0.15 percent to 0.24 percent during the same period. On the aggregate level, the share of domestic and foreign value added in China's final demand stood at 83 percent and 17 percent in 2009, respectively (OECD 2013a). The share of foreign content in China's exports further rose to about one-third by 2011, the second highest among G20 countries, after South Korea (OECD-WTO 2015a).

Figures 2.6 presents China's average backward and forward GVC linkages between 1995 and 2011 by country. The bottom panel of figure 2.6, which presents China's backward GVC linkages, reveals the importance of Asian countries such as Cambodia, Vietnam, South Korea, Thailand, and Singapore as major suppliers of foreign inputs for Chinese exports. The top panel of figure 2.6, showing China's forward GVC linkages, in turn suggests that more developed countries, such as the United States, Japan, France, and the United Kingdom, tend to draw on a higher share of DVA from China in their exports.

Several characteristics of China's GVC participation are worth noting. First, while China is not the only country with a high level of GVC integration, what distinguishes it from other GVC-embedded countries such as

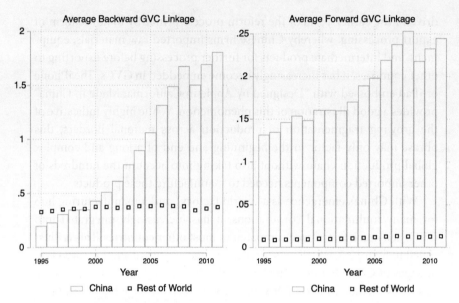

Fig. 2.5. Average Backward and Forward GVC Linkages of China and Other
Countries in the TiVA Dataset, 1995–2011 (%)
Source: OECD, TiVA dataset.
Note: The GVC linkages for China are the average between China and the rest of the coun-
tries included in the TiVA dataset. GVC linkages for "ROW (rest of the world)" are the aver-
age of the forward and backward GVCs of all the other bilateral pairs (excluding China).

Japan, South Korea, Singapore, and Malaysia is its sheer size and its relatively high level of export-to-GDP ratio, which has stood at around 35 percent in past years, compared to 8 percent for the United States and 13 percent for India (Koopman, Wang, and Wei 2008).

Second, in terms of sectoral variation, the electrical equipment industry
stands out as having a particularly high level of GVC integration, in large
part due to its extensive assembly activities and high level of reliance on
foreign inputs. According to the TiVA database, the electrical and optical
equipment sector had the highest average share (65 percent) of FVA in
gross exports among all sectors between 1995 and 2011. Only the textiles
and footwear industry had a greater share of re-exported intermediate
imports in intermediate exports (68 percent). In addition to having strong
backward GVC linkages, this sector has extensive forward GVC linkages,
with its DVA embodied in foreign exports accounting for 3.22 percent of
gross exports. Besides the electrical and optical equipment sector, the tex-

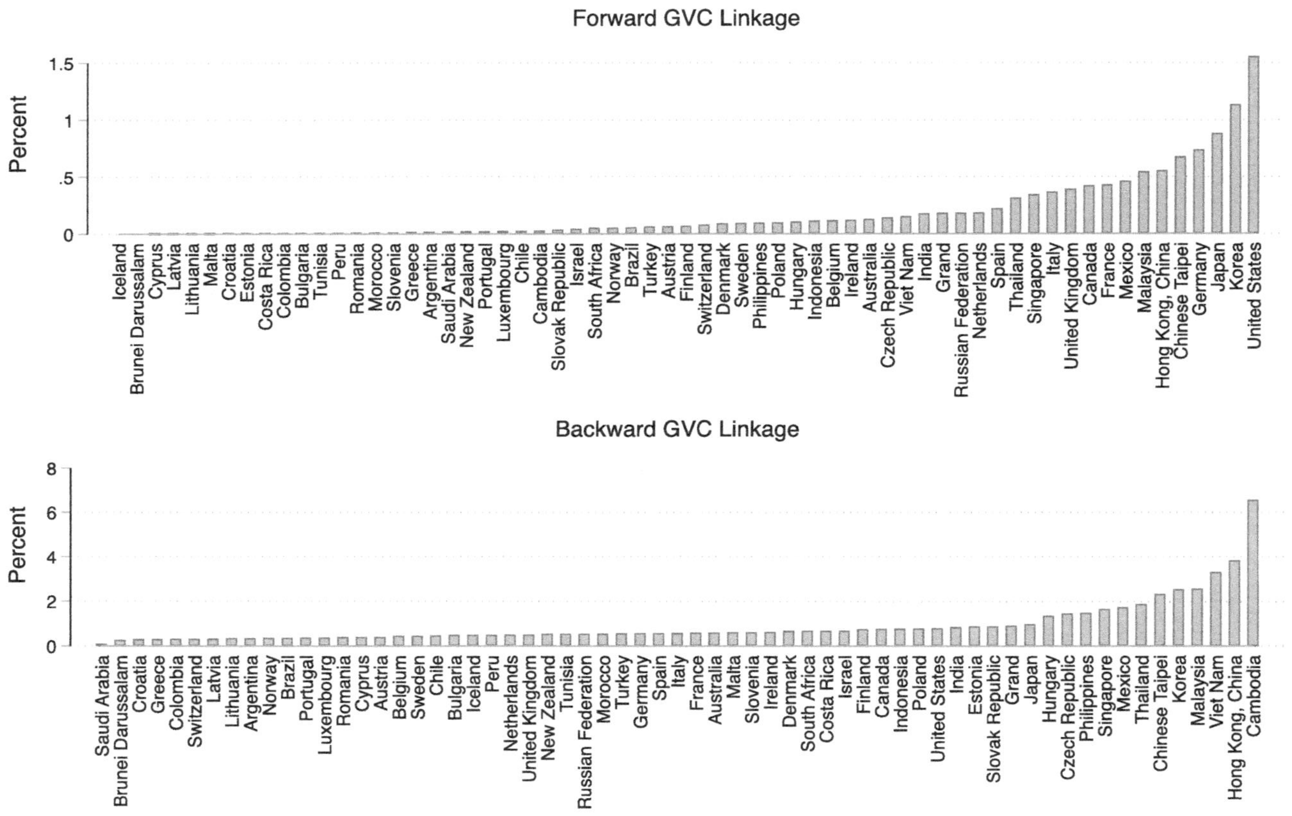

Forward GVC Linkage

Backward GVC Linkage

Fig. 2.6. China's Average Backward and Forward GVC Linkage by Partner Country, 1995–2011 (%)

Source: OECD, TiVA dataset, https://stats.oecd.org

tiles, leather, and footwear sector also stands out as having both strong backward and forward GVC linkages; this may reflect the salience of processing trade for labor-intensive manufacturing industries in China, especially during the early years of reform. For manufacturing industries as a whole, imports of intermediates represent key drivers of China's backward GVC participation.

Third, in examining a country's GVC integration, it is important to take into consideration not only the level of its GVC participation but also its ability to promote domestic economic growth by creating value in GVCs. In other words, it is necessary for us to look at the relative share of foreign versus domestic value added in a country's final demand, or sales, within its domestic market, as many developing countries have sought to capture a greater share of DVA per dollar of exports, or to "move up the value chain" through growing GVC participation.

Here it is interesting to note that while most countries have experienced declines in the DVA embedded in their exports with growing GVC participation, China has defied this trend, with the share of DVA in its exports rising from 65 percent in 2000 to 70 percent in 2007. The increase was particularly pronounced in the processing sector, which saw this share increasing from 46 percent to 55 percent during the same period.[20] In contrast to the important role of DVA, FVA constituted a much smaller share of China's total final demand, amounting to just 17 percent of total final demand in 2009.[21] Whereas foreign content constituted about three-quarters of China's total exports in the information and communications technology (ICT) sector in 1995, that number dropped to a little over a half by 2011, a trend that can also be observed in other high-tech sectors, such as electrical machinery and transport equipment (OECD-WTO 2015). Kee and Tang (2016) suggest that the growing importance of domestic relative to foreign activities for China's exports can best be explained by the fact that Chinese exporters are increasingly substituting domestic for imported materials in terms of both volume and varieties, rather than by other factors such as rising wages or the growing share of high-DVA or nonprocessing industries in China's total exports.

The apparel industry provides a particularly good example of China's success in upgrading along GVCs. According to Frederick (2016), the industry successfully upgraded along several dimensions, such as process, product, end-market, and function, by offering a wide variety of product categories, developing a good reputation, emphasizing product affordability and reliability, and engaging in an acceptable level of compliance. She further attributes this success to a combination of micro- and macro-level dynamics. At the micro-level, these include the industry's ability to: cultivate a functional division between production and sales and establish sourcing offices in the Greater China area so as to forge closer relationships with global buyers; continuously engage in technological and production process upgrading to reduce the cost of production; and effectively anticipate possible shifts in suppliers and make the necessary adjustment to business strategy accordingly. At the macrolevel, industrial policies that encourage upgrading and the development of global competitiveness—including providing loans and grants and other forms of support, targeting markets in the developing world without established buyer-supplier relationships under the Go Out policy, and identifying and creating niches in a diversified industry—also played an important role in the industry's ability to capitalize on the opportunities brought about by growing GVC integration (Fredrick 2016).

Finally, another important dimension of China's GVC participation concerns the role of services in the value chain. As manufacturing exports now increasingly involve value added from services industries (e.g., logistics, communication services, business services, design, marketing, and after-sales care), we are now witnessing a growing trend toward servicification, or "the increase of purchases, production, sale, and export of services" in manufacturing (Lodefalk 2015). In China's case, services value added has grown in importance during the past decades, with the services sector's share of total exports of DVA reaching 41.9 percent in 2011. Services value added accounted for about 31.1 percent of China's manufactured exports in the same year, slightly lower than the average for the Organisation for Economic Co-operation and Development (OECD) of 36.9 percent. The wholesale, retail, and hotels sector took up a relatively large share of total gross exports (12.2 percent), followed by business services (6.6 percent) and transport and telecommunications services (5.6 percent) (OECD-WTO 2015).

China and Its FTAs

The development of FTAs in China, and in East Asia more broadly, tends to lag behind that elsewhere in the world, such as the United States or Europe. By the end of 2002, all five of the world's 30 leading economies that did not yet belong to any FTAs were found in East Asia: China, Hong Kong, Japan, South Korea, and Taiwan. According to Gao (2011) and Nakagawa and Liang (2015), resource constraints, hostility toward FTAs in the pre-reform era, strategic considerations relating to the imperative of WTO entry, and China's relatively heavy dependence on the U.S. export market and hence on an open world economy may explain why regional trade liberalization was not high on the country's negotiation agenda early on in the process.

However, since becoming a member of the WTO in 2001, China has been actively exploring trade opportunities in global markets through bilateral and regional free trade agreements. In light of the slow progress toward multilateral trade negotiations under the WTO, the emergence and proliferation of RTAs elsewhere in the world, and the need to search for new markets, the Chinese leadership has gradually come to see preferential trade liberalization as a useful supplement to multilateral trade liberalization (Gao 2011). The increasing competition Chinese exports posed to developing countries also led Chinese leaders to increasingly realize the importance of promoting regional economic cooperation in order to reassure China's neighbors of the nonpredatory nature of China's "peaceful development" (Katada and Solís 2010).

It was against this background that China signed its first FTA, the Framework Agreement on China-ASEAN Comprehensive Economic Cooperation, in November 2002. Since then China has signed a total of 16 bilateral or regional FTAs with almost 30 countries and regions in both the developed and developing worlds, including the Asia-Pacific Trade Agreement (Bangladesh, India, Laos, South Korea, and Sri Lanka, 2002) and trade agreements with Hong Kong (2003), Macao (2003), Chile (2007), Pakistan (2007), New Zealand (2008), Singapore (2009), Peru (2010), Taiwan (2010), Costa Rica (2011), Iceland (2014), Switzerland (2014), Australia (2015), South Korea (2015), Maldives (2017), and Georgia (2018). Currently, China is negotiating FTAs with the Gulf Cooperation Council, Australia, Israel, Mauritius, Moldova, Norway, and Sri Lanka. It has also entered into upgrade or second-phase FTA negotiations with ASEAN, New Zealand, and Pakistan, and negotiations are under way toward the conclusion of a China-Japan-Korea FTA as well as the RCEP. In addition, China has proposed FTA joint feasibility studies with countries such as Bengal, Canada, Colombia, Fiji, Mongolia, Nepal, Palestine, Panama, and Papua New Guinea.[22] Appendix 2.1 presents an overview of China's bilateral and regional FTA activities.

An important characteristic of Chinese FTAs is that they entail a relatively low level of trade liberalization and legal obligations. According to Antkiewicz and Whalley (2005, 1554), China's FTAs are characterized by diversity in terms of form and coverage, brevity and "hence the inevitable vagueness of the texts involved," and the "absence of explicit and clear dispute resolution procedures with conciliation between the parties being relied upon." Focusing mainly on liberalizing trade in goods and services, these agreements tend to exclude sensitive sectors and issues that may be difficult to deal with, such as intellectual property protection, dispute settlement mechanisms, special sectoral liberalization, environment, and labor standards (Hufbauer and Wong 2005). Furthermore, Chinese negotiators have tended to adopt a gradual and piecemeal approach to FTA negotiations, initially focusing on trade liberalization in goods, to be extended to broader issues such as trade liberalization in services and investment promotion at a later stage.[23] Similarly, China's FTA negotiations have proceeded gradually, starting with smaller partners in the developing world, followed by negotiations with developed countries.

The diversity and varying coverage of China's FTAs can be seen by comparing its agreements with developing and developed countries such as those with ASEAN and New Zealand. While ACFTA incorporates commitments to the general principles of development cooperation in addition to targeted and precise tariff liberalization commitments, the FTA with New Zealand in turn puts greater emphasis on the latter than the former, in a way that reflects New Zealand's developed country status (Whalley and Li 2014).

Slight variation may be discerned even among China's FTAs with developed countries. For example, while both the China-Korea FTA and the China-Australia FTA (ChAFTA), which we will discuss in more detail in chapter 3, go beyond tariff liberalization in agriculture and manufactured goods to include expanded coverage in areas such as services and investment, telecommunications, e-commerce, and government procurement, the China-Korea FTA includes a stand-alone competition chapter that is not in ChAFTA and is only seen in a handful of China's FTAs with other countries such as Switzerland and Iceland. It also includes provisions on nontrade issues such as environment policy that are absent in ChAFTA (Jiang 2019; Li et al. 2017; SSCC 2018).

There are a few potential explanations for why China's FTAs, especially those signed in earlier years, tend to be of lower quality and "economically less meaningful" (Bergsten et al. 2008). First, the rather comprehensive trade liberalization concessions Beijing has made in its WTO accession negotiations have led many Chinese officials to believe that the country needs some breathing room to adjust to its WTO commitments before it can take on additional deep trade liberalization measures (Nakagawa and Liang 2017). Second, China's piecemeal approach to FTA negotiations may have reflected Chinese negotiators' desire to gradually develop the requisite experience and skills so as to gain leverage with larger economic partners in future negotiations (Hufbauer and Wong 2005; Katada and Solís 2010). Third, the incremental process of trade negotiation and the shallow trade liberalization underlying China's FTAs may serve a political purpose by allowing the leadership to carve out areas of special protection for vested domestic interests and provide domestic opponents with more time to adjust to more extensive and potentially painful trade liberalization measures in the future (Jiang 2008; Zeng 2010). Finally, and perhaps most importantly, a number of studies (e.g., Bergsten 2008; Kwei 2006; Chin and Stubbs 2008) have noted the primacy that Chinese FTAs place on geopolitical and strategic interests. From such a perspective, the predominance of strategic and noneconomic objectives in China's FTA diplomacy has led Chinese officials to negotiate agreements with low levels of obligation, and this may in turn complicate the prospect of creating a broader framework for regional trade liberalization.

The United States: GVC and PTA Participation

As a large economy, the United States has a lower GVC participation rate than many other developed countries, particularly with regard to backward GVC linkages, as it sources only a small share of intermediate inputs from abroad. In other words, only a relatively small share of the final demand for manufactured goods and market services in the United States derives from foreign value added, while the majority represents domestic value added created within the country. In 2016, the share of foreign value added in gross exports was only 9.04 percent for the United States, compared to 16.48 percent for the Euro area, 13.54 percent for East Asia, and 28.19 percent for ASEAN. In contrast, the share of domestic value added in gross exports reached 90.96 percent for the United States, compared to 83.52 percent, 86.46 percent, and 71.81 percent for the Euro area, East Asia, and ASEAN, respectively.[24]

In terms of sectoral distribution, chemical and business services lead other sectors in forward GVC participation due to the relatively large share of intermediate goods produced by these sectors that end up in the exports of other countries. Business services, for example, have the highest level of domestic value added, at 96.05 percent in 2016. In contrast, manufacturing industries such as coke and petroleum products, motor vehicles, transport equipment, and machinery and equipment have the highest levels of foreign value added share in gross exports, reaching 26.82 percent, 23.77 percent, 18.26 percent, and 18.04 percent, respectively, in 2016.[25] Certain manufacturing industries, such as textiles, are only marginally involved in GVCs.

One important feature that differentiates the United States from China is the greater importance of the service sector in facilitating the efficient functioning of GVCs. As manufacturing exports now extend beyond goods production to include significant value added from service industries such as design, development, marketing, and after-sales care, services have emerged as important links for connecting firms' globally dispersed production processes (Jones and Kierzkowski 2001). In addition to serving as critical links in GVCs, services may also constitute important inputs in manufacturing activities. For example, outsourced research, design, and engineering activities are often indispensable to the early stages of production processes, while marketing and distribution services play important roles in connecting the product to the consumer (Heuser and Mattoo 2017). Furthermore, services are increasingly provided not only through arm's-length market-based transactions but also in-house, leading to "servicification" even within manufacturing firms (Kelle 2013; Miroudot and Cadestin 2017).

The increasingly important role of services in enabling GVCs is reflected in the rising share of services value added in U.S. manufacturing exports. In 2011, services value added—including business services, distribution services, transport and telecommunications, and financial services—represented about 32.1 percent of U.S. manufacturing exports, slightly below the OECD average of 36.9 percent. The wholesale, retail, and hotel sectors, business services, and transportation and telecoms have the highest levels of value added in total gross exports, at 12.2 percent, 11.3 percent, and 3.9 percent, respectively (OECD-WTO 2015b).

In chapter 5, we examine how the rise of GVCs is shaping the U.S. approach to FTA negotiations, using the TPP negotiations as the main case. It should be noted, however, that far from being a leader, the United States has often been a follower in bilateral and RTA negotiations. Given America's long-standing preoccupation with global trade liberalization, it was only in the early 1980s that Washington belatedly jumped onto the RTA bandwagon in view of the "demonstration effects" of such agreements (Baldwin 1997). Still, Washington started off slowly, with the negotiation of free trade accords with Israel (1985) and Canada (1988), justified on the grounds of strategic relations, geographic proximity, or close economic ties through intra-industry trade and investment (Feinberg 2003). When Mexico later sought a similar agreement, the Clinton administration managed to bring NAFTA to fruition, despite substantial domestic concerns about the threat that the agreement might pose to labor-intensive industries in the United States (Destler 2016).

The move toward FTAs accelerated in the early years of the Clinton administration, with the United States joining other Asia-Pacific Economic Cooperation (APEC) nations as well as Western Hemisphere nations to negotiate what would be some of the world's largest free trade areas. However, this stream of activities was largely scuttled by domestic opposition stemming from within the president's own party, as Congress' refusal to extend to the president the fast-track negotiation authority that was very much needed to bring FTA negotiations to a conclusion left President Clinton with only one, largely uncontroversial, FTA with Jordan concluded when he left office.

The pace of regionalization gained momentum again under the George W. Bush administration, when bilateral and regional trade negotiations came to be viewed by key trade officials such as U.S. Trade Representative (USTR) Robert Zoellick as a useful supplement to multilateral trade negotiations (Zoellick 2001a, 2001b). The fact that President Bush managed to secure fast-track negotiation authority—renamed trade promotion authority—from Congress facilitated this process, leading to the signing of FTAs with Chile and Singapore in 2003. This was followed by the conclusion or ratification of more FTAs with U.S. trading partners, including with Morocco, Australia, Central America, and the Dominican Republic (CAFTA-DR),[26] Bahrain, Oman, Peru, Colombia, Panama, and South Korea.

Overall, as Destler (2016) pointed out, while the debate over free trade in the earlier decades pitted the winners of trade, in particular exporters and international investors, against the losers of trade in the import-competing sectors, such a pattern had shifted by the 1990s as most large U.S. industries had internationalized their production and come to see FTAs as serving their interests. Opposition to trade liberalization instead stemmed largely from an anti-globalization coalition composed mainly of labor and environmental groups who saw free trade as exacerbating the income gap between the rich and poor and inflicting serious damage on the environment.

In this uncertain political environment, President Obama—who took little initiative on trade in his first term—became a strong advocate for mega-regional trade agreements such as the TPP and TTIP in his second term. However, dwindling political support for free trade among not only rank-and-file Republicans but also establishment Republicans, reinforced by widespread discontent among labor leaders with the negative effect of globalization on manufacturing jobs and wages, cast a shadow over the future of these agreements. The fate of the TPP was doomed when President Trump, who viewed the TPP as a poorly negotiated agreement that gave away U.S. power, pulled the United States out of the agreement.

While political circumstances prevented the TPP from coming to fruition, the negotiations over this agreement nevertheless offered a valuable opportunity for us to examine our arguments regarding how variation in firms' GVC positions may shape their negotiation preferences and strategies. We will show that while GVC linkage does not explain the actual negotiation outcome, it does explain why businesses with strong GVC ties were able to influence the articles and texts of TPP agreements in a way that broadly reflected their interests, a story that will be the focus of chapter 5.

Conclusion

In this chapter, we have defined the two key concepts that will inform the rest of our analyses: GVCs and PTAs. We have shown that most existing works on the nexus between the two focus on the effect of PTAs in stimulating intermediate goods trade instead of how GVC integration may affect the formation and depth of PTAs. As we test our key theoretical propositions mainly based on the experiences of China and the United States—the world's two largest economies that simultaneously occupy important positions in global supply chain activities—we also provided an overview of their growing enmeshment in GVCs and recent moves to embrace FTAs.

Overall, this chapter sets the stage for the subsequent analyses of the role of GVCs in shaping firm preferences and lobbying for preferential trade liberalization and the pattern of PTA formation. In chapter 3, we begin our empirical inquiries by zooming in on the individual firms. Drawing on in-depth fieldwork in China, we will examine how the different GVC positions of Chinese firms affect their experiences with and attitudes toward preferential trade agreements.

CHAPTER 3

GVCs and PTA Utilization

Evidence from Chinese Firms

On a particularly sweltering afternoon in the summer of 2018, a small conference room of the Jiangsu Department of Commerce in Nanjing was packed with people for a consultation meeting on how firms in Jiangsu could benefit from China's existing and future free trade agreements (FTAs). In attendance were officials from the department, the provincial Administration of Quality Supervision, Inspection and Quarantine (AQSIQ), and the local branch of the China Council for the Promotion of International Trade (CCPIT), as well as dozens of representatives from firms and industry associations across the province.

During the first part of the meeting, managers from a number of firms told stories about their experiences with China's recently signed FTAs, including those with Australia and South Korea, and credited these agreements with being crucial in helping them increase sales, expand into new markets, and reduce the costs of input materials in spite of rising labor costs, exchange rate fluctuations, and heightened protectionist policies adopted by countries such as the United States. These firms came from a diverse range of industries and localities and included a carpet manufacturer in Nantong, an integrated circuit producer in Suzhou, a supplier of heat-sink materials for cell phones in Zhenjiang, and a trading firm in Nanjing.

A casual observer at the meeting may have come away with the impression that firms in Jiangsu were benefiting greatly from China's FTAs, but the reality was far from that. In fact, one of the main goals of this meeting was for officials to gather information from import and export firms and figure out how the government could "help firms step up their usage of FTAs," according to the deputy director of the provincial AQSIQ.[1] The aforementioned firms were invited to share their success stories with other firms that had "failed to take full advantage of the potential gains from these FTAs."[2]

A closer examination of these FTA users reveals that all of them are well plugged into global value chains (GVCs) in one way or another. The carpet manufacturer, a subsidiary of a multinational firm headquartered in Dalton, Georgia, imports wool from Australia, turns it into carpets, and exports the carpets to the United States. The firms making integrated circuits and heat-sink materials are suppliers for major global electronics brands. The trading firm imports and exports over $1 billion worth of both intermediate and finished goods annually, serving clients in China and more than 50 other countries.

Why are GVC-embedded firms more likely to take advantage of preferential trade agreements (PTAs) and become their vocal advocates? The answer to this question is important, as it lays the foundation for our theoretical arguments linking GVC integration and firm preferences and support for PTAs. After all, why would a firm care about preferential trade liberalization if it sees little benefit in PTAs or has no plans to ever use a PTA in the first place? In chapter 1, we argued that the way in which GVC networks operate can lead to more substantial gains from preferential trade liberalization for firms embedded in these networks. We also presented a number of reasons why, compared to those with few or no GVC linkages, firms with either strong backward or forward linkages should be more likely to benefit from PTAs, become their active users, and in turn support preferential trade liberalization more broadly.

This chapter validates these mechanisms by drawing on qualitative research from our fieldwork in China between 2017 and 2018. We conducted more than 60 in-depth interviews with managers of internationally oriented firms (i.e., firms that import, export, or do both), most of which can be grouped into four categories: those not embedded in GVCs (exporters or importers of finished goods), those backward linked to GVCs (firms that use imported parts or components in their production and exports), those forward linked to GVCs (firms that export intermediate products), and those with both backward and forward GVC linkages.

We structured the firm interviews around questions regarding the firms' experiences with China's two recent FTAs with Australia (ChAFTA) and South Korea (China-ROK FTA). More specifically, we asked firms the following questions: whether and how these FTAs have impacted on their business activities; what kind of obstacles they have encountered in using the FTAs and how they overcame them; and how the FTAs have shaped their sourcing and market strategies. Evidence from our fieldwork corroborated our expectation that firms with GVC linkages should be more likely to benefit from and use these two FTAs, which in turn form the basis of their preferences for PTAs more generally, including ones currently being negotiated. In addition to illuminating firm preferences, our interviews with local customs offices and trade bureaus as well as industry association representatives and scholars yielded valuable insights into the role of firms in FTA policymaking, suggesting that firms do have avenues for influencing trade policy, despite China's authoritarian political system.

The remainder of this chapter proceeds as follows. First, we briefly survey the existing research on the scope of and explanations for PTA utilization, which provides a good indication of firm preferences toward PTAs. Next, we describe our fieldwork research design in more detail, discussing our choice of fieldwork site, the types of firms we interviewed, the topics of our interviews, and how these choices allow us to effectively account for alternative explanations of PTA utilization. In the second half of the chapter, we report findings from the fieldwork, detailing how firms with varying levels of GVC integration view the costs and benefits of these PTAs and why such linkages can incentivize firms to overcome the obstacles that otherwise would have prevented them from making use of such agreements. Additionally, we offer some preliminary evidence on the role of these firms in China's FTA policymaking. These findings help set the stage for the more systematic empirical tests that will follow in the subsequent chapters.

Why Do Firms (Not) Use PTAs?

While we are primarily interested in firm preference and support for preferential trade liberalization, we are aware that preferences can be endogenously affected by the economic, social, legal, and cultural structures of a society (Palacios-Huerta and Santos 2004). An important part of the process of endogenous preference formation is learning by experience and observation. In our case, if a firm does not understand what a PTA is or what kind of benefits it may offer, then the firm may not have an opinion on these agreements, let alone support them. Only after using PTAs for their imports and exports can firms begin to form their preferences, depending on the outcome of their experiences. Therefore in this chapter we focus on establishing the link between the GVC position of the firms and their PTA utilization rate, or the frequency with which firms actually use PTAs for imports and exports, which is an important precondition for their support (or lack thereof) for preferential trade liberalization.

Despite the proliferation of PTAs around the world, it has been widely recognized that most firms do not actually use these agreements in their trade transactions, forgoing potential gains from tariff and nontariff barrier reductions. Many studies have documented this problem of FTA underutilization.[3] In a survey of 1,688 Japanese firms by the Japan Chamber of Commerce and Industry in 2008, only 33 percent, 12 percent, and 24 percent of the firms reported having used Japan's FTAs with Mexico, Malaysia, and Chile, respectively (Takahashi and Urata 2010). A series of surveys conducted by the Japan External Trade Organization between 2009 and 2011 similarly show that approximately 20 percent of Japanese overseas affiliates in ASEAN were using FTA schemes for exporting to ASEAN countries or Japan (Hayakawa 2015). This pattern can be observed elsewhere in Asia. A study by the Asian Development Bank based on a sample of 841 firms in China, the Philippines, Singapore, South Korea, and Thailand found that only around 28 percent of the firms were importing or exporting under the various preferential tariff arrangements (Kawai and Wignaraja 2011).

The issue of FTA underutilization goes beyond Asia. The Swiss Chinese Chamber of Commerce (SwissCham) reported that three years after the implementation of the FTA between China and Switzerland, only 38 percent of the surveyed Swiss firms indicated that they had used the agreement in 2016, though that number increased to 54 percent in the following year (SwissCham 2016, 2017). More broadly, in 2015, Thomson Reuters and KPMG International conducted a global trade and management survey with 446 trade professionals in 11 countries.[4] Only 30 percent of the respondents indicated that their companies fully used all of the FTAs available to them (Thompson Reuters and KPMG 2015).[5] In the 2016 version of the survey, which was expanded to include more than 1,700 trade professionals from 30 countries, the reported utilization rate was even lower, at 23 percent (Thompson Reuters and KPMG 2016).[6]

One may think that firms are not making full use of FTAs because they do not see much value added in doing so, or they have tried to use FTAs but find the costs outweigh the benefits. But this is not the case. In the KPMG trade management survey, for example, the majority of the firms considered identifying and leveraging FTAs as an investment rather than an expense, with 74 percent of them stating that the benefits of full FTA utilization could compensate for its potential risks and efforts (KPMG 2015). Furthermore, when asked about approximately how much in import duties their company could save on an annual basis through the use of FTAs, only 8 percent of the firms that indicated having used FTAs reported the absence of any savings, whereas 52 percent reported savings of more than $1 million (KPMG 2016).

What then prevents firms from taking advantage of the 400-plus FTAs around the world? One of the reasons most frequently cited by both firms and scholars for underutilization is the administrative costs associated with rules of origin (ROOs) and other administrative procedures relating to FTAs, an issue aptly summarized by *The Economist* (2009):

> Bilateral deals come laden with complicated rules about where products originate—rules which impose substantial costs of labelling and certification on firms. The more overlapping deals there are, the more complex the rules and the higher the costs. *No wonder few firms actually want to use FTAs.* (emphasis added)

While the above observation was made in reference to the ever-expanding web of FTAs in Asia that some have dubbed the "noodle bowl" (Baldwin 2008), it applies to firms in other parts of the world as well. In both rounds of the KPMG surveys, the top answer given by firms when asked about their biggest challenges in using FTAs for import or export was "complexity of rules of origin" (41 percent in 2015 and 23 percent in 2016). This was closely followed by "challenges in gathering raw material origin documentation from vendors" (38 percent in 2015 and 20 percent in 2016), an issue closely related to ROOs. Similarly, in the 2017 SwissCham survey, firms cited "procedures too complicated" (27 percent) as the top reason for not using the China-Switzerland FTA, while 43 percent of those firms that did try to use the FTA mentioned problems of "red tape/increased administrative expenditure" (18 percent), "elaborate and complex administrative process" (19 percent), or "extra costs for documents" (19 percent) (Swiss-Cham 2017).

In addition to the administrative and financial costs involved in dealing with complex ROO requirements in PTAs, other factors that deter firms from taking advantage of the FTAs available to them include lack of internal expertise to manage FTA compliance, insufficient margins of preferences, and bureaucratic red tape (Bernard et al. 2012; Cruz et al. 2018; Dai et al. 2018; Kawai and Wignaraja 2011; SwissCham 2016, 2018).

For each individual firm, ultimately, the decision on whether or not to use FTAs for their imports and/or exports may come down to a simple question of cost-benefit analysis. Firms are unlikely to learn about PTA provisions, tailor business plans to tariff schedules, or invest in human capital to deal with preferential tariff compliance unless the potential benefits outweigh the costs of these investments.

Our argument suggests that one distinction between firms that use FTAs frequently and those that use them rarely or not at all is the degree of their GVC linkages. Compared to firms not constrained by GVCs in their trade transactions, firms with either backward or forward GVC linkages are more likely to rely on suppliers or clients in specific countries shaped by the value chain. This should make it more difficult for them to shift to different markets and, consequently, increase the benefits that can be derived from preferential trade liberalization. These benefits should in turn incentivize GVC-linked firms to overcome the financial and administrative costs associated with using PTAs that often deter firms without such linkages to more proactively embrace such agreements. As a result, these firms should be more active users of PTAs, leading to their increased support for preferential trade liberalization over time.

Fieldwork Research Design

In order to validate the above mechanisms linking PTA usage to support for preferential trade liberalization, it is important that we account for other alternative explanations. Scholars have identified three factors as the main drivers of FTA utilization, each relating to the firm, the agreement, and the government. First, firm size has consistently been found to be one of the most important predictors for FTA utilization (Cadot et al. 2006; Hakobyan 2015; Keck and Lendle 2012). Larger firms are better equipped than smaller ones to muster the necessary financial and human resources to pay for the aforementioned costs. Furthermore, as larger firms tend to engage more in global trade than smaller firms, the potential savings from tariff reductions are often more substantial.

Second, the scope and depth of the FTAs matter. Previous studies have found that FTA utilization is higher for products with larger tariff margins and less-restrictive ROOs in the case of the Generalized System of Prefer-ences (e.g., Bureau et al. 2007; Cadot et al. 2006; Hakobyan 2015; Keck and Lendle 2012) or the Cotonou Agreement, the treaty between the European Union and the African, Caribbean, and Pacific Group of States (Francois et al. 2006; Manchin 2006). In the surveys cited above, many firms unsurpris-ingly attributed their decisions not to use PTAs to "small preference mar-gins" (Zhao 2011), "products not being covered by the FTA" (SwissCham 2016), or "products already enjoying duty-free access" (KPMG 2016).

Last but not least, the role of the government cannot be overlooked. On the one hand, the government and its relevant agencies can facilitate FTA utilization by providing firms, especially the small and medium ones, with more information—the lack of which constitutes a major deterrent, accord-ing to various surveys (KPMG 2016; SwissCham 2017); streamlining the ROO certification systems (for example, replacing the manual calculation-based system to an automatic one); and improving the capacities of customs agencies.[7] On the other hand, firms may have even fewer reasons to use FTAs if they expect to encounter additional bureaucratic red tape and potential rent-seeking behavior from custom officials (Kawai and Wig-naraja 2011).

Our sample selection and choice of interview topics reflect an effort to rule out these alternative explanations. First, rather than structuring our interviews around all of China's FTAs, we focused on China's FTAs with South Korea and Australia because these two agreements can be distin-guished from the rest in a number of important ways. As detailed in appen-dix 3.1, both agreements took more than a decade to negotiate, and when they were ratified (on the same day, coincidentally), the two countries were ranked the third- and fifth-largest trading partners of China, respectively. Furthermore, both FTAs have been billed as the most comprehensive of their kind among China's existing FTAs, with the government and media hyping their potential in the respective countries.

Table 3.1 summarizes the scope and depth of the ChAFTA and China-ROK FTA. The results are based on text analyses of the provisions in the final agreements (SSCC 2018). It can be seen that in WTO-plus areas such as market access, trade remedy (antidumping, countervailing, and safe-guard measures), services (trade in services, financial services, natural per-son movement), intellectual property rights (IPR), and public procurement, both agreements contain provisions with commitment levels higher or much higher than the WTO. Also covered in the agreements were WTO-X

Table 3.1. Scope and Depth of China-KOR FTA and ChAFTA

FTA Date of entry into force		China-ROK FTA December 20, 2015	ChAFTA December 20, 2015
	Bilateral trade in 2015	$275.8 billion	$113.8 billion
WTO-plus Areas	% zero-tariff trade (after N years) for China	44% (0) to 85% (20)	85% (0) to 97% (15)
	% zero-tariff trade (after N years) for partner	52% (0) to 91% (20)	81.5% (0) to 100% (5)
	Market access of goods	**Medium**	**High**
	Sanitary and phytosanitary measures (SPS)	Low	Low
	Technical barriers to trade (TBT)	Low	Low
	Antidumping measures	**Medium**	**Low**
	Countervailing measures	**Low**	**Low**
	Safeguard measures	**Medium**	**Medium**
	Cross-border trade in services	**Medium**	**Medium**
	Financial services	**Medium**	**Medium**
	Natural person movement	**High**	**Medium**
	Intellectual property rights	**Medium**	**Medium**
	Public procurement	Low	Low
WTO-X Areas	Market access for investment	**Low**	**Medium**
	Treatment of investment	**Low**	**Medium**
	Protection of investment	**Medium**	**Low**
	Investment and environmental measures	**Low**	None
	Investor–state dispute settlement	Medium	High
	Competition policy	Medium	None
	Labor standards	None	None
	Environmental policy	Medium	None
	E-commerce	Low	Low
	Telecommunication	**Low**	**Medium**

Notes: This table is adapted from figure 3.2 in SSCC (2018). "High" means the FTA contains provisions with commitment levels much higher than those in the WTO (in the case of WTO-plus areas) or with very substantial requirements (in the case of WTO-X areas); "Medium" means the FTA contains provisions with commitment levels higher than those in the WTO or with substantial requirements; "Low" means the FTA contains provisions with commitment levels no higher than the WTO or with general requirements; "None" means the FTA does not mention such provisions. Bold type denotes that the provision is subject to the dispute settlement provisions of the FTA (legally enforceable). Additional notes can be found in SSCC (2018, 37). Bilateral trade data are drawn from "11–6 Value of Imports and Exports by Country (Region) of Origin/Destination," *China Statistical Yearbook 2016*, National Bureau of Statistics of China.

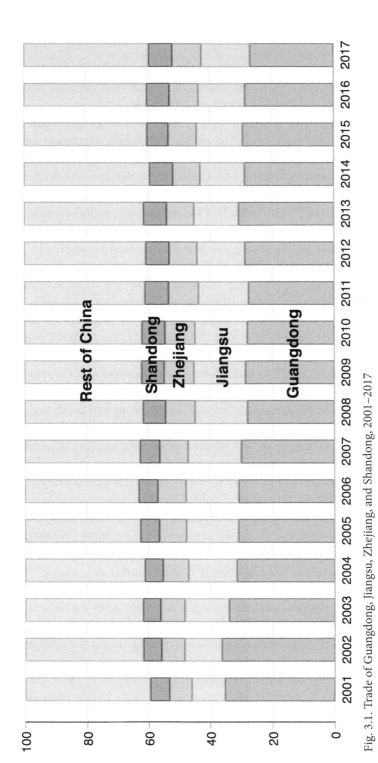

Fig. 3.1. Trade of Guangdong, Jiangsu, Zhejiang, and Shandong, 2001–2017

Source: China Statistical Yearbook, various years.

Note: The bars represent total imports and exports of each province as a share of China's total annual trade.

provisions, often with substantial requirements, in areas such as investment protection, competition policy, environmental policy, e-commerce, and telecommunication, especially in the China-ROK FTA.

Though both agreements still fall short in depth of coverage in comparison to the as yet unratified Comprehensive and Progressive Agreement for Trans-Pacific Partnership (CPTPP), signed by the original 11 members of the Trans-Pacific Partnership minus the United States, they are both deeper and much more comprehensive than many of the earlier FTAs entered into by the three countries. The China-ROK FTA, for example, includes a separate chapter on economic cooperation, which is absent from Korea's previous FTAs with major trading partners such as the United States and the EU. Similarly, ChAFTA contains chapters dedicated to issues of intellectual property and e-commerce, which are absent in China's early FTAs, such as with Pakistan or Singapore. Steven Ciobo, Australia's minister for international development and the Pacific, praised ChAFTA as "the trade agreement of a generation" and "a landmark deal that will bring Australia and China even closer together" (Hurst 2015).

Focusing on these two FTAs thus allows us to rule out some of the alternative explanations of PTA (under)utilization discussed above that are related to features of the agreement, such as limited scope and depth (e.g., China's FTAs with Chile and Iceland), the complexity of the ROOs (e.g., China's FTA with ASEAN), or low bilateral trade volumes (e.g., China's most recent FTAs with Georgia and Maldives).

Second, we picked the four coastal provinces of Guangdong, Jiangsu, Shandong, and Zhejiang as the sites of our fieldwork to account for the role of the government. These are the four largest provinces (excluding the municipalities of Beijing and Shanghai) in terms of trade volume. Together, they make up over half of China's overall trade since 2001 (see figure 3.1). Guangdong in particular has consistently ranked number one among all Chinese provinces, with RMB 6.3 trillion in imports and exports in 2016, or 25.9 percent of the national total. According to data released by the General Administration of Customs, nearly half of the top 50 cities in 2016 are from these four provinces—eight in Guangdong, six in Jiangsu, and five each in Zhejiang and Shandong (The State Council 2017).

More importantly, the provincial and local governments of these four provinces have been among the most active in providing a wide range of policy supports to increase the ease for their firms to use the FTAs. For example, Guangdong was one of the first provinces to implement the "rules of origin priority entry and exit thousand enterprise assistance program (原产地助力优进优出千企帮扶计划)" initiated by the AQSIQ in 2017, aimed at helping firms take advantage of the FTAs in their effort to "go out (走出去)" (China News Net 2017). In Jiangsu, the provincial Commerce Bureau launched a comprehensive campaign called "FTA Benefiting Jiangsu Firms (FTA惠苏企)," holding consultation meetings (such as the one described at the beginning of this chapter), collaborating with both traditional and social media to promote new policies and formulating targeted programs and green channels for key import and export firms.[8] In Shandong, local customs bureaus streamlined the process of applying for the ROO certificates by implementing new paperless systems and waiving application fees for firms applying for certificates pertaining to ChAFTA and the China-ROK FTA.[9] In Zhejiang, the provincial AQSIQ implemented a program called "FTA Country Compass (自贸协定国检指南针)" and compiled "rules of origin tariff reduction manuals (自贸协定原产地证书关税减免手册)," detailing the procedures and available FTAs for each city's top 100 export and import goods.[10] As a result, firms in these provinces are the most frequent users of PTAs in China. In Jiangsu, for example, the utilization rates of ChAFTA and the China-ROK FTA were close to 60 percent in 2016, which was higher than the average nation-wide utilization rate of about 30 percent (China FTA Network 2016a).

Finally, in these provinces we targeted large and internationally oriented firms with extensive import or export activities (or both) with South Korea and/or Australia in a wide range of industries, as opposed to a representative sample of firms in a few industries. This way, we were able to control for other firm-specific features found to be determinants of PTA utilization, such as size and trade profile.

Overall, our sampled firms should be the most likely ones in China to benefit from FTAs and have the highest capacity and government support to do so. Consequently, it should be safer for us to draw the conclusion that any differences in PTA utilization result from their varying degrees of GVC integration.

The Broader Effects of ChAFTA and China-ROK FTA

On the broader scale, the effects of ChAFTA and the China-ROK FTA were immediate, as eligible firms rushed to apply for certificates of origins.

According to the AQSIQ, merely a month after the ratifications of the FTAs in December 2015, the AQSIQ's National Inspection and Quarantine System and the CCPIT issued a record 40,700 certificates of origin, covering $4.439 billion worth of goods for the China-ROK FTA and 56,300 certificates of origin covering $2.144 billion worth of goods under ChAFTA. The total savings from tariff reductions were estimated at $284 million (China FTA Network 2016b).

By the end of 2016, more than 1.11 million certificates of origin pertaining to the two FTAs had been issued, covering imports and exports of $32.2 billion for an estimated total tariff savings of $2.4 billion. The average utilization rate of the two agreements reached 41 percent, which was 7 percent higher than the average utilization rate of China's other FTAs and 19 percent higher than the global average (China FTA Network 2017a). According to the Ministry of Commerce, nearly 50 percent of its surveyed companies indicated that their exports to South Korea had increased or increased substantially since the agreement came into effect, and 57 percent reported that their volume of consultations or orders had increased or increased significantly (Xinhua 2016).

Bilateral trade between China and the two countries also saw substantial increases. Two years after ChAFTA came into effect, Australian exports to China rose 25 percent in the first nine months of 2017 to a record AUD110 billion ($84.3 billion). Among them, Australia's exports to China were $57.36 billion, an increase of 38.2 percent, accounting for 33.3 percent of Australia's total exports (China FTA Network 2017b). Meanwhile, while bilateral trade between China and South Korea in 2016 continued its downward trend that had started in 2014, exports of South Korean goods that earned tariff favors through the China-ROK FTA declined by only 4 percent from 2015, while those of nonbeneficiary products tumbled by 12.8 percent. This led the Korea Ministry of Trade, Industry and Energy to credit the FTA with "shoring up exports to China" (The Hankyoreh, 2016). As more tariffs were eliminated in 2017, bilateral trade rebounded to reach $280.26 billion, an increase of 10.9 percent from one year earlier.

In addition to trade, ChAFTA and the China-ROK FTA also promoted investments. In the first nine months of 2016, China's nonfinancial foreign investment in Australia amounted to $2.79 billion, an increase of 73.3 percent from the same period in 2015 and higher than China's average growth rate of outward investments by nearly 20 percentage points. Similarly, during the first 11 months of 2016, China's investments in South Korea reached

$770 million, a substantial increase of 60.7 percent year-on-year, and South Korea's investments in China amounted to $4.37 billion, a year-on-year increase of 17.8 percent (China FTA Network 2018). The increase in bilateral investments is particularly impressive considering the slowdown of trade in 2016, prompting the following remark from a scholar at the China Institute of Contemporary International Relations:

> The China-ROK FTA is the "stabilizer" of the economies of China and South Korea. If the Sino-Korea trade is likened to a big ship, then the FTA is its "anchor." When it comes to wind and sea, the ship may sway, but it can't sink with an anchor.[11]

Findings from Fieldwork

The overall success of ChAFTA and the China-ROK FTA belies the fact that the vast majority of Chinese firms have yet to capture the potential benefits. In fact, most firms were not even aware of these FTAs until told by customs officials or their foreign clients.[12] In what follows, we will show that GVC-linked firms are more likely to benefit from the preferential trade liberalization made possible by PTAs, in terms of both tariff barrier reduction and trade liberalization in areas beyond tariffs. Many of our surveyed firms subsequently became frequent users of PTAs and had an interest in seeing the upgrade and expansion of China's FTA network.

Preferential Tariffs

As we discussed earlier, the most direct benefits of PTAs are preferential tariffs, but taking advantage of these benefits comes with costs; the most common ones, according to our interviewees, are "extra paperwork," "complex application procedure to apply for certificate of origin," and "shipment delays for products benefiting from preferential tariffs."[13] For firms without GVC linkages, the benefits from tariff reductions may not be sufficient to cover these costs. On the one hand, in comparison with what firms already enjoy through most-favored nation (MFN) tariffs, the margins of preferences in PTAs are often "small and will take too long to realize."[14] On the other hand, the fact that these firms do not rely on suppliers or clients in specific geographic locations shaped by the value chain means that it would be easier for them to divert trade to other MFN markets, especially if the countries in the free trade zones start putting up nontrade barriers.

A pesticide manufacturer in Zhenjiang illustrates this logic for exporters of final goods for foreign consumption. The firm exports more than 40 varieties of insecticides, fungicides, and herbicides to more than 20 different countries. Thus the firm did not bother to apply for certificates of origin for their exports to Australia when ChAFTA went into force. It was, in fact, the local customs official who came to the firm and helped reissue the certificates after several of their shipments had already left for Melbourne. "We appreciated the efforts of the local customs for helping us save some money," the firm said, "but in the grand scheme of things it does not matter that much."[15] It turns out that, with the recent controversy over glyphosate, the primary ingredient in pesticides, and the rising technical barriers in advanced economies, the firm was already in the process of reorienting their exports to Latin America. "ChAFTA lowers the tariff of pesticides by 3 percent, making it lower than the MFN rates in other markets, but you never know when you will be hit by antidumping duties, which happened a few years ago. Thus, we have decided to look elsewhere."[16]

For importers of final goods for domestic consumption, the preferential margins are often dwarfed by other import-related taxes. The experience of a Hangzhou firm is quite representative. The firm is a major online retailer of skincare products from South Korea, which have recently become very popular among young urbanites in China. When the China-ROK FTA was ratified, the firm was disappointed to see that only 14 cosmetics products were included in the tariff reduction schedule, which excluded some of their most popular items. Furthermore, the firm's imports that did qualify for preferential tariffs would get "a measly 1.3 percent reduction over five years," which was "negligible" given that on top of the tariffs, it needed to pay 30 percent sales tax and 17 percent value-added tax (VAT) for all imported cosmetics.[17] In fact, the firm was more concerned about increased competition from new online retailers, as the China-ROK FTA was predicted to generate huge growth in cross-border e-commerce.

In contrast to firms that import or export final goods only, firms embedded in GVCs have more reasons to invest in using the PTAs, depending on whether they are backward or forward linked to global supply chains. Firms with backward GVC linkages rely on foreign inputs to produce the intermediate or final goods they export. Because these inputs (e.g., raw materials or high-value components) are frequently essential parts of GVCs and cannot be easily substituted by sourcing from domestic or other foreign markets at a competitive price, the gains from preferential tariffs can be substantial. The carpet firm mentioned earlier, for example, uses Australian wool exclusively for its high-end products that are exported to Europe and the United States. Not surprisingly, the firm was very pleased with the additional duty-free import quota on Australian wool, introduced by ChAFTA.[18] "For years we were forced to spend a ton of money buying import quotas from other companies so that we would have enough wool to keep the machines running and fulfill the orders," the manager explained. "Those days are gone now thanks to ChAFTA!"[19] A number of textile firms in Tongxiang shared similar experiences, reporting substantial increases in the imports of Australian wool since ChAFTA had gone into force.[20]

A special case of backward GVC linkage is processing trade whereby goods produced with foreign intermediates are exported back to those same countries, oftentimes between affiliates and parent firms in the form of intra-firm trade. In these instances, firms are able to recuperate savings both ways through preferential tariffs with the partner country. A firm in Suzhou exemplifies this benefit of "double savings." Founded as a joint venture with Samsung in 1995, the firm is one of Samsung's largest overseas production facilities for household appliances such as refrigerators and air conditioners. Nearly 70 percent of the firm's raw materials and key components have to be imported from South Korea to meet the technical standards set by Samsung. A large share of the finished products is then exported back to South Korea. The company has been using the Asia-Pacific Trade Agreement (APTA) for its imports since 2003, but since the China-ROK FTA provides even lower tariffs on those imports, as well as reduced tariffs on the finished products sold in South Korea, the firm quickly made the switch, saving millions in both imports and exports.[21]

Also contributing to the increased use of PTAs among backward-linked firms is the fact that the vast majority of them are joint ventures or wholly owned subsidiaries of multinational corporations that as a result of their extensive supply chain networks are more cognizant of the cost-saving opportunities of preferential tariffs and hence more experienced in utilizing PTAs. Many of these firms we interviewed have dedicated personnel specializing in trade compliance to ensure that "every possible saving is realized."[22] In some cases, headquarters would send specialists to their Chinese affiliates to conduct training sessions on the procedures to apply for certificates of origin.[23]

It is worth noting that many of these backward-linked firms also serve consumers or other firms in the home market. For instance, about 60 percent of the refrigerators made by the joint venture with Samsung are sold in China.[24] Similarly, it is quite common for original-equipment-manufacturing firms to have separate lines of products exclusively targeting the domestic market. While traditional import-competing firms would be categorically worse off with the influx of foreign goods under preferential tariffs, the use of cheaper foreign inputs for domestically oriented production may offset such adverse effects for these firms.

In the case of forward GVC linkages—that is, when a firm's domestic value added ends up in the production and exports of foreign intermediate or final goods—the logic is similar: preferential tariffs make their products cheaper in partner countries, driving up demand and increasing sales. Furthermore, since many of these forward-linked firms have been integrated into the global supply chains of major foreign brands, the more competitive import prices resulting from preferential tariffs would allow these firms to maintain and solidify their supply chain relationships with foreign clients. This is especially valuable for firms that face increased competition from suppliers in countries with cheaper labor and production costs, as demonstrated by the experiences of a firm in Rizhao, Shandong province.

Located close to the port of Qingdao, the firm has been a major exporter of yarn, greige cloth, and other unfinished fabrics to South Korea. Around mid-2015, the firm encountered a difficult dilemma when one of its biggest clients in Seoul indicated that it might redirect portions of its order to suppliers in Thailand or Malaysia in an attempt to cut costs. The firm could reduce the prices below production costs to retain that order, worth $8 million, but it would essentially be operating at a loss. If not, the firm would risk more of its orders being switched to Southeast Asian suppliers. Things turned for the better when the firm learned that most of its exports would qualify for duty-free tariff the moment the China-ROK FTA went into effect later that year. "[The FTA] was a game-changer," recalled the director of foreign trade, who led the negotiations. "When we presented them with our new quotes [with the duty-free tariff], which were only slightly higher than what they got from the Malaysians, they decided to stay with us. After all, they know that our products are better!"[25]

Beyond Tariffs

Many firms likened certificates of origin to "paper gold (纸黄金)"[26] or "passports (通行证)"[27] that helped them optimize and expand their business by reducing tariffs and saving costs, but preferential tariffs are not the only benefits. As we discussed earlier, PTAs cover a range of WTO-plus and WTO-X issues, such as investment regulations and IPR protection, that are particularly attractive to GVC-embedded firms exporting knowledge-intensive products or services. This is the case for a firm in Dongguan that makes patented, high-end elastic fabrics supplied to brands such as Triumph and Lululemon. In 2012, the firm was looking to expand its production by opening new plants in Vietnam or Malaysia. After conducting research in those markets, however, the firm decided not to proceed, citing "poor business environment and industrial support" as the main reasons. "Many firms are moving to Southeast Asia for its low labor costs. This is not much of a concern for us. Rather, we need to know that our investments can be protected. That's why we are closely following the latest round of negotiations [between China and South Korea] on services and investment," revealed the firm's manager.[28]

Common challenges facing many Chinese firms are nontariff barriers and behind-the-border measures. When a firm is slapped with antidumping duties, it needs to either find other export markets or relocate its production to the destination country, also known as "tariff-jumping foreign direct investment (FDI)" (Blonigen et al. 2004).[29] Whereas firms without GVC linkages have both options, GVC-linked firms may have no choice but to relocate their production due to their supply chain constraints. PTAs can facilitate such tariff-jumping FDI by making it easier and safer for firms to invest, especially when they have more comprehensive terms for investment facilitation and protection. Following the China-ROK FTA, for example, South Korea created the Saemangeum Korea-China Industrial Cooperation Complex (新万金韩中经济合作园区) to attract Chinese investors by offering a wide range of incentives, including tax benefits, assistance with leases, and subsidies (BusinessKorea 2018). Similar to the Dongguan firm above, many of the GVC-linked firms we spoke to either were actively planning or had been advised by local governments to look into these opportunities to "sail across the ocean with borrowed boats (借船出海)."[30]

When firms invest in PTA partners, their overseas subsidiaries can also gain preferential access to third countries through the PTA network of the partner country, indirectly expanding their business to those markets.[31] This can be illustrated by a major manufacturer in Wuxi of biotherapeutic materials made from mammalian cell cultures. The firm exports 60 percent of its products to the United States. Given that an FTA or a bilateral investment treaty (BIT) between China and the United States is unlikely to materialize anytime soon, the firm was scouting other potential locations to expand its foreign operations. With a newly signed FTA with the United States in September 2018, South Korea has become the front runner. The firm reasoned that "the new FTA, together with the China-ROK FTA, means that [its] entire production process can enjoy preferential tariffs, from China to South Korea and to the United States."[32]

On the flip side, the potential of PTAs to attract FDI into the home country also creates opportunities for firms embedded in GVCs to climb up the value chain as they form joint ventures with their technologically more advanced partners. An example of this is a joint venture established recently in the new Sino-Australian Modern Industrial Park in Zhoushan, Zhejiang province by a Ningbo firm and a leading new materials company from Australia that makes veneer fibers widely used in furniture and construction. The Chinese firm agreed to finance all of the capital investments in the new factory plant in exchange for the license to use the patented technology from the Australian firm for its own production and sales. "On the face it appears that we got the short end of the stick in this deal," the firm explained, "but we are looking long term and see this as an investment for us to learn new technologies from a leading firm, which will be crucial for us to stay competitive in both domestic and foreign markets."[33]

Thus far we have mostly focused on manufacturing firms, but they are certainly not the only ones using the PTAs. A fair share of China's trade is conducted by trading firms and agencies that do not actually produce any goods. Instead they play a more facilitative role for firms (with varying degrees of GVC linkages) by covering all aspects of trade, from customs declaration and commodity inspection to warehousing and transportation. As such, these firms are often more familiar with PTA rules relating to domestic content and labeling requirements than many manufacturers, especially the small and medium ones that lack such expertise. In a way, these firms are also embedded in GVCs by providing the necessary services that connect the different stages of the global supply chains represented by their client firms. Not surprisingly, they are frequent users of PTAs because, in the words of one large trading firm in Qingdao, "more PTAs mean more business."[34]

The above logic also applies to manufacturers that are beginning to engage more in the production, sales, and export of services, also known as the servicification of manufacturing (Lodefalk 2013). A textile firm in Guangzhou represents such a case. The firm was established in 1994, when it was spun off from the Guangdong Textile Import and Export Group, China's first textile- and apparel-trading enterprise, founded more than 60 years ago. With its expertise in foreign trade gained over time, the firm has reinvented itself as a "supply chain organizer (供应链服务平台)."[35] Drawing on its extensive network of clients up and down the supply chain, the firm connects textile manufacturers of both finished and intermediate goods across China with the capacity and qualification to serve foreign clients, providing these manufacturers with the necessary logistical and administrative support. In doing so, the firm pays close attention to China's evolving PTA networks, constantly looking for new opportunities to "establish, join and manage international production networks and value chains for textile firms in Guangdong and beyond."[36]

Firm Influence in PTA Policymaking

Unlike firms with little or no involvement in GVCs who might have tried to use PTAs but eventually gave up—such as the pesticide firm above—the GVC-linked firms we talked to share one thing in common: they have all become repeat users of PTAs.[37] When asked why, an auto parts firm in Rizhao put it best: "once you go with a free trade agreement, you don't go back!"[38] Some firms even adapted their business strategies around existing and future FTAs. "Our next market will be wherever China signs the next FTA," proclaimed a textile firm in Weifang, Shandong province.[39]

Not surprisingly, the more these firms use PTAs, the more likely they are to develop a stake in the expansion and upgrade of China's FTA network. But do firms play any role in the negotiations of existing and future FTAs? Conventional wisdom suggests that nonstate actors in an authoritarian country such as China do not have much input in the domestic policymaking process. When it comes to trade policymaking in China, most scholars have taken a top-down approach by focusing on the preferences of Chinese leaders, Beijing's overall foreign policy goals and domestic political concerns, or international market pressures (see, for example, Hsueh 2016). These analyses build on the assumption that trade policies are designed by Chinese leaders to meet their political and economic objectives, given certain domestic and international constraints.

While such an assumption is still true, the policymaking process in China has become increasingly pluralized. The gradual devolution of decision-making power during the reform era, which accelerated after China's entry into the WTO, has led to increased political fragmentation, with bargaining among bureaucratic actors at various levels generating policies that increasingly reflect the distinct cleavages between the center and localities (Huang 1996; Lieberthal and Lampton 1992). The proliferation of both central and local government officials in the policymaking process has, in turn, created more access points for societal actors. In fact, the growing consensus among China scholars is that while the contours of the policymaking process are still defined by the state, actors outside of the state—such as the media, nongovernmental organizations, intellectuals, and activists—are now increasingly active in shaping policy outcomes (e.g., Jakobson and Knox 2011; Mertha 2010).

The pluralization of the policymaking process is particularly prominent in the economic realm, where firms have become more vocal in shaping the process of policy initiation, deliberation, and implementation. A growing body of literature on business lobbying in China (e.g., Kennedy 2005, 2009; Yu et al. 2014; Zeng 2007) has shown that while domestic companies were largely peripheral to the policymaking process prior to the onset of economic reform, they have become increasingly active in "every stage of the policy process, from setting the agenda to identifying policy options and shaping regulatory implementation," during the reform era (Deng and Kennedy 2010, 101). Examples of this include Kennedy's study (2005b) of how lobbying by domestic and foreign firms in China has led to different outcomes in antidumping cases, Steinberg and Shih's (2012) documentation of China's use of currency undervaluation as a response to demands from powerful tradable industries, Li's analysis (2013) of the influence of firms and business associations during China's WTO accession negotiations, and Naoi et al.'s use of firm surveys (2019) to illustrate how Chinese companies interact with the government regarding regulatory policies for FDI entry.

How exactly do firms participate in the economic policymaking process? Adapting insights drawn from earlier research on the political strategies of firms in market economies (e.g., Hillman and Hitt 1999; Shirodkar and Mohr 2015; Yoffie 1987) and on business-government relations in the Chinese context, some scholars (e.g., He and Che 2018; Kennedy and Deng 2012; Tian and Gao 2006; Tian et al. 2003) have documented the wide range of political or nonmarket strategies adopted by Chinese firms to lobby for preferential policies, support, or protection from the government. Such strategies have included direct participation (e.g., managers running for local or national people's congresses), the use of proxies (e.g., hiring retired officials as consultants), information consulting (e.g., submitting comments to online consultation portals), mobilizing social forces (e.g., issuing statements to the media), institutional innovation (e.g., forming coalitions with other firms in the same industry), building political connections (e.g., socializing with government officials), and offering financial incentives (e.g., gift giving), to name a few. Others (e.g., Zhang and Zhang 2005) have divided the political strategies of Chinese firms into preemptive (to gain preferential benefits from government policies) and reactive (to counteract potential negative impacts of government policies), drawing parallels with the relational and transactional strategies of firms in market economies.

Our fieldwork confirms that when interacting with the government, companies employ a combination of many of the political and nonmarket strategies identified by previous research, which can be broadly grouped into four categories, depending on (a) their preferences for a collective versus an individual approach and (b) their preferences for formal versus informal channels: individual informal lobby, individual formal lobby, collective informal lobby, and collective formal lobby. Furthermore, we find evidence that GVC-linked firms are generally more active and spend more time and resources on lobbying efforts than firms without GVC linkages.

Many firms in China nowadays engage with the central and local governments directly through personal relations and networks they have cultivated over time (informal lobbying) to "speak for the firm (为企业说话)."[40] One would expect larger and state-owned firms to have an advantage over small and private ones in this regard, given their superior resource endowment and ties to the state. However, our interviews with firm managers suggest that this is not necessarily the case. Instead, GVC-linked firms in our sample, regardless of size and ownership type, seem to have better direct access to policymakers. For example, many of the firms described earlier in this chapter have recruited retired government officials in trade-related departments to serve on their board of directors or as consultants so as to tap into their networks with former employers. Others have sought opportunities to speak with or send letters to current government officials through close family members or mutual friends. Some firms even acknowledged using financial instruments to establish and maintain ties to these officials. Almost all of the firms in our interviews mentioned the importance of personal relations in getting access to the government. "There are limited direct communication channels between the government and the individual firms," according to one firm, "it's mostly about interpersonal communication and your *guanxi* network."[41]

The target of informal lobbying does not have to be government officials. Firms sometimes go through nongovernmental actors such as scholars and think tanks that they know would be involved in the policymaking process to act as their surrogates. Other times, they call attention to their issues of concern by reporting to the media or attending public forums or conferences. Many of the GVC-linked firms we spoke to, for example, have dedicated public relations specialists that actively engage with these nongovernmental actors and look for every opportunity that can help protect and advance their interests.

Instead of, and sometimes in addition to, lobbying on their own, all of the informal activities described above can be a collective effort. This is mostly done through industry and business associations. The All-China Federation of Industry and Commerce (ACFIC), for example, which served as an agency of the United Front's work to regulate domestic firms, has now become a major platform for facilitating the bottom-up process of policy input as a result of the party's "open policy-making" initiative (Huang et al. 2017). Besides the ACFIC, firms are also often members of multiple industry and business associations at the national and local levels. These associations have assumed an increasingly important role in forming bridges between expanding business communities and the government in the reform era (Deng and Kennedy 2010). This can be seen in a number of official documents promulgated by the government. In May 2007, the General Office of the State Council issued "Several Opinions on Accelerating the Reform and Development of Industry Associations and Chambers of Commerce," which stated that these associations should "conduct in-depth industry research, actively report to the government the demands of member firms, put forward opinions and suggestions on industry development and legislation, and actively participate in the research and formulation of relevant laws, regulations, and industrial policies."[42] Most recently, in March 2019, the State Council issued the "Notice on Fully Hearing the Opinions of

Enterprise and Industry Associations in the Process of Formulating Administrative Regulations and Administrative Documents," further confirming the importance of industry and business associations.[43]

Previous studies (e.g., Kennedy 2009) have shown that large firms are more inclined to act individually by making use of their personal relationships with local, regional, or even central leaders, whereas medium and smaller firms lacking such networks or patronage protection tend to take collective action via industry and business associations. Our fieldwork suggests this may no longer be the case, as almost all of the firms we spoke to have joined at least one industry or business association. Once again, firms' GVC position seems to influence their level of activity in these associations. Managers of firms embedded in GVCs often assume association leadership roles and tend to invoke these roles to "add additional legitimacy" to their claims in their own informal lobbying efforts. As a result, many managers of such firms agreed that for trade-related issues that affect the entire industry, going through associations is in fact more effective than lobbying on their own.

Interestingly, when it comes to issues related to PTAs, informal lobbying through either trade and business associations or individual firms appears to be mostly reactive. That is, firms and their representative associations inform governments of potential improvements or changes after a PTA has been signed, one example being the application and approval processes for ROO certificates. While effective in bringing changes to PTA implementation (e.g., faster approval of ROO certificates), such reactive lobbying has had no effect on new PTAs under negotiation, although it could have an impact on the renegotiation of existing PTAs.

Formal lobbying, on the other hand, allows firms to influence the terms of future PTAs through official channels and platforms established specifically for the purpose of garnering feedback from relevant stakeholders. A prominent example of such formal lobbying is online consultation, which has become an increasingly standard feature of policy and law making in China (Balla 2014, 2017; Horsley 2009). In 2008, a year after the decision to include public consultation in the policy-drafting process was pronounced, the plan to reform the health system announced by the central government through the National Development and Reform Commission (NDRC) in October 2008 garnered nearly 30,000 online comments (Balla and Liao 2013). More recently, between December 26, 2018, and February 24, 2019, the draft Foreign Investment Law was open for public consultation through the NPC online portal, resulting in a total of 1,139 comments from 391 stakeholders, nearly a third of which were from firms and business associations (Li 2020).

In the case of PTAs, firms from our interviews have mentioned leaving comments during online consultations about proposed FTAs such as the ones with Australia and South Korea conducted by the Ministry of Commerce and its various local branches. Firms were also encouraged to attend consultation meetings offline and express their opinions and concerns. As the case at the beginning of this chapter shows, individual firms, especially those having extensive value-chain connections with the relevant countries under consideration, now routinely participate in government-led consultations on FTAs. In the second half of that meeting, for instance, after the firms had shared their experiences with the existing FTAs, the officials began taking questions on what the government could do to increase the utilization rates and invited firms to offer suggestions about what they would like to see in China's future FTAs. The firms were told that their views would be taken into account by the negotiators because one of the latter's main objectives is to "allow firms to deeply participate in international rulemaking (让企业深度参与国际规则制定)."[44] Similar meetings had been held in other localities, according to our interviewees, and the general impressions were quite positive—"the officials did a great job explaining how we can more fully tap the benefits brought by the FTAs and also went the extra mile in hearing what we had to say," said a manager from one firm that attended a similar consultation meeting in Zibo, Shandong province.[45]

Similarly, industry and business associations play a key part in carrying the voices of firms to policymakers, especially during the feasibility analysis stage of future FTAs. Before the official negotiations of the China-ROK FTA were launched, for example, the two countries conducted a series of government-business-academic joint study meetings (官产学联合研究) designed to "involve as many relevant parties as possible."[46] For the various feasibility studies and exploratory discussions of China's earlier and future FTAs, the CCPIT and its various local branches have organized multiple rounds of public and industry consultations through various forums, seminars, and workshops. Regarding how the CCPIT provides a bridge between firms and the government, it is worth quoting a senior official of the CCPIT:

> It is crucial for firms to participate in these feasibility studies. Our role is to collect data and draft reports to the relevant government departments on

the policy demands from related industries, especially suggestions and recommendations from firms on intellectual property, environmental protection, e-commerce, competition policy, and government procurement. These can be used as reference points for the negotiations and preparation for a high-level free trade agreement between China and its trading partners.[47]

Conclusion

In this chapter, we have unpacked the micro-foundation of our theory by documenting the experiences of Chinese firms in four coastal provinces with two recent FTAs signed by China, one with South Korea and the other with Australia. We have shown that firms embedded in GVCs are more likely to benefit from PTAs than firms without such linkages. Consequently, these firms have become a core constituency for supporting preferential trade liberalization. We have also provided additional evidence that even in an authoritarian context, GVC-linked firms can use both formal and informal institutions to provide input and exert influence on the PTA policy-making process.

The results from our qualitative fieldwork provide important validity checks for the causal mechanisms of our theory linking GVC integration with preferential trade liberalization. The next natural question to ask is how generalizable these findings are to a broader, more representative set of firms. We take up this question in the next chapter, drawing on a unique firm-level survey we designed and implemented in China.

CHAPTER 4

GVCs and the Trade Policy Preferences of Chinese Firms

A Firm-Level Survey

The previous chapter provided qualitative evidence from four coastal provinces that firms with extensive global value chain (GVC) linkages have benefited from China's expanding preferential trade agreement (PTA) networks and are more likely to support the government in signing new agreements with countries that are current or intended trading partners. In this chapter, we will explore whether these findings can be generalized to other Chinese firms. To do so, we designed and implemented an original survey that included a set of questions aimed at tapping firms' position in GVCs, including their backward and forward GVC linkages as well as their attitudes toward international trade generally and preferential trade liberalization specifically. We expect that after accounting for other factors that may affect a firm's trade policy position, including firm age, size, ownership, productivity, and product substitutability, firms with strong GVC linkages should be more likely to demonstrate a favorable attitude toward preferential trade liberalization.

In addition to the attitudinal questions, we also embedded in the survey a conjoint experiment to explore firms' preferences for the design of PTAs, including the degree of tariff reduction, the time required for the PTA to enter into force, the presence and content of dispute settlement mechanisms, investor protection, intellectual property rights (IPR) protection, and provisions for trade remedies. We use the experimental design to explore whether GVC-integrated firms are more likely to prefer deeper PTAs that address nontariff barriers and behind-the-border issues.

The rest of this chapter is organized as follows. In the next section, we detail the design and implementation of our survey, in particular the sample of respondents that forms the basis of the following analysis. We then describe how we constructed our GVC measures based on the survey questions, the design of the conjoint experiment, and the testable hypotheses based on these measures. This is followed by a discussion of the main results. We conclude by summarizing the findings.

A Survey of Chinese Firms

Business surveys have become an increasingly popular tool for both scholars and policymakers to gain insights into the preferences and decision-making processes of entrepreneurs and senior managers. Some of the most well-known examples of firm-level surveys are the World Bank's Enterprise Surveys (WBES), which cover a broad range of business environment topics—including access to finance, corruption, infrastructure, crime, competition, and performance measures—administered to a representative sample of an economy's private sector. With over 131,000 interviews in 139 countries, the WBES have generated hundreds of studies and reports on a wide range of topics.

In China, scholars have used firm-level surveys to study investments in research and development, corporate restructuring, and industrial upgrading (e.g., An and Shi 2006; Dai and Zhang 2013; Lu 2003; Zhou and Lu 2002). Most of these surveys, however, are small in scale, often implemented in one province or even one city, and provide scant details about the sampling scheme, design, and implementation of the surveys, making it difficult to draw inferences on the external validity of the findings.

There are, however, several exceptions. The China module of the WBES was implemented by the Enterprise Survey Organization of China's National Bureau of Statistics (NBS) in 2005. The survey interviewed 12,400 firms located in 120 cities across all Chinese provinces except Tibet. In each province, the provincial capital was automatically surveyed and additional cities were selected based on the economic size of a province. A total of 100 firms were randomly sampled in each city, with the exception of the four province-level cities (Beijing, Tianjin, Shanghai, and Chongqing), where 200 firms were surveyed (Mako 2006). A similar nationwide survey on corporate social responsibility was conducted jointly by the China Center for Economic Research (CCER) and the NBS in 2006, covering 1,268 firms in 12

Chinese cities (Shen and Yao 2009). Similar to the WBES, in each city, 100 firms were randomly selected from those with an annual sales volume larger than RMB 5 million, or $640,311, using a two-stage stratified sampling strategy with respect to ownership and size.

A more recent example is the Chinese Outward Direct Investment Survey, an annual national business survey conducted by Weiyi Shi and Boliang Zhu in collaboration with the China Council for the Promotion of Investment and Trade (CCPIT) and Tsinghua University. The most recent available version of the survey was fielded between June and August 2014. The researchers employed CCPIT's local councils to recruit subjects from a list of randomly selected firms, stratified by industry, ownership, size, and overseas investment status. In addition, local councils were permitted to include from their jurisdictions firms not on the list. The survey collected 601 responses in total, spread over 17 Chinese provinces (Zhu and Shi 2019).

There are several reasons why so few large-scale, nationwide, firm-level surveys have been conducted in China. First, they are costly. For the WEBS and CCER surveys, the NBS dispatched hundreds of trained enumerators to conduct face-to-face interviews with business owners. Second, firm-level surveys in China require support from local agencies to help with implementation, which may be difficult to obtain for most researchers. Last but not least, the ability to conduct a firm-level survey, or any survey for that matter, is subject to the vagaries of the political environment in China, especially when researchers are working with government agencies such as the NBS, who may terminate the collaboration without notice.

We tried to overcome these challenges by implementing our firm-level survey through an online marketing research company, which has recently become a cost-effective tool for subject recruitment in China (Alkon and Wang 2018; Burzo and Li 2018; Fang and Li 2020; Li and Zeng 2017; Truex 2017). These firms maintain an online panel of potential subjects, often in the millions, who receive invitations to fill out questionnaires in exchange for cash or points that can be used for merchandise. The company we employed is one of the leading players in China, with an online subject pool of more than 2.6 million and a daily active user base of more than one million.

The company has collected basic demographic information on all of the subjects, making it possible to aim a survey at particular subsamples of the subject pool. For our purposes, we targeted our survey at firm managers, defined as those holding managerial positions, such as general managers, vice presidents, directors, and chief executive officers (CEOs). The company used a variety of methods to recruit these people into the subject pool, mostly by inviting managers who had enlisted the company to help with their own marketing research. The incentives provided to these managers are much higher than those offered to ordinary citizens, but they are still considerably lower than the costs involved in traditional firm-level surveys.[1]

Importantly, the marketing research company was only responsible for subject recruitment, not the design of the questionnaire, which was distributed as a link directing the respondent to an external website, where the survey is hosted. On the introductory page of the survey, the firm managers read general information about the survey, reviewed the consent form, and decided whether or not to participate. The survey was designed to be completed in 10–15 minutes. At the end of the survey, the managers were redirected back to the research company to claim their completion code. The full survey questionnaire can be found in appendix 4.7.

The survey was in the field between April and June 2017. During this period, the company sent out batches of invitations to a random sample of the manager pool to reach our target sample size of 500. With such an "opt-in" method of subject recruitment, all of the potential respondents that met the eligibility criteria were invited to take part in the survey, and the survey link expired once a preset number of responses was reached. This made it difficult to calculate response rate as in traditional surveys, since the invitations were rolled out in phases rather than based on a predetermined size. In total, 569 firm managers successfully completed the survey.

The left panel of figure 4.1 shows the geographical distribution of the number of firms in our sample, which includes 27 of the 32 provincial-level administrative units in China. The five regions not represented in our sample are Hainan, Inner Mongolia, Ningxia, Qinghai, and Tibet. The top four regions are Guangdong (19.6 percent), Shanghai (13.4 percent), Beijing (12.5 percent), and Jiangsu (7.9 percent). The right panel of figure 4.1 presents the differences between the percentage of firms in each region for our sample with those calculated from the total number of firms in the *China Statistical Yearbook* (2017). The differences are color-coded according to the absolute differences between the two. Not surprisingly, the top four regions all have large positive differences, with the percentage of firms in Guangdong, the city of our fieldwork, overrepresented by 10.6 percent. For the majority of the provinces, however, the differences are within 5 percent.

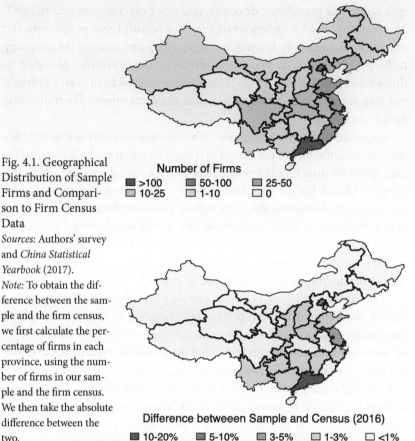

Fig. 4.1. Geographical Distribution of Sample Firms and Comparison to Firm Census Data
Sources: Authors' survey and *China Statistical Yearbook* (2017).
Note: To obtain the difference between the sample and the firm census, we first calculate the percentage of firms in each province, using the number of firms in our sample and the firm census. We then take the absolute difference between the two.

Number of Firms
■ >100   ■ 50-100   ■ 25-50
□ 10-25   □ 1-10   □ 0

Difference betweeen Sample and Census (2016)
■ 10-20%   ■ 5-10%   ■ 3-5%   □ 1-3%   □ <1%

Overall, this urban bias is consistent with the geographical composition of other samples drawn from online panels, as well as the distribution of the level of economic development across Chinese provinces.

More than half of the firms (57.1 percent) were founded in or after 2000, and the average age of the firms is 19.9 years. The majority of the firms are private (60.3 percent), followed by state-owned firms (16.9 percent), foreign-invested firms (14.4 percent), joint ventures (6.7 percent), and collective firms (1.8 percent). In terms of the sectoral composition of our sample, the majority of the firms are in manufacturing industries (35.8 percent), followed by the machinery (17.1 percent), textile (7.9 percent), basic metal (5.5 percent), and rubber and plastic (4.8 percent) industries. With regard to size, 34 percent of the firms have more than 500 employees, 29.4

percent employ between 201 and 500 employees, and 7.1 percent have fewer than 50 employees. These firms are also fairly engaged in international trade and investment, with about a third (30.6 percent) owning a facility or having investments in another country.

In terms of their trade activities, 50 percent and 73.1 percent of the firms reported having imported and exported in the past year, respectively. On average, the sample firms exported to 2.5 countries, which are, in descending order, the United States (36 percent), South Korea (29 percent), Japan (28.1 percent), Indonesia (27.9 percent), Vietnam (25.6 percent), Germany (22.8 percent), Australia (20.4 percent), Russia (19.5 percent), Brazil (17.6 percent), Canada (17.2 percent), and Mexico (11.6 percent). They also imported from an average of 1.3 countries, which are, in descending order, the United States (25.6 percent), Germany (20.7 percent), Japan (18.8 percent), South Korea (12.3 percent), Australia (9.5 percent), Indonesia (8.9 percent), Vietnam (8.1 percent), Canada (7.2 percent), Russia (6.3 percent), Brazil (6.2 percent), and Mexico (3.3 percent).

Critics of this recruitment method argue that random samples drawn from online panels in China such as the one we use are not nationally representative. Nevertheless, recent research has demonstrated that they are comparable, across a range of covariates, with the much larger population of Internet users (Li, Shi, and Zhu, 2018). Similarly, to establish the external validity of our findings, it is crucial for us to show that the sample of firms we draw on is at least comparable to the national average.[2] We do so by comparing the attributes of firms in our sample with those from the Chinese Firm-level Industrial Survey (CFIS), an annual survey conducted by the NBS that includes the universe of "above-scale" industrial firms in China, defined as all state-owned enterprises (SOEs) and non-SOEs with sales exceeding RMB 20 million. Even though this threshold excludes the vast majority of small firms in China, the CFIS is often regarded as representing the Chinese manufacturing sector as a whole (Brandt, Van Biesebroeck, and Zhang 2014). The 2008 national economic census, which sampled every firm in China irrespective of size, counted 2.41 million firms in China. Although the size of the CFIS sample is only 17 percent of the 2008 census, the total assets of the firms in the CFIS sample amounted to RMB 43.1 trillion, accounting for 91.1 percent of the total assets in the national census.

Table 4.1 compares the most recent CFIS, conducted in 2013 and covering a total of 345,101 firms, with our sample in a number of indicators. We can see that our sample firms (column B), especially those in the "above-scale" subsample (column C), are fairly representative of the national average in terms of regional location, registration type, industry breakdown, and sales. That the two surveys were conducted four years apart could explain the small discrepancies. For example, there are fewer SOEs in our sample, but this is most likely due to China's SOE reform, which has continuously reduced the number of state firms, small ones in particular, over time. Overall, the broad similarities between the two samples should increase our confidence in making (cautious) inferences about the population of Chinese firms using results from our sample firms.

Several additional steps were taken to increase our confidence in the internal validity of our sample. First, the marketing research company

Table 4.1. Sample Comparison

Variable/Sample	A	B	C
Region			
Eastern	75.9	80.7	79.3
Central	16.7	12.3	13.2
Western	7.4	7	7.5
Registration Type			
SOE	23.6	16.9	20.2
Private	59.7	60.3	54.4
Foreign	9.9	14.4	16.5
Collective	1	1.8	1.8
Joint Venture	5.8	6.7	7
Industry			
Textiles and Textile Products	10	7.9	8.4
Leather, Leather and Footwear	2.3	2.5	1.8
Wood and Products of Wood and Cork	2.5	1.2	0.9
Pulp, Paper, Printing and Publishing	1.9	1.9	0.7
Coke, Refined Petroleum and Nuclear Fuel	0.6	0.9	1.1
Chemicals and Chemical Products	6.9	4.6	5
Rubber and Plastics	4.8	4.8	4.8
Machinery	11.5	17	18.3
Electrical and Optical Equipment	10	5	5.2
Other	49.5	54.2	53.8
Sales (CNY)			
< 20 million	—	22.9	—
20–40 million	24.4	15	19.4
40–80 million	23.7	20.1	27.1
80–200 million	27	19.3	25
>200 million	24.9	22	28.5
Sample Size	345,101	569	441

Note: The three samples are (A) 2013 CFIS, (B) 2017 GVC survey, and (C) 2017 GVC survey with firm sales greater than 20 million RMB.

double-checked every potential subject during prescreening to ensure they meet the survey's inclusion requirements. The vast majority (89.7 percent) of the sampled managers have worked in their firms for more than 24 months and thus should be quite familiar with the firms' operational, financial, and long-term strategic plans. Second, when the survey was in the field, we carefully monitored the collected responses and removed those who completed the survey in less than five minutes, as well as those who failed an attention check built into two of the survey questions. Much to our relief, unlike ordinary citizens recruited online—who routinely speed through surveys and fail attention checks—very few of our initial respondents fell into these two categories. Finally, during our fieldwork in Guangdong in the summer of 2017, we sent the same survey link to the firms for completion by a member of the management team prior to the interviews. We then compare the results from the interview respondents with the overall responses from the 112 Guangdong firms in the firm-level survey. The responses are broadly consistent with each other, suggesting that the survey instruments are generally valid.

Measuring GVC Position and Preferential Trade Preferences

As we discussed in chapter 2, firm-level GVC measures are often hard to come by. In the case of China, there have been efforts to capture the different stages of production in trade by taking advantage of newly released firm census and customs data. The latter, which is compiled by the General Administration of Customs, contains detailed firm-level data on the universe of import and export shipments classified as either processing trade or regular trade.[3] On the assumption that firms engage in processing trade only if they are part of GVCs, Gangnes et al. (2014) distinguish GVC trade from regular trade based on the trade regimes with which a Chinese firm is associated. In their study on credit constraints, Manova et al. (2015) further break down processing trade into pure assembly and processing with imports to capture the different GVC segments in a firm's trade activity.

Since we are fielding our own survey, we have the opportunity to adopt the bottom-up approach by directly asking the firms about their GVC positions. To do so, ideally one needs information on the domestic and foreign value added that is embodied in every input and output used by the firm. Furthermore, as we saw in the National Organizations Survey (NOS) in chapter 2, one also needs to acquire information on the firm's outsourcing and offshoring activities beyond its primary business function—such as research and development, marketing, and customer service—to capture the increasing servicification of manufacturing. In the setting of online surveys, however, it is difficult to ask respondents to answer these cognitively challenging and complex questions, especially since it is not feasible for respondents to ask researchers clarifying or follow-up questions, which would be common in face-to-face interviews.

In designing the survey instruments in the questionnaire, we therefore tried to make the questions as simple and straightforward as possible. This is underscored by respondents giving very few "don't knows" in the responses to questions regarding firm-specific characteristics, such as employment and sales, even though that option was available for all of these questions. Obviously, this required us to make compromises by leaving out certain questions that respondents might not have been able to answer on the fly. Most notably, we did not include any questions on the outsourcing and offshoring of the service component in manufacturing. This is primarily because the degree of servicification among Chinese firms is still relatively low (Simola 2017).

We used two sets of questions to capture the firms' GVC position. First, for each firm in our survey, we asked its managers whether or not the firm had sold products abroad (exported) or purchased goods from abroad (imported) in the last year. The possible answers to both questions were "yes," "no," and "don't know." Depending on the responses to these two questions, we can divide the firms into four groups, merging the small number of "don't know" responses with the "no" category.

Out of the 569 firms, 121 (21.3 percent) are "*domestic firms*" that have neither exported nor imported in the past year. Another 32 (5.6 percent) of our sample firms are "*exclusive importers*" that imported products in the past year to be either directly sold or used in the production of goods for the domestic market. Both types of firms are directly outside the GVCs, as they do not engage in exports, though they might indirectly be part of the GVCs of the next two types of firms if they supply inputs for their production. Nevertheless, given that these firms conduct their business exclusively within the Chinese border, our theory suggests that they should be the least likely to support preferential trade liberalization.

Firms that engage in exports are more likely to be directly embedded in GVCs, depending on what they sell to foreign markets. The 163 "*exclu-*

sive exporters" (28.7 percent) that reported having exported but not imported in the past year will have forward GVC linkages as long as they do not *exclusively* export final goods, with the linkage being stronger the more the firm exports intermediates and raw materials. These firms may also have backward GVC linkages if they use inputs from the *exclusive importers* that contain foreign materials. For example, a foreign automaker in China may rely exclusively on a joint venture supplier for parts and components, most of which are produced from imported foreign materials, rather than importing them directly from abroad. Compared to domestic firms and importers, these firms should be more likely to support preferential trade liberalization.

Finally, the majority of our sample firms (44.5 percent) reported having both exported and imported in the past year. We label these firms "*traders*" to distinguish them from those that only engage in either exports or imports. Like *exclusive exporters*, these firms can have forward GVC linkages as long as they supply intermediates and raw materials to foreign producers. They can also have backward GVC linkages if their exports of final products contain imported parts and components, which can be from their own imports or from their suppliers that use imported materials. The processing firms ubiquitous in China fall into this category.

The above classification provides a crude measure of GVC position among our sampled firms. For example, firms that only export final products are lumped together with firms that primarily export intermediate products and raw materials, but the former has no forward GVC linkages. Nevertheless, such firms can still have backward linkages through their use of inputs sourced from domestic importers. Overall, therefore, it is safe to assume that both traders and exclusive exporters should be more embedded in GVCs than domestic firms and exclusive importers. This leads to the following testable hypothesis:

Hypothesis 4.1: *All else being equal, traders and exclusive exporters are more likely to support preferential trade liberalization than domestic firms and exclusive importers.*

For the last two types of firms (exclusive exporters and traders), we use a second set of questions to tap their degree of forward and backward GVC linkages. First, we asked firms that have exported to indicate the share of intermediate products or raw materials in their exports (*I%E*). We then multiplied this by the firm's exports as a share of its total sales (*E%S*) to get the share of a firm's intermediate exports in sales (*IE%S*). The resulting quantity (normalized by sales) can be regarded as an approximate measure of a firm's *degree of forward GVC linkage*, as indicated in equation 4.1 below.[4]

Degree of Forward GVC Linkages (IE%S) =

share of intermediate products in exports (*I%E*) × (exports/sales) (*E%S*)   (4.1)

Using a concrete example to illustrate, let's consider two textile firms in the sample: an SOE in Shandong (firm ID 13) and a foreign-invested firm in Beijing (firm ID 569). Both firms reported having exported in the previous year, which accounted for 30 percent and 80 percent of their respective annual sales. However, 50 percent of the exports of the Shandong firm were intermediate products, compared to only 10 percent in the case of the firm in Beijing. Using the formula above, we calculate the forward GVC linkages of these firms to be 15 percent and 8 percent, respectively. In other words, even though the Beijing firm exports more, it has weaker forward GVC linkages. This can be validated by examining the two firms' primary products: cotton yarn (Shandong) and shirts (Beijing).

Similarly, we asked firms who had purchased goods from abroad the share of imported parts and components in their final products (*I%F*). These final products are either exported or sold on the domestic market, but only the former count toward the firm's backward GVC linkage. To compute this measure, we first calculate the share of a firm's final exports in sales (*FE%S*) by subtracting *IE%S* (calculated using equation 4.1) from *E%S*. We then multiply *I%F* by *FE%S* to obtain the share of a firm's final exports with foreign content in its sales (*FF%S*), on the assumption that the final products for both foreign and domestic markets have the same amount of foreign content. The calculation is derived from equation (4.2) below.

Degree of Backward GVC Linkages (FF%S) =

share of intermediate products in final exports (*I%F*) × (final exports/sales) (*FE%S*)   (4.2)

where

$FE\%S = E\%S - IE\%S$

Once again, we illustrate the calculation of this measure using two concrete examples from the survey, an SOE in Fujian (firm ID 118) and a private firm in Hebei (firm ID 132), both making electrical equipment. The Fujian firm reported that 39 percent of its annual sales were from exports, 27 percent of the exports were in intermediate goods, and imported intermediates accounted for 43 percent of its final products. Using the formula above, we first calculate the final exports in sales (*FE%S*) of the firm to be 28.5 percent, which is then multiplied by the firm's share of intermediate products in final exports. The result is 12.2 percent. For the Hebei firm, the three numbers are 42 percent, 32 percent, and 39 percent, respectively. Applying the same formula, this firm's share of final exports in sales is almost the same as for the firm in Fujian, but since the former reported a lower percentage of imported intermediates in its final products, the firm's resulting degree of backward GVC linkages is slightly lower.

Figure 4.2 plots the distribution of the forward and backward GVC measures for the traders and exclusive exporters in our sample. In the left panel, we can see that nearly half of these firms only sell final products and thus do not have forward GVC linkages, compared to firms who export more intermediate goods, including a few that almost exclusively export intermediates that may end up in products sold to third countries. The right panel plots the measure of backward GVC linkages for the traders only (exclusive exporters do not have backward GVC linkages by construction). Like the measure of forward GVC linkages, the distribution is skewed, with nearly 40 percent of the firms not using any of the imported parts and components for the final products they export. Our theory suggests that firms with higher backward and/or forward GVC linkages should be more likely to support preferential trade liberalization.

Hypothesis 4.2: *All else being equal, firms with higher backward and/or forward GVC linkages are more likely to support preferential trade liberalization.*

To map each firm's GVC position onto its attitudes toward preferential trade liberalization, we asked the firm managers whether or not they agreed with the statement that "PTAs such as the China-ASEAN Free Trade Agreement are good for my firm's business." We also presented statements about other forms of trade liberalization, phrased in the same way: (1) "Free trade is good for my firm's business"; (2) "Trade agreements are good for my firm's business"; and (3) "The World Trade Organization is good for my firm's business." Responses to these questions were coded on a five-point Likert scale from "strongly disagree" to "strongly agree."

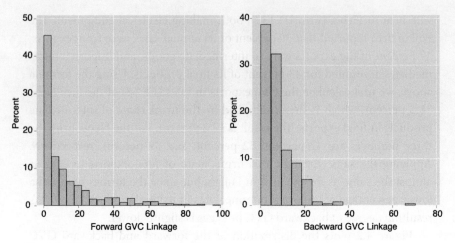

Fig. 4.2. GVC Linkages of Sample Firms

Source: Authors' survey.

Note: The degrees of forward and backward GVC linkages are calculated using Equations 4.1 and 4.2 with responses from the survey questions.

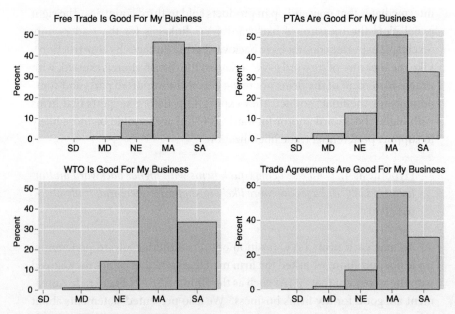

Fig. 4.3. Firm Preferences for Trade Liberalization

Source: Authors' survey.

Note: SD denotes "strongly disagree"; MD denotes "moderately disagree"; NE denotes "neither disagree nor agree"; MA denotes "moderately agree"; and SA denotes "strongly agree."

Figure 4.3 plots the distribution of the responses to these four questions. A couple of things are worth noting. First, the firms in our sample are extremely supportive of free trade. The vast majority of the respondents either moderately or strongly agree that free trade is good for their business. This high level of support, however, is not surprising, as other studies have found similarly high numbers (e.g., Li and Zeng 2017). In the 2014 Pew Global Attitudes Survey, for example, 89 percent of the respondents in China agreed that "growing trade and business ties between China and other countries" is a good thing, compared to 68 percent in the United States (Pew 2014). Enthusiasm over free trade appears to be shared by ordinary citizens and business elites alike.

Second, the responses to the three statements on trade agreements display a similar pattern, with the "moderately agree," "strongly agree," and neutral respondents in a roughly 4:2:1 ratio. Given the similar patterns in the responses, one might expect them to be highly correlated, but they are not: the highest pairwise correlation among the responses is 0.43, suggesting that the differences in the responses could be driven by firm-specific characteristics such as their GVC linkages. We examine whether this is indeed the case in the next section.

Findings

To test the above two hypotheses about the relationship between GVC linkages and support for preferential trade liberalization, we run a series of ordinary least squares (OLS) regressions using the responses to the four questions as the dependent variables. Although these measures are ordinal, we employ OLS rather than ordered probit for ease of interpretation.[5] The first set of independent variables comprises the firms' GVC positions, which we construct using the import and export profiles. Specifically, we create three dummy variables, each representing one of the three types of firms— traders, exclusive exporters, and exclusive importers—with domestic firms as the reference category.

We further include in all of the models a battery of control variables that may influence firm trade preferences. These variables are constructed from questions in the survey that asked about the firm's age (calculated from the year it was founded), registration type (SOE, private, foreign, or joint venture), number of employees, annual sales, productivity, political connec-

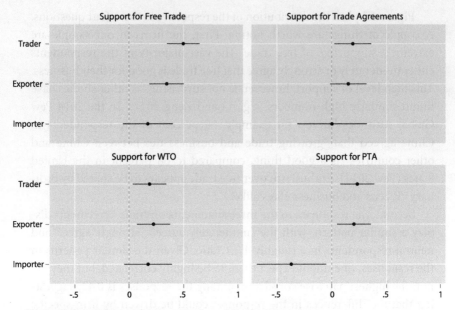

Fig. 4.4. Firm Support for Free Trade and Trade Agreements
Source: Authors' survey.
Note: Full model estimates can be found in appendix 4.3.

tions, the substitutability of its products, and whether the firm owns a facility or has investments abroad. Appendix 4.1 provides details on how we measured these control variables as well as the summary statistics of all the variables used in the models.

Figure 4.4 plots the coefficient estimates from the four regression models, each corresponding to one of the statements. For brevity, we omit the control variables and present only the three measures on GVC positions.[6] The results are broadly consistent with hypothesis 4.1. Traders and exclusive exporters, who are more embedded in GVCs, are more likely to support free trade, the World Trade Organization (WTO), and PTAs. The only insignificant results are regarding the statement on trade agreements in general, though the coefficients are correctly signed. We can also observe from the statistically insignificant coefficients for exclusive importers that they have similar preferences to domestic firms' except in the case of PTAs, which appear to have the least support from exclusive importers. It is possible that these firms primarily serve the domestic market and thus worry about the competition that could arise with the influx of foreign imports after the signing of PTAs.

While the coefficients themselves may seem small, the substantive effects are large, especially considering the strong level of support among our sampled firms. For example, traders and exclusive exporters respectively score 0.23 and 0.2 points higher on the 5-point Likert scale in terms of their support for PTAs, even though the average level of support is already very high (4.14 out of 5). And as we noted earlier, the effects might be even stronger, as these coefficients should present the lower bound of the effects of GVC position because both traders and exclusive exporters may include firms that are not embedded in GVCs (e.g., firms that exclusively export final products).

We now turn to hypotheses 4.2 by replacing the GVC dummy variables in the same model specification above with more granulated GVC measures available for firms that engage in exports. Recall that exclusive exporters are defined as firms that have exported but not imported, and the more intermediate goods they export, the stronger their forward GVC linkage. While these firms can also have backward GVC linkage if they use imported inputs from their suppliers (e.g., exclusive importers), we were not able to obtain such information using questions from the survey. Thus we look at them separately from traders for whom we have both backward and forward GVC measures.

Panel (a) of Figure 4.5 plots the coefficient estimates of forward GVC linkages from the four models. Consistent with hypothesis 4.2, the results suggest that forward GVC linkages are positively correlated with firm support for PTAs. The effect is substantively significant as well, as can be seen in the marginal plot in panel (b) of figure 4.5. Moving from no forward GVC linkage (i.e., exporting final goods only) to maximum forward GVC linkage (i.e., exporting intermediate goods only) will switch a firm from moderately agreeing to strongly agreeing with the statement that PTAs are good for their business. For traders, we combine the measures of their forward and backward GVC linkages to create a measure of general GVC embeddedness. The results, plotted in panel (c) of figure 4.5, are similar to previous ones. Firms with higher backward and forward GVC linkages are more supportive of PTAs, though the substantive effects in panel (d) of figure 4.5 are smaller. Interestingly, neither backward nor forward GVC linkage seems to have any impact on firm support for the WTO, pointing to the possibility that firms may perceive multilateral trade liberalization, which involves a greater number of countries, as less effective in promoting trade liberalization than regional trade liberalization.

Finally, we use information on the source and destination of the firms' imports and exports to see whether or not firms are more likely to support

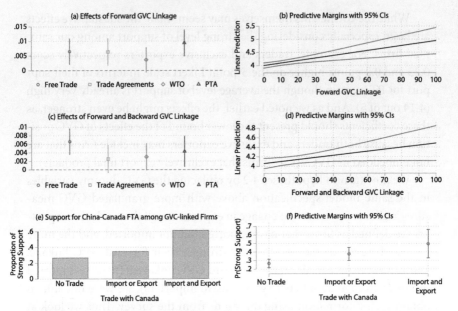

Fig. 4.5. Effects of Forward and Backward GVC Linkages
Source: Authors' survey.
Note: Full model estimates can be found in appendix 4.4.

preferential trade liberalization with a country with which they have strong backward or forward GVC linkages (proposition 1.1). In particular, our survey included one such question asking firm managers about their support for the China-Canada Free Trade Agreement, currently being considered by the governments of both countries. Similar to the questions on preferences for trade liberalization, there was a high level of enthusiasm among our sample firms for the proposed China-Canada FTA, with 26.9 percent and 64.3 percent of the respondents stating that they would "strongly" or "moderately" support the endeavor, respectively.

Of the 416 traders and exclusive exporters in the sample (i.e., firms with some degree of backward or forward GVC linkage), 85 stated they had exported to Canada and 28 indicated they had imported from Canada. Assuming these firms are more embedded in GVCs that involve Canada, we should expect them to have even more reason to support the agreement with Canada. Panel (e) of figure 4.5 plots the raw percentage of firms that "strongly support" the China-Canada FTA among the three groups of firms, depending on how they trade with Canada. Consistent with proposition

1.1, we see that more than 60 percent of the firms that have both exported to and imported from Canada strongly support the FTA, compared to 33 percent of firms that have either imported or exported, and 24 percent for firms that do not trade with Canada. The same pattern can be observed in panel (f) of figure 4.5, where we plot the marginal effects of the firms' trade with Canada on the probability that they would pick the "strongly support" option using estimates from a probit model with the same set of control variables.

GVCs and PTA Depth

The analyses so far demonstrate that Chinese firms with higher backward and forward GVC linkages are more likely to support preferential trade liberalization. Furthermore, these firms are also more likely to support preferential trade liberalization with a country with which they have strong GVC linkages. But do they have any preferences regarding the content of PTAs? Our theory suggests they should favor terms that result in deeper integration, which leads to the following hypothesis:

Hypothesis 4.3: *Firms with strong GVC linkages, either backward or forward, should be more likely to support deep PTAs that contain more rigorous provisions regarding behind-the-border measures than shallow PTAs.*

To test this hypothesis, we implemented a series of conjoint experiments in the second half of the survey. Developed in marketing and psychology to analyze multidimensional choices, conjoint analysis involves having respondents evaluate two or more hypothetical options (e.g., several political candidates) with multiple attributes (e.g., race, party, and ideology) and then estimating how each attribute affects a respondent's preferences for different options. While the conjoint design has increasingly been used in studies of politics and international political economy (e.g., Bechtel and Scheve 2014; Hainmueller and Hopkins 2015; Hansen et al. 2015; Umaña et al. 2014), it has some added benefits when applied to citizens in an authoritarian country. By presenting realistic scenarios bundled with multiple dimensions, the conjoint design increases the chances that the results will reveal the true preferences of the respondents, whose answers could otherwise be biased due to self-censorship or pressure to conform if we were to ask them for their preferences directly.

For the purpose of this study, we created hypothetical PTA proposals with detailed information on six design features: the degree of tariff reductions, the level of IPR and investor protection, the terms on trade remedy measures and dispute settlement mechanisms, and the time frame for the implementation of tariff and other liberalization policies. For each of these design features, we include three different values on the level of integration, from shallow to deep (see table 4.2). Hypothesis 4.3 suggests that a PTA that reduces tariffs to zero, provides strict intellectual property (IP) and investment protection, contains flexible terms on the use of trade remedies and dispute settlement, and requires the signatories to implement these liberalization policies within one year of the ratification of the PTA would be the most popular for firms with strong backward and/or forward GVC linkages.

The conjoint experiment proceeded as follows. First, each respondent read a short introductory text and some instructions on how to complete the choice-tasks:

Table 4.2. Deep versus Shallow PTAs: PTA Features Used in the Conjoint Experiment

PTA Attributes	Shallow	Medium	Deep
Level of tariff reductions on the company's major products	No change from the current level	A 10% cut in tariffs from the current level	Reduced to zero
Investor protection	No terms on investor protection	Generic terms on investor protection	High-standard terms on investor protection
IP rights protection	No terms on IP protection	Generic terms on IP protection	Strict terms on IP protection
Trade remedy measures (e.g., antidumping and countervailing duties)	No terms on trade remedies	Contains terms on trade remedies but can only be invoked after mandatory mediation fails	Contains terms on trade remedies and can be invoked with no restrictions
Time frame for the liberalization of tariff and other trade barriers	Within five years after the signing of the PTA	Within three years after the signing of the PTA	Within one year after the signing of the PTA
Dispute settlement mechanism	No dispute settlement mechanism	Contains dispute settlement mechanism but strict conditions apply	Contains dispute settlement mechanism but some conditions apply

Source: Authors' own survey.

Suppose that the Chinese government will sign a preferential trade agreement with [(a) the countries with which your company has the most business OR (b) some of its largest trading partners].[7] We will show you five sets of PTA design, each with a pair of proposals with comparable attributes such as the level of tariff reduction, dispute settlement mechanism, IPR protection, and so on. Please carefully compare the attributes in each pair before making your selection.

After the introduction, respondents were presented with two hypothetical PTAs, with the five attributes described above side by side in a table. To minimize primacy and recency effects, the ordering and contents of the attributes were fully randomized. We repeated this binary comparison five times for every respondent, and each time respondents were asked, "In comparison, which of the two PTAs do you prefer?" This forced choice yielded a variable for each of the ten (2×5) PTAs, coded "1" if the respondent chose that agreement and "0" if not.

For conjoint experiments (and discrete choice experiments in general), the rule of thumb in the literature as proposed by Orme (1998) suggests that the sample size (N) required to achieve adequate power for the main effects depends on the number of choice tasks (t), the number of alternatives (a), and the number of analysis cells (c) according to the following equation, $N > 500c / (t \times a)$. In our case, the number of tasks is 5 and the number of alternatives is 2 (each respondent was asked to rate 5 pairs of PTA proposals). The number of analysis cells is equal to the largest number of levels in any of the attributes, which is 3 in our design. Plugging these numbers into the equation above, we conclude that the minimum number of observations for our design is 150. Our sample size of 569 thus is substantially larger.

This design yields a total of 5,690 (569 × 2 × 5) PTAs to be evaluated.[8] To obtain the average marginal component effect (AMCE) of each attribute value on the probability that a particular PTA will be chosen, we use a linear probability model that regresses the choice of PTA on a set of dummy variables corresponding to the values of each feature, with the middle value (medium level of depth) excluded as the baseline. We also include the same set of control variables used above. Standard errors are clustered on the respondent to account for within-respondent correlations in their responses. The regression coefficient for each dummy variable thus represents the AMCE of that value of the feature relative to the omitted baseline value.[9]

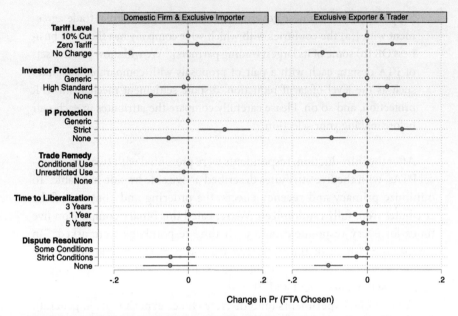

Fig. 4.6. GVC Linkages and Preferences for PTA Design

Source: Authors' survey.

Note: This plot presents the AMCE of randomly assigned FTA features on the probability that a respondent would choose the FTA for GVC-embedded firms ($N = 3,974$) and non-embedded firms ($N = 1,354$). All estimates in this figure are based on a linear probability regression with the binary choice as the dependent variable and PTA features as independent variables along with the control variables (not reported). The bars denote 95 percent confidence intervals (CIs) based on robust standard errors clustered by respondent. Points without bars indicate the reference category for a given feature.

We present the main findings of the conjoint analysis in figure 4.6, which illustrates the marginal effect associated with each attribute on an individual's probability of choosing the PTA for firms with and without GVC linkages. The dots are coefficient estimates, and the horizontal lines represent the 95 percent confidence intervals, which are longer for domestic firms and exclusive importers because we have fewer observations in this category. Each attribute can be interpreted relative to the (omitted) baseline category, which is depicted as the dot on the vertical zero line.

We first examine GVC-embedded firms (i.e., exclusive exporters and traders) on the right panel of figure 4.6. Since the baseline category for each of the PTA design features is the medium one, we should expect to see the two coefficient estimates corresponding to the deep/shallow one to fall on the right/left side of the vertical line at zero. This is indeed the case for tariff level, investor protection, and IPR protection, and the differences are both statistically significant and substantively large. For the other three design features, however, the results are mixed. It appears that GVC-embedded firms don't really care about how soon the policies called for by the PTA are implemented. In addition, while they prefer PTAs with trade remedy and dispute settlement mechanisms, they are indifferent to the strictness of the conditions attached to their use.

Firms not embedded in GVCs, on the other hand, are not so discerning when it comes to evaluating the PTAs. While they prefer the inclusion of investor protection and trade remedy in the PTA to nothing at all, the depth of such measures does not appear to matter that much. Likewise, as long as the PTA cuts tariffs, a 10 percent reduction works equally well as zero tariff. Furthermore, they do not seem to care about the implementation schedule of the PTA or the inclusion of a dispute settlement mechanism. The one exception is IPR protection: firms with no GVC linkages are more likely to favor PTAs with stricter IPR protection than those with generic or no protection.

The finding that Chinese firms, especially those without GVC linkages, value stricter IPR protection may seem puzzling, as poor IPR protection has often been flagged as one of the most significant challenges for doing business in China. However, this picture may no longer be accurate. Scholars (e.g., Zhang 2019) have noted that China has gradually but steadily improved its IPR regime since the State Council issued China's National Intellectual Property Strategy in 2008. In the most recent member survey published by the U.S.-China Business Council, released in August 2019, 58 percent of the firms reported modest to substantial improvement in IPR protection in the China market (USCBC 2019).[10] A few months later, in November 2019, the general offices of the Central Committee of the Chinese Communist Party and the State Council jointly issued the "Guideline on Strengthening Intellectual Property Rights Protection," further demonstrating Beijing's commitment to stepping up in this area.

Meanwhile, newspaper reports, academic studies, as well as our own experience in the field suggest that Chinese firms, including those without deep foreign partnerships, are increasingly cognizant of the importance of IPR protection, especially at a time when more Chinese firms are engaged in indigenous innovation and industrial upgrading that call for greater IPR protection (Economist 2019; Rosen 2019). This can be seen in the explosion of patent applications in China over time, which reached 1.54 million in 2018, accounting for almost half of the global total according to a report released by the World Intellectual Property Organization (Yu 2019). All of these factors—improvements in the IPR regime, the central government's issuance of a formal guideline, and demand from Chinese firms, along with rising international pressure—likely contributed to the preference in favor of stricter IPR protection among our sampled firms.

Overall, comparison between the two types of firms lends support to hypothesis 4.3—that is, firms with strong GVC linkages, either backward or forward, should be more likely to favor deep PTAs than shallow ones. Specifically, the odds ratio that a GVC-embedded firm will choose the deepest PTA (i.e., zero tariff, strict IP and investment protection, flexible use of trade remedies and dispute settlement, and one year to implement) over a PTA offering medium-level integration (i.e., all the design features set at the baseline level) is 1.8. The same odds ratio for a firm without GVC linkage is 1.1.

GVC and Firm Lobbying through Business Associations

Our survey focused mainly on the role of GVCs in shaping firm trade preferences, but questions remain as to whether firms have been able to influence the government's PTA policy. To address this question, we incorporated in the survey a set of questions to assess firms' lobbying behavior. Given the sensitivity of the issue and the somewhat negative connotation of the word "lobbying" in the Chinese context, we did not ask firms directly about the political strategies they utilized when interacting with the government. Instead we included in the survey a series of questions that asked firms about their memberships in and views of industry or trade associations. In the absence of in-depth interviews with firm managers in the survey, these questions allow us to establish plausible links between firms' GVC positions and their potential use of business associations to provide input during the trade policymaking process. The focus on business associations is also informed by our fieldwork. As we showed in chapter 3, in the area of foreign economic policymaking, firms increasingly rely on business associations to informally or formally voice their preferences and opinions on trade-related policies, including the contents and processes of proposed PTAs.

The first two questions examined firm membership in business associations. Firms need to have membership in their respective industry or trade associations in the first place to coordinate their lobbying efforts with other firms through these associations. To gauge the extent of membership, we asked the firm managers whether or not their firms joined either local or national associations representing their industries. The membership ratio of our sample firms is quite high. Across the entire sample of 569 firms, 462 (81.2 percent) and 342 (60.1 percent) are members of either local or national business associations. Furthermore, 320 firms (56.2 percent) have joined both, leaving only 85 firms (14.9 percent) without any associational affiliation.

An interesting pattern emerges when we cross-tabulate the membership ratios with the firms' GVC positions. Notably, there is a positive relationship between a firm's GVC linkage and its membership in business associations, whereas other features of the firms, such as size and ownership, do not correlate with membership. In particular, firms that both import and export (traders)—i.e., those that are mostly likely to be embedded in GVCs—have the highest membership ratio in such associations: 89.7 percent for local ones and 69.6 percent for national ones. In contrast, firms that are most likely outside of GVCs (i.e., domestic firms and exclusive importers) have the lowest membership ratio—69.9 percent for local business associations and 43.1 percent for national ones. Furthermore, using the backward and forward GVC linkage measures calculated above, we find that firms with higher linkages in both are more likely to be members of local or national associations. While we have no way of knowing whether membership in business associations makes a firm more likely to lobby for its preferred policy, at least the GVC-linked firms are more likely to have that option than firms not embedded in GVCs.

For the 484 firms that are members of local or national business associations (or both), we followed up with a question asking the managers to rank the importance of the main functions of these associations, including (1) "representing the common interests of all companies in the industry"; (2) "acting as a bridge between the government and the industry by communicating the common interests of the member firms to the government"; (3) "coordinating business operations among firms in the industry"; (4) "supervising the quality of products and services in the industry"; (5) "conducting qualification review and issuing certificates on behalf of the government"; (6) "collecting and releasing statistics on the basic situation of the industry"; and (7) "tracking the development of the industry both at home and abroad for the reference of enterprises and governments."

Among these seven main functions, the second is the most relevant to lobbying. Once again, here we see divergent responses from firms with varying GVC linkages. On average, managers of domestic firms and exclusive importers rank the functions associated with domestic business operations such as certificate issuance, quality supervision, and business coordination more highly, whereas managers of GVC-embedded firms rank "communicating the common interests of the member firms to the government" as the most important function of business associations, tied with the general mandate of "representing the common interests of all companies in the industry."

Finally, we asked firm managers to rate how satisfied they are with each of the functions of the associations in which they are members, using an 11-point scale from 0 (least satisfied) to 10 (most satisfied). Overall, the average rating for the seven main functions ranges from 6.4 to 7.0, suggesting that the firms are generally satisfied with the business associations. There are no statistically significant differences between the ratings given by managers of firms with different levels of GVC linkages. That said, GVC-linked firms are slightly less satisfied with the ability of the associations to serve as a "bridge between the government and the industry by communicating the common interests of the member firms to the government." This result is somewhat puzzling but could be explained by the fact that the demands of GVC-linked firms may be more complex, given their nature (e.g., tariff reduction), as opposed to a request to revise a domestically issued standard, for example.

Overall, the evidence from our survey suggests that GVC-linked firms are more likely to avail themselves of the opportunities provided by associational memberships to influence the policymaking process and are also more likely to value the role of associations in conveying their preferences and representing their interests to the government. Combined with the qualitative evidence from chapter 3, the analysis in this chapter suggests that collective lobbying through business associations could be an effective way for GVC-linked firms to push for their interests in PTA policymaking in China.

Conclusion

In this chapter, we have used a survey of Chinese firm managers to examine the relationship between firms' GVC linkages and their inclinations about preferential trade liberalization. Specifically, we constructed two measures of GVC position, using information on the import and export activities of the firms, the products they produce, and their views on multilateral as well as preferential trade liberalization. We found that after accounting for other factors that could affect a firm's trade policy position, including firm age, size, ownership, productivity, and product substitutability, firms more deeply embedded in GVCs via either backward or forward linkages held more favorable attitudes toward trade liberalization in general and PTAs in particular. In addition, we found that these firms were also more likely to support a PTA signed with a country with which they had strong GVC linkages. Finally, we used a conjoint experiment to examine the relationship between GVC linkage and a firm's preferences for the design of PTAs. The results showed that firms with strong backward or forward GVC linkages preferred deep PTAs that contain more rigorous provisions for the protection of IP and investor rights, and more flexible use of dispute resolution mechanisms and trade remedy measures.

Combined with the qualitative evidence in chapter 3, results from the survey analysis lend considerable support to our hypotheses about GVC-embedded firms being favorably disposed to PTAs that reduce tariffs and nontariff barriers to trade as well as other behind-the-border measures that impede business operations. Overall, these findings contribute to a growing body of research on firm heterogeneity (e.g., Bernard et al. 2007; Melitz 2003), especially regarding heterogeneous firm preferences arising from different levels of involvement in GVCs (e.g., Blanchard et al. 2016; Kim et al. 2018; Osgood 2018). The empirical evidence, drawn from a country that has emerged as a major manufacturing center where businesses have extensive supply chain linkages across the globe, thus provides additional support for our argument about how GVCs may be moving the main cleavage in trade politics away from the divide between export-oriented and import-competing interests to increasingly pit GVC-embedded firms against those without such linkages.

CHAPTER 5

GVCs and Corporate Lobbying for Preferential Trade Liberalization in the United States

The Case of the Trans-Pacific Partnership

In the preceding chapters, we provided micro-level evidence in support of our main theoretical propositions that firms heavily embedded in global value chains (GVCs) are more likely to favor preferential trade agreements (PTAs), especially those with deeper and more rigorous terms. The next natural question one might ask is that, given such preferences, are these firms also more likely to actively pursue and lobby for such agreements to be signed with the partner countries that they are linked with? The qualitative and survey evidence presented in chapters 3 and 4 suggests that this may indeed be the case for both backward- and forward-linked firms even in China's authoritarian context. This chapter more directly addresses this question by examining the implications of growing GVC integration for the pattern of corporate lobbying for preferential trade liberalization in the United States, where firms constantly seek to influence policies either directly through lobbying and campaign contributions or indirectly through associations or via verbal messages (Ludema, Mayda, and Mishra 2018)."[1]

Our empirical examinations leverage newly available data on business lobbying by the Fortune 500 companies in the United States for what would have been the world's largest free trade agreement, the Trans-Pacific Partnership (TPP). In our analysis, we focus on the period from 2006 onward not only because the deepening of GVCs after 2000 provides us with a better opportunity to highlight its impact on business preferences and behavior but also because this is the period during which lobbying for the TPP was most active, leading to the conclusion of the final agreement by 12 countries in Atlanta, Georgia, on October 5, 2015. We focus on the political implications of growing foreign content in exports (i.e., backward GVC linkages) in our analysis due to data limitation.

Although zeroing in on Fortune 500 companies may invite concerns about selection bias, studies of corporate lobbying that look at both randomly generated samples and large firms have shown that results from the two sample types do not reveal systematic differences (see, e.g., Drope and Hansen 2006). Further, a new wave of research on the politics of trade lobbying inspired by the "new new trade theory" (e.g., Bernard et al. 2007; Ciruriak et al. 2014; Melitz 2003; Osgood et al. 2017) has demonstrated that it is often the biggest firms—particularly those with high levels of export intensity—that are more likely to have the motivation and means to influence trade policy. Such observations should, we hope, assuage concerns about our use of the largest U.S. firms for our empirical analysis.

This chapter proceeds as follows. First, we provide some background information on the TPP and examples of lobbying by the U.S. Coalition for TPP, a group of U.S. companies and associations representing a wide variety of sectors of the U.S. economy that explicitly supported and worked to secure the passage of the TPP.[2] We also show how our theory would predict divergent patterns of corporate lobbying as a function of the GVC linkages of the firms with TPP countries and with China. Second, we introduce our measurement of the GVC linkage of the Fortune 500 firms using the metrics derived from the Trade in Value Added (TiVA) database. Using these measures, we then select two industries—one having low GVC linkage with TPP countries and high GVC linkage with China and the other having high GVC linkage with TPP countries and low GVC linkage with China—in a most-likely case design to examine whether the preferences and behaviors of firms in these industries are consistent with our theoretical expectations. Finally, we generalize the findings from the "most-likely" cases in a multivariate analysis that combines GVC position measures with information about lobbying for the TPP by the Fortune 500 companies (such as donations, trade report submissions, and general support for the TPP) that we constructed using lobbying reports and other publicly available data.

The TPP and Corporate Lobbying in the United States

This section presents an overview of corporate lobbying activities related to the TPP. It should be noted, however, that while the empirical focus of this book is on preferential trade liberalization, this does not mean that formal treaties are the only or even the main channels through which firms can influence trade liberalization in the contemporary era. Firms can also seek to open foreign markets by lobbying the government to bring a trade dispute to the World Trade Organization (WTO) or to unilaterally address foreign market access barriers negatively impinging on their interests.

With regard to multilateral trade dispute resolution, the WTO Understanding on Rules and Procedures Governing the Settlement of Disputes provides member countries with a recourse to address grievances arising from trade practices inconsistent with WTO agreements. In the United States, the U.S. Trade Representative (USTR) is authorized under Section 301 of the Trade Act of 1974 to file a formal WTO complaint against the trade practices of another WTO member believed to have nullified or impaired benefits accruing to the complainant "either by petition of an 'interested party' or on its own accord" (Shedd et al. 2012). The USTR is further authorized to undertake retaliatory action in the event the defendant has failed to comply with adverse WTO rulings. Once the USTR files a WTO dispute, the case then goes through the formal WTO dispute settlement process, whereby the parties first engage in bilateral consultations to reach a mutually agreed solution. If consultations fail, the case is then subject to adjudication by panels and, if applicable, by the Appellate Body, whose reports are binding upon the parties once adopted by the Dispute Settlement Body (DSB). In the event that the losing party fails to implement the ruling, the complainant can adopt WTO-authorized countermeasures to rebalance reciprocal trade benefits and induce compliance.[3]

Beside regional and multilateral trade liberalization, businesses in the United States can also petition the USTR to launch an investigation under Section 301 into unreasonable or discriminatory policies and practices of a foreign government that burden or restrict U.S. commerce. Following the initiation of a Section 301 investigation, the USTR has 12 to 18 months to reach a negotiated settlement with the foreign country through either compensation or the elimination of the alleged trade barrier. If a case involves a trade agreement, such as those under the WTO's Uruguay Round agreements, the USTR is required to pursue formal dispute proceedings as provided by the agreement. With the exception of those cases involving a trade agreement on issues related to intellectual property rights (IPR), the USTR has 12 to 18 months to negotiate a settlement with a foreign country. If an agreement is not reached, the USTR may retaliate against the foreign country, usually by raising import duties on foreign products, to rebalance lost concessions (Morrison 2019).

During the 1980s and early 1990s, the United States frequently resorted to the unilateral approach to trade disputes, a tactic dubbed "aggressive unilateralism" by economist Jagdish Bhagwati (Bhagwati and Patrick 1990). After the GATT was replaced by the WTO in 1995 with a much strengthened DSB, the USTR has increasingly shifted away from unilateral to multilateral approaches by bringing more cases to the WTO for dispute resolution. However, while the rise of an internationally agreed system of dispute resolution under the WTO has largely rendered Section 301 obsolete since 2010, President Trump recently revived unilateral trade negotiation approaches by launching Section 301 investigations, mostly against China and the European Union, to address Washington's trade concerns (Bown 2017b).

Overall, while businesses have multiple channels through which to push for trade liberalization, it is beyond the scope of this book to provide an exhaustive account of the lobbying activities conducted through all possible avenues. Instead we choose to focus on preferential trade liberalization, which has remained an important part of the global trading system, in view of the proliferation of PTAs and the recent trends toward the negotiation of mega-regional trade agreements among the major economies. This leads us to a more in-depth analysis of one of the proposed mega-regional trade agreements, the TPP.

The TPP was from its outset hailed as a "21st-century, high-quality" agreement that would provide American goods and services businesses with better market access and a more level playing field, as well as raise the bar for future trade rules. Had it been implemented, the TPP would have represented the largest free trade area ever created (Lim et al. 2012), with its 12 participating countries accounting for approximately 40 percent of the world's gross domestic product (GDP). However, while the U.S. Congress granted President Barack Obama "fast-track" authority to negotiate the agreement in 2015, the deal never made its way to Capitol Hill for ratification due to shifting domestic political sentiments, and it was eventually abandoned by President Donald J. Trump when he signed an executive order withdrawing the United States from the TPP early in his administration in 2017. The remaining 11 TPP countries have since agreed in May 2017 to revive negotiations for a similar agreement without U.S. participation.

U.S. businesses have actively lobbied for the conclusion and contents of the agreement ever since TPP negotiations first began as an expansion of the Trans-Pacific Strategic Economic Partnership Agreement (TPSEP or P4) in 2008.[4] According to the Center for Responsive Politics (CRP), between 2008 and 2015, 487 clients paid lobbyists up to $2.6 billion to meet with or contact lawmakers and administration officials to discuss the TPP (Tucker 2015). In addition, many firms sent comment letters to the Office of the USTR regarding the TPP. In a comment letter submitted in 2009, for example, Ford Motor Company listed 10 specific guiding policies that it wished to see in the TPP, including "dismantling non-tariff barriers as well as tariffs," "promoting an accelerated tariff reduction mechanism or sectoral agreement for trade for environmental goods," and "requir[ing] our part- ners to pursue market-based currency policies" (Drutman 2014).

Often, firms organize and lobby through their representative industry associations. For example, Pharmaceutical Research and Manufacturers of America, the largest drug lobby group in the United States, has spent more than $110 million since 2009 seeking to add in the TPP a 12-year patent protection period on drugs treating Alzheimer's, cancer, and other major diseases. Another example is the dairy sector, which has been keen on opening up the Canadian and Japanese markets to expanded dairy imports from the United States. The National Milk Producers Federation, in par- ticular, saw the TPP as presenting "a critical opportunity for [dairy produc- ers] to finally liberalize U.S.-Canada dairy trade—an issue that has taken on increasing importance in light of the robust efforts by Canada to impede even the limited access currently available to U.S. dairy exporters" (National Milk Producers Federation 2013). In 2010, the Federation wrote a 10-page letter to the USTR stating that while it would "continue to work with USTR and the United States Department of Agriculture (USDA) as part of the consultation process for this initiative," it "hopes that the final agreement will result in one that provides net benefits to U.S. dairy producers and opening the Canadian dairy market is a linchpin to achieving that result" (National Milk Producers Federation 2013).

Some of the organizations lobbying for the TPP represented interests spanning multiple industries. The U.S. Chamber of Commerce, which rep- resents the interests of more than three million businesses of all sizes, sec- tors, and regions, considered advocating for the TPP one of its top priori- ties. Beginning in 2011, the Chamber sent staff members to "attend every

TPP negotiation round" and raised the importance of TPP "at every meeting . . . with the administration and members of Congress on trade." According to the Chamber's director for Asia, there were "eight policy staff and five communications staff any given day working on how to get the message of the importance of TPP across [to the policymakers]" (Ho 2013).

There is much evidence that lobbying was paying off for these firms and organizations. For example, the textile industry successfully lobbied U.S. negotiators to include a "yarn-forward" rule in the TPP, which would have required all important production steps of textile products to take place in a TPP country, preventing China from supplying cheap textile components to other Asian countries (Ikenson 2013). Pharmaceutical Research and Manufacturers of America, the biggest spender in terms of campaign donations related to the TPP, made sure that U.S. proposals in the TPP negotiations would strengthen patent exclusivity for drug companies and limit the ability of national regulatory agencies to support generic drug development (Brandom 2013). The International Intellectual Property Alliance, a trade group that represents the film and music industry, helped Hollywood put on the negotiation agenda terms that would extend corporate-owned copyrights to life plus 95 years (Farrell 2013).

However, while lobbying can be a fruitful activity, and the potential rewards to be gained by influencing policymakers who have the capacity to develop favorable policies and legislation are large, few companies actually participate in this activity. A review of the general lobbying pattern of publicly traded firms suggests that less than 10 percent of these firms actually engage in lobbying activities (Kerr et al. 2014). The firms that do lobby tend to be larger and their efforts are persistent: if they lobby one year, they are 92 percent likely to lobby the next (Kerr et al. 2014).

Our analysis of the TPP lobbying pattern of the Fortune 500 companies in the United States during the TPP negotiations similarly shows that only a little more than 100 unique firms have lobbied in favor of the TPP. This raises the question of why only a fraction of the businesses engaged in lobbying activities while the remaining ones largely remained silent. What induces divergent corporate behavior over a trade agreement such as the TPP? Our answer to this question centers on the different GVC positions of these firms with TPP countries and China. In the following section, we more specifically lay out our key expectations based on the theory developed in chapter 1.

Lobbying for and against the TPP in the United States

The determinants of firm lobbying activities over trade issues, including preferential trade liberalization, have received considerable scholarly attention, with existing theories emphasizing the importance of export orientation versus import competition for the industry, geographical concentration, or the capacity to organize for collective action as explanations for the variation in firms' lobbying activities (Barber, Pierskalla, and Weschle 2014; Busch and Reinhardt 2000; Drope and Hansen 2009; Milner 1989; Schonhardt-Bailey 1991). While acknowledging these alternative explanations, our argument focuses on how growing GVC linkages may have influenced a firm's lobbying regarding the TPP.

To recap, our theory predicts that GVC integration will influence business support for preferential trade liberalization for two main reasons. First, businesses with supply chains have more reasons to push for lower tariffs in countries that are part of their GVC network so as to prevent disruption to their supplies of production materials and intermediate inputs. Second, firms embedded in GVCs should be strongly motivated to support agreements that allow them to move goods across national borders more cheaply. A preferential trade agreement such as the TPP would both lower trade barriers and address concerns about transborder costs through instruments that facilitate trade by permitting the fast, reliable import of goods.

The importance of the TPP for businesses with strong GVC linkages was reflected in the lobbying activities of the U.S. semiconductor industry, the nation's third-largest industry for manufactured goods export, after automobiles and airplanes. In its testimony to the U.S. International Trade Commission (USITC) in 2016, the Semiconductor Industry Association (SIA) made a strong argument about the importance of the agreement for enhancing the industry's market access in Asia; strengthening the global semiconductor supply chain, which has been and continues to be crucial to the industry's competitiveness; and aligning global trade rules with evolving trade patterns in today's digital economy.

According to the SIA, U.S. exports of semiconductors to TPP countries represented 41 percent of total U.S. semiconductor goods exports to the world in 2014. The elimination of tariffs and nontariff barriers therefore promised to provide the industry with even greater access to this important market, thus encouraging further technological development and growth.

Furthermore, while U.S. companies manufacture the majority of semiconductors in the United States, they rely heavily on the global supply chain for raw materials, manufacturing equipment, assembly, packaging and testing, and distribution, with TPP countries such as Japan, Malaysia, Singapore, and Vietnam occupying diverse segments of this global supply chain. In addition, as many U.S. semiconductor firms have significant design, manufacturing, research and development (R&D), and other services activities in these countries, TPP provisions such as "tariff elimination on semiconductor-rich applications (i.e., autos and auto parts), simplification and harmonization of customs and trade procedures, regulatory coherence, removal of impediments to E-commerce, and requirements to eliminate tariffs on tech products" could therefore "strengthen the semiconductor supply chain and better enable companies to achieve efficiency, lower costs, and reduce costs" (SIA 2016).

The experience of the semiconductor industry, which should be indicative of others that are also linked to TPP countries, leads to the following testable hypothesis in the context of TPP negotiations:

Hypothesis 5.1: *Firms in industries with a high level of GVC linkages with TPP countries should be more likely to support the agreement.*

In addition to emphasizing the positive effect that backward GVC linkages with TPP countries may have had on industry support for the TPP, we also examine the flip side of the story: the trade policy preferences of those industries with strong supply chain linkages with China, a country excluded from TPP negotiations. The theoretical argument developed in chapter 1 leads us to expect that firms in industries with substantial GVC linkages to China should have been less likely to support (and may even have openly opposed) the TPP because of the substantial adjustment costs they would have incurred due to the trade and investment discrimination that would have arisen under the TPP. Given the rise of China as a global center of manufacturing and supply chain activities for many of these firms, such adjustment costs could have been particularly consequential. This discussion of the effect of backward GVC linkages with excluded members leads to the following hypothesis.

Hypothesis 5.2: *Firms in industries with a high level of GVC linkages with China should be less likely to support the TPP.*

Mapping the GVC Positions of Fortune 500 Firms

To empirically evaluate the hypotheses proposed in the previous section, we ideally need a GVC measure for each of the Fortune 500 firms, using information on the firm's entire supply chain from design to distribution. Unfortunately, such information is not publicly available. We therefore use the GVC linkage of the industry to which the firm belongs to approximate that of the firm. The underlying assumption is that Fortune 500 firms, being the largest in their respective industries, are likely to have more extensive production networks than most other firms. Thus the GVC linkages of the industry are more likely to represent the lower threshold of the GVC linkages of the Fortune 500 firms, especially if these firms account for a large share of the imports and exports of the industry.

For reasons discussed in chapter 2, we use the TiVA dataset to construct measures of the GVC linkages of industries with both TPP countries and China. While it would be desirable to analyze both the industry's backward GVC position (foreign value added from China or TPP countries in the American industry's gross exports) and its forward GVC position (i.e., the value added of U.S. content in the gross exports of China and TPP countries), to the best of our knowledge, forward GVC linkage data specific to TPP countries are not available from TiVA or any other dataset. We are therefore limited to backward GVC linkages in our analysis. Nevertheless, such an approach should be conducive to our hypothesis testing given that the vast majority of the Fortune 500 firms are higher up in GVCs and thus are likely to be backward linked to countries located downstream in GVCs such as China and Vietnam.

Using the TiVA dataset, we compute for each industry the foreign value added from TPP countries and from China in its gross exports, respectively. We then take the natural log of these values to smooth out the skewness in the distributions. Finally, we match the six-digit North American Industrial Classification System codes of the Fortune 500 firms to the industries using a concordance table with the two-digit International Standard Industrial Classification (ISIC) codes of the TiVA dataset. We also manually check the firms and the ISIC codes to correct any apparent mismatches.[5]

Figure 5.1 is the scatterplot of the two GVC measures in the most recent year (2011) of the industries covering firms in our sample. The size of the dots indicates the number of firms that belong to the industry, which is represented with the two-digit ISIC codes. We then calculate the average of

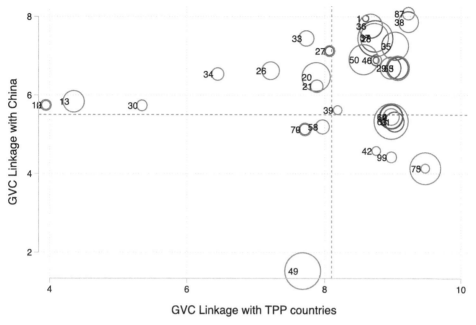

Fig. 5.1. Industry GVC Linkages of Fortune 500 Companies in 2011
Source: TiVA database with authors' own calculations. *Note:* Each dot represents an industry, and the size of the dot is proportional to the number of Fortune 500 firms in that industry. The numbers are two-digit ISIC codes.

these two measures, which are represented as the two dashed lines in the figure. This creates a two-dimensional Cartesian system with four quadrants, each corresponding to whether or not the GVC linkages of the industry with TPP countries and China are higher or lower than the average.

The two diagonal quadrants are industries that have higher than average GVC linkages with TPP countries but lower than average GVC linkages with China, and vice versa. Our hypotheses suggest that firms in the former group should have been more likely to support and lobby for the TPP, while those in the latter group should have been less likely to do so. Moving on to the two off-diagonal quadrants, we should expect firms with lower than average GVC linkages to both TPP countries and China not to have taken any particular stance on the TPP, and certainly not to have done anything to either facilitate or sabotage its conclusion. The attitudes and behaviors of firms in the last quadrant are more ambiguous. On the one hand, their higher than average GVC linkages to TPP countries should have motivated these firms to support and lobby for the agreement. On the other hand, they may not have been as enthusiastic in supporting the TPP as firms with strong GVC linkages to TPP countries and weak linkages to China.

To corroborate whether or not firms act in a way that is consistent with the above expectations, we adopt a most-likely case research design (Eckstein 1975), which has been deemed to provide "the strongest sort of evidence possible in a nonexperimental, single-case study" (Gerring 2007, 115). The inferential leverage of the most-likely case design is that if a case is believed likely to fit the theory, and if the data confound the expectations, that result can be taken as a falsification of the theory. The design is most effective when one can generate precise predictions from the theory and when the cases selected can maximize the leverage on the theory (Levy 2008).

In our case, applying the most-likely case design means that we should focus on the two diagonal quadrants because they provide the more precise and theoretically more interesting predictions on the relationship between GVC linkages and support for the TPP (corresponding to our two hypotheses). In each quadrant, we pick our "most-likely" cases, following an iterative process. First, we identify the most-likely cases in each of the quadrants for our theoretical expectation—e.g., an industry having the highest/lowest GVC linkage with China and lowest/highest GVC linkage with TPP countries. Next, we use public domain information such as annual corporate reports to ascertain whether the GVC linkages of the Fortune 500 firms roughly match that of the two measures we calculated for their corresponding industries. If it does not, or if we are unable to obtain such information, we move to the next most-likely industry, e.g., the one having the second-highest/lowest GVC linkages to China and the lowest/highest GVC linkages to TPP countries, and repeat these two steps. This procedure yields two industries: transportation and warehousing (high GVC linkages with TPP countries and low GVC linkages with China) and rubber products (low GVC linkages with TPP countries and high GVC linkages with China). In the following sections, we take a closer look at the firms in these two industries to ascertain whether their attitudes and behaviors are consistent with our theoretical expectations.

Transportation and Warehousing: UPS and FedEx

There are two Fortune 500 firms in the transportation and warehousing industries: United Parcel Service (UPS) and FedEx Corporation. UPS was founded in 1907 as a messenger company and has since grown into the world's largest package delivery company. As a major global provider of specialized transportation and logistics services, the company's businesses span more than 200 countries and territories worldwide (UPS Fact Sheet 2018). Founded in 1971, FedEx is the world's largest express transportation company. The company provides services for more than 3.6 million shipments to more than 220 countries and territories each business day, connecting markets that comprise more than 90 percent of the world's GDP within one to three business days (FedEx 2018).

UPS and FedEx are playing an increasingly important role in the rise of global supply chains as companies around the world expand their reach into new regions. This is because it is too costly for most globally oriented companies to organize in-house transportation services, given the complexity of shipping components and products across multiple borders. Instead they rely on firms such as UPS and FedEx to be third-party logistics providers, or "3PLs," using their expertise in international trade rules, their ability to reach suppliers in remote locations, and their reliability in delivering goods on time. In other words, while 3PLs do not produce any goods on their own, they are an integral part of the GVCs of the companies they serve. As a matter of fact, a recent study found that 90 percent of the U.S. Fortune 500 companies rely on 3PL providers for outsourced logistics and supply chain services (Berman 2017).

A closer look at the operations of both companies reveals that their value-chain positions are much more closely linked to TPP countries than to China. While in their annual reports both companies have repeatedly highlighted China for its growth potential, their market shares in the country have remained small, largely due to the fierce competition from homegrown Chinese logistics companies such as SF Express and ZTO Express. According to a 2014 report on the express parcel and delivery industry, released by the Development and Research Center of China's State Post Bureau, UPS, FedEx, and other international firms accounted for a mere 1.2 percent of total packages and 12.3 percent of the total revenue of the industry in 2013 (Deloitte 2014).

Not surprisingly, both UPS and FedEx were strong advocates for the TPP from the beginning of the negotiations. There were at least three reasons why the TPP could have benefited these 3PL providers. First, the elimination of 18,000 duties, including all duties on manufactured goods, likely would have created thousands of new and improved export opportunities (Carter 2016). Second, the TPP addressed the need for clear, transparent, and harmonized regulations across multiple sectors, which could have helped ensure the efficient operation of supply chains in TPP countries.[6] Finally, the TPP could have bolstered the already booming e-commerce industry, with an entire chapter that ensured "non-discriminatory market access for electronic payment systems, as well as express delivery services."[7] All of these benefits—lower tariffs, streamlined regulations, and opportunities for e-commerce—would have led to more trade in a market of more than 800 million people that accounted for 40 percent of global GDP, and consequently higher package volumes for UPS and FedEx. "[The] TPP will help UPS customers across multiple sectors by bringing down tariffs, accelerating the release of goods through customs, and supporting the participation of small businesses in regional and global supply chains," said David Abney, chief executive officer (CEO) of UPS (UPS Pressroom 2015). Echoing that sentiment, Fred Smith, founder of FedEx, described the TPP as "an important step toward achieving free trade agreements between the United States and 11 other countries in the Pacific Rim" and declared UPS to be "100% behind the TPP," which would "unlock more trade opportunities with the other fast-growing TPP countries" (Dries 2016).

Given the strong vested interests of these firms in the TPP, UPS and FedEx, both members of the U.S. Coalition for TPP, actively lobbied Congress for its passage. According to data from the Federal Election Commission (FEC), between January and March 2015, when the U.S. Senate was debating fast-tracking the TPP, UPS and FedEx were among the top five spenders of all members in the coalition, donating $80,000 and $40,000 in campaign contributions, respectively (the average member donation during this period was $21,678). Major recipients of these donations were three Democratic fence-sitters that eventually gave President Obama the majority he needed to push through the fast-track vote: senators Michael Bennet of Colorado, Patty Murray of Washington, and Ron Wyden of Oregon.

Even after the TPP negotiations were completed, both firms continued lobbying in an effort to push Congress into ratifying the deal and voiced their strong concerns when both presidential candidates, Donald J. Trump and Hillary Clinton, threatened to withdraw from the TPP. In August 2016, UPS was reportedly focusing its lobbying efforts on members of Congress who were opposing the deal during the summer recess, hoping to get the TPP approved in the lame-duck session after the U.S. presidential election. "We think there's a sense of urgency there," UPS CEO David Abney told Reuters (Carey 2016). On November 25, 2016, after Donald J. Trump won the presidential election, Michael Ducker, president and CEO of FedEx Freight, joined a chorus of logistics and transportation interests calling for the president-elect to honor America's commitment to the TPP and bolster extant trade ties. "Trade agreements are the solution, not the problem," Ducker told the 2016 JOC Inland Distribution Conference, adding that his company was "100 percent committed to the Trans-Pacific Partnership" (King 2016).

Rubber Products: Goodyear

Goodyear Tire & Rubber Company, founded in 1898 by Frank Seiberling and based in Akron, Ohio, is the only Fortune 500 firm in the rubber products industry. As one of the world's largest tire companies, with annual sales of more than $15 billion, Goodyear employs approximately 66,000 people and manufactures its tires for automobiles, commercial trucks, motorcycles, sport utility vehicles (SUVs), race cars, airplanes, farm equipment, and heavy earth-mover machinery in 50 facilities located in 22 countries around the world (Goodyear Corporate 2018). The history of the company in the last 25 years, however, shows that Goodyear has higher GVC linkages with China than with TPP countries.

Goodyear was the first global tire manufacturer to set foot in China, when in 1994 it purchased a 60 percent stake in Gold Lion (subsequently renamed Goodyear Qingdao Engineered Elastomers Company Ltd.), an automotive hose factory based in Qingdao of Shandong province, as well as a 75 percent stake in Dalian International Nordic Tire Co. (later known as Goodyear Dalian Tire Company Ltd.), based in Dalian of Liaoning province. Between 1995 and 2002, Goodyear experienced a period of stagnant global sales that saw its compound annual growth rate dip to less than 1 percent, bringing the company to the brink of bankruptcy with a record net loss of $1.25 billion in 2002 (*Rubber & Plastic News* 2003).

As the company struggled to recover, it made a big bet on China on the heels of the country's accession to the WTO. Between 2002 and 2006, Goodyear rapidly built its presence in China from fewer than 100 aftermarket outlets to a franchise network of more than 1,000 outlets to capitalize on surging demand. In addition to growing sales, Goodyear also leveraged China as a sourcing base for its local and global operations, moving its Asia headquarters to Shanghai in 2005. The goal, according to the company, was to take advantage of the lower labor and material costs in China and its geographic proximity to major rubber-producing countries such as Thailand and Indonesia.[8] The success of this strategy was reflected by an annual sales growth of 10 percent and $35 million annual cost savings, as well as other top-line gains obtained through sourcing raw materials, equipment, and finished goods from China (Bliss and Haddock 2008).

In 2007, Goodyear announced that it would further reorganize its business model to take advantage of growing opportunities in China and other emerging markets. The company subsequently made plans to increase its presence in China through a $500 million expansion of its manufacturing plant in Dalian, which was already accounting for about 10 percent of Goodyear's global tire production, to facilitate increased production of high-value-added consumer and commercial tires (Chow 2007).

Around the same time, Goodyear began to downsize its operations in other parts of the world. In the same year the new plant broke ground in Dalian, for example, Goodyear announced that it would end tire production in Valleyfield, Québec, Canada, shedding the majority of its 1,000 workers there in an attempt to reduce excess high-cost manufacturing—"one of those necessary steps to make Goodyear more competitive in an increasingly global business environment" (CBC News 2007). A year later, in 2008, with the planned closure of its manufacturing plant in Somerton, Australia, Goodyear revised its cost-savings target upward to more than $2 billion by 2009, citing improved efficiency throughout the supply chain and in back-office operations as a result of investments in high-value-added, low-cost production capacities in China as well as other emerging markets (Selko 2008).

By integrating China into its global supply chain, Goodyear also built lasting partnerships with its suppliers in China to help them reach higher standards in product quality and management processes, an issue that often plagues companies sourcing and exporting from China. Thanks to these measures, Goodyear's China plant is capable of producing high-end, high-value tires that receive the company's highest rating in quality audits for global markets across all Goodyear facilities worldwide. In 2015, Goodyear opened its new China Development Center, further incorporating China into its global network of innovation centers, with the aim of increasing the speed and efficiency of developing high-quality premium tires for China-based auto manufacturers (Goodyear Corporate 2015).

Given that Goodyear had been relocating its production networks to

China from countries such as Canada, one would not have expected the company to be enthusiastic about the TPP. Indeed, Goodyear was not a member of any of the organizations that supported the agreement, such as the U.S. Coalition for TPP. In fact, given the importance of China in Goodyear's supply chains for sourcing and production on a global scale, it was very unlikely that the company would have been on board with an agreement explicitly concocted to exclude China. This was evident in 2014, when the U.S. Commerce Department imposed antidumping duties on tire imports from China. This case was unusual in the sense that the antidumping investigation was brought by United Steelworkers, the largest industrial labor union in North America, which claimed that Chinese tire manufacturers enjoyed subsidies from the Chinese government, allowing them to sell their tires below market prices in the United States (Overy 2015). The Rubber Manufacturers Association, representing Goodyear, which would normally have been the petitioner for the investigation, instead remained silent. Nor did Goodyear, or any of the seven other big tire manufacturers in the United States, side with the union. "We take no position at Goodyear on the trade case, a sentiment similar to that of other manufacturers," said Goodyear's executive vice president at an auto industry conference early in 2004: "we are a global tire company and we play globally" (Davis 2015). What she didn't say was that Goodyear could be hurt by the antidumping tariffs, too, as some of their original equipment manufacturer (OEM) tires for foreign vehicles were made in its China plant and exported to the United States (Aguilar 2017).

While companies such as UPS and FedEx applauded the TPP negotiators for finally reaching an agreement in Atlanta, Goodyear went in the other direction. On November 2, 2016, a year after the conclusion of the TPP negotiations and a week before the 2016 U.S. presidential election, in which both candidates had been critical of the TPP, Goodyear announced that it had broken ground on a $485 million expansion of its tire factory in Dalian, which would raise the plant's capacity by about five million tires a year when completed in 2020. "Goodyear's latest investment in Pulandian [a district in Dalian] strengthens our presence in China. As one of our most important and key growth markets, our global brand and innovative product portfolio in China will gives us a competitive edge," said Chris Delaney, president of Goodyear's Asia Pacific branch (*Plastics and Rubber Newswire* 2016). With the U.S. withdrawal from the TPP, Goodyear's bet on China seemed to have paid off.

Multivariate Analysis

The most-likely case design from the previous section offers confirmatory evidence for our hypotheses that firms having higher GVC linkages with TPP countries should have been more likely to support the agreement, while firms having higher GVC linkages with China should have been less supportive. Furthermore, our case-study evidence demonstrates that traditional theories of trade, which focus on the division between exporters and importers, are not sufficient for explaining the lobbying activities (or lack thereof) of firms that do not import or export but are part of the supply chains of other firms (UPS and FedEx) or of multinational corporations with extended supply chains across the world (Goodyear).

We now explore whether these findings can be generalized to the full sample of the Fortune 500 firms—that is, whether firms having stronger GVC linkages with TPP countries/China would have been more/less likely to support and lobby for the agreement.[9] To do so, we first identify firms that actively lobbied on the TPP, using lobbying reports made public by the CRP (OpenSecrets.org 2018). Founded in 1983, the CRP focuses on collecting data on money in politics, including lobbying and contributions from interest groups, major industries and firms, and super political action committees (PACs). Specifically, we used the keywords "TPP" and "Trans-Pacific Partnership" as the issue area to filter through the CRP's online database. We focused on lobbying reports, with the caveat that these reports are based on voluntary disclosures, and that the parties submitting the reports specifically mentioned the agreement by name in their lobbying disclosure forms. Still, these lobbying reports should largely reflect the firms that were most likely to be affected by the TPP *and* that actively sought to influence the outcome of the agreement in their favor.

Figure 5.2 provides two examples of these lobbying reports. The first one (fig. 5.2a) was submitted by Sandler, Travis & Rosenberg, the world's largest international trade, customs, and export law firm, who lobbied on behalf of Walmart in the second quarter of 2013 for issues on "TPP rules of origin and horizontal trade issues." The second lobbying report (fig. 5.2b) was submitted by Nike on behalf of itself for lobbying activities in the last quarter of 2013 on the TPP and other trade-related issues. The lobbying reports also contained information regarding the income/expenses related to the lobbying activities, the government agencies targeted by the lobby, as well as the names of the individuals who acted as lobbyists in the specific issue area.

Using the information in the lobbying reports, we created three measures of the level of support for the TPP for each of the Fortune 500 firms. The first measure is the number of lobbying reports by the firm. Between 2006 and 2016, a total of 4,010 lobbying reports listed the TPP (or its variants) as (part of) the specific lobbying issue(s). Sifting through these reports, we identified 110 of the Fortune 500 firms appearing as clients either on their own or as members of an association in at least one of these lobbying reports. The first two columns of table 5.1 present the top 10 firms in terms of their appearances in the lobbying reports during this period. The average of this measure is 2.1, with a standard deviation of 7.3, indicating a highly skewed distribution. Nike tops the list with 71 reports, followed by Ford Motor, Comcast, Seaboard Corporation, Biogen Idec, Walmart (formerly Wal-Mart Stores), Eli Lilly and Company, IBM, Intel, and Pfizer. All else being equal, more lobbying reports indicate that a firm was more mobilized to influence the outcome of the negotiation.

Second, we look at how much these firms were spending in terms of their lobbying contributions, which can be understood as a costly instrument for transmitting information about the value of trade liberalization for the firm (Ludema, Mayda, and Mishra 2018). To obtain this information, we could simply tally up the "expenses" disclosed in the lobbying reports (e.g., fig. 5.2b), but these data are only available for firms that lobby for themselves, whereas the majority of the lobbying reports list "income" earned by the organizations employed to conduct the lobbying on behalf of the firm (e.g., fig. 5.2a). These data also do not allow us to break down firm spending by issue area and so do not specifically capture firm contributions

Table 5.1. Top 10 Fortune 500 Firms Lobbying for the TPP, 2006–2016

Company	Lobbying Reports	Company	Donations ($)
Nike, Inc.	71	Comcast	7,103,731
Ford Motor	62	United Parcel Service	5,225,806
Comcast	58	Aflac Incorporated	4,831,590
Seaboard Corporation	40	Boeing	4,626,583
Biogen Idec Inc.	31	Microsoft	4,009,915
Wal-Mart Stores	30	Pfizer	3,936,930
Eli Lilly and Company	29	Wal-Mart Stores	3,671,009
IBM	29	Morgan Stanley	3,539,160
Intel Corporation	29	Amgen Inc.	3,345,125
Pfizer	29	Exxon Mobil	3,257,913

Source: CRP and FEC with authors' own calculations.
Note: Number of lobbying reports and amount of donations are summed over the entire period.

Clerk of the House of Representatives
Legislative Resource Center
135 Cannon Building
Washington, DC 20515
http://lobbyingdisclosure.house.gov

Secretary of the Senate
Office of Public Records
232 Hart Building
Washington, DC 20510
http://www.senate.gov/lobby

LOBBYING REPORT

Lobbying Disclosure Act of 1995 (Section 5) - **All Filers Are Required to Complete This Page**

1. Registrant Name ☑ Organization/Lobbying Firm ☐ Self Employed Individual
SANDLER, TRAVIS & ROSENBERG, P.A.

2. Address
Address1 1300 PENNSYLVANIA AVE., N.W. SUITE 400   Address2
City WASHINGTON   State DC   Zip Code 20004   Country USA

3. Principal place of business (if different than line 2)
City _____   State _____   Zip Code _____   Country _____

4a. Contact Name	b. Telephone Number	c. E-mail	5. Senate ID#
Mr. DAVID COHEN	2022169307	dcohen@strtrade.com	34295-330

7. Client Name ☐ Self   ☐ Check if client is a state or local government or instrumentality   **6. House ID#** 301270034
WAL-MART STORES, INC.

TYPE OF REPORT   8. Year 2013   Q1 (1/1 - 3/31) ☐   Q2 (4/1 - 6/30) ☐   Q3 (7/1 - 9/30) ☐   Q4 (10/1 - 12/31) ☑

9. Check if this filing amends a previously filed version of this report ☐
10. Check if this is a Termination Report ☐   Termination Date _____   11. No Lobbying Issue Activity ☐

INCOME OR EXPENSES - YOU MUST complete either Line 12 or Line 13

12. Lobbying	13. Organizations
INCOME relating to lobbying activities for this reporting period was:	**EXPENSE** relating to lobbying activities for this reporting period were:
Less than $5,000 ☐	Less than $5,000 ☐
$5,000 or more ☑ $ 30,000.00	$5,000 or more ☐ $ _____
Provide a good faith estimate, rounded to the nearest $10,000, of all lobbying related income for the client (including all payments to the registrant by any other entity for lobbying activities on behalf of the client).	**14. REPORTING** Check box to indicate expense accounting method. See instructions for description of options.
	☐ **Method A.** Reporting amounts using LDA definitions only
	☐ **Method B.** Reporting amounts under section 6033(b)(8) of the Internal Revenue Code
	☐ **Method C.** Reporting amounts under section 162(e) of the Internal Revenue Code

Signature   Digitally Signed By: Mr. David Cohen   Date   01/22/2014

LOBBYING ACTIVITY. Select as many codes as necessary to reflect the general issue areas in which the registrant engaged in lobbying on behalf of the client during the reporting period. Using a separate page for each code, provide information as requested. Add additional page(s) as needed.

15. General issue area code TRD

16. Specific lobbying issues

Discussions on TPP rules of origin and horizontal trade issues

17. House(s) of Congress and Federal agencies ☐ Check if None

U.S. HOUSE OF REPRESENTATIVES, U.S. SENATE, U.S. Trade Representative (USTR)

18. Name of each individual who acted as a lobbyist in this issue area

First Name	Last Name	Suffix	Covered Official Position (if applicable)	New
Nicole	Bivens Collinson		Assistant Textile Negotiator, USTR	☐
Edward	Steiner		Legislative Director, Representative L. Sanchez	☐
Edward	Steiner		Legislative Assistant, Representative Farr	☐
Elise	Shibles			☐

Fig. 5.2a. Lobbying Firm: Sandler, Travis & Rosenberg on behalf of Walmart.
Source: CRP, OpenSecrets.org

<table>
<tr><td>Clerk of the House of Representatives
Legislative Resource Center
135 Cannon Building
Washington, DC 20515
http://lobbyingdisclosure.house.gov</td><td>Secretary of the Senate
Office of Public Records
232 Hart Building
Washington, DC 20510
http://www.senate.gov/lobby</td><td>**LOBBYING REPORT**</td></tr>
</table>

Lobbying Disclosure Act of 1995 (Section 5) - **All Filers Are Required to Complete This Page**

1. Registrant Name ☑ Organization/Lobbying Firm ☐ Self Employed Individual
NIKE, INC

2. Address
Address1 507 SECOND STREET, NE   Address2
City WASHINGTON   State DC   Zip Code 20002   Country USA

3. Principal place of business (if different than line 2)
City   State   Zip Code   Country

4a. Contact Name	b. Telephone Number	c. E-mail	5. Senate ID#
Ms. JENNIFER BENDALL	2025436453	Jennifer.bendall@nike.com	29334-12

7. Client Name   ☑ Self   Check if client is a state or local government or instrumentality
NIKE, INC

6. House ID#
314330000

TYPE OF REPORT
8. Year 2013   Q1 (1/1 - 3/31)   Q2 (4/1 - 6/30)   Q3 (7/1 - 9/30)   Q4 (10/1 - 12/31) ☑

9. Check if this filing amends a previously filed version of this report ☐
10. Check if this is a Termination Report   Termination Date _____   11. No Lobbying Issue Activity ☐

INCOME OR EXPENSES - YOU MUST complete either Line 12 or Line 13

12. Lobbying	13. Organizations
INCOME relating to lobbying activities for this reporting period was:	**EXPENSE** relating to lobbying activities for this reporting period were:
Less than $5,000 ☐	Less than $5,000 ☐
$5,000 or more ☐ $ _____	$5,000 or more ☑ $ 280,000.00
Provide a good faith estimate, rounded to the nearest $10,000, of all lobbying related income for the client (including all payments to the registrant by any other entity for lobbying activities on behalf of the client).	**14. REPORTING** Check box to indicate expense accounting method. See instructions for description of options. ☑ **Method A.** Reporting amounts using LDA definitions only ☐ **Method B.** Reporting amounts under section 6033(b)(8) of the Internal Revenue Code ☐ **Method C.** Reporting amounts under section 162(e) of the Internal Revenue Code

Signature | Digitally Signed By: Jennifer Bendall, Sr. Director of Government and Public Affairs | Date   01/17/2014

LOBBYING ACTIVITY. Select as many codes as necessary to reflect the general issue areas in which the registrant engaged in lobbying on behalf of the client during the reporting period. Using a separate page for each code, provide information as requested. Add additional page(s) as needed.

15. General issue area code TRD

16. Specific lobbying issues

Trans-Pacific Partnership (TPP) Agreement; Issues related to Customs Reauthorization; National Defense Authorization Act of 2014, Berry Amendment.

17. House(s) of Congress and Federal agencies   Check if None

U.S. HOUSE OF REPRESENTATIVES, U.S. SENATE, State - Dept of (DOS), U.S. Trade Representative (USTR)

18. Name of each individual who acted as a lobbyist in this issue area

First Name	Last Name	Suffix	Covered Official Position (if applicable)	New
Jennifer	Bendall			
Jesse	McCollum			

Fig. 5.2b. Self-Lobbying: Nike.
Source: CRP, OpenSecrets.org

to influence trade issues. Furthermore, it is not feasible to uncover the individual contributions of firms when they lobby together as members of an association.

Given these limitations, we took a different approach by looking at the campaign finance reports released by the CRP. Firms are legally required to report their campaign finance contributions to the FEC, including the recipient of the contribution, their office held or contested, and the amount of the contribution. Specifically, we identified three congressional committees and two subcommittees in Congress that had primary jurisdiction over matters of trade during the 109th–112th sessions of Congress,[10] when the TPP negotiations were under way, and collected data on the total amount of donations that a firm made to members of these committees.

We focus on these committees with primary jurisdiction over trade because Congress delegates to them broad authority over the markup of legislation related to trade matters, including the TPP and fast-tracking the president's trade deals. Congressional committees are the legislative trenches where big bills on trade are handled, and often the stakes are high, so Fortune 500 firms have huge incentives to donate to elected officials who have power to influence these decisions—which will affect foreign commerce by, for example, establishing tariffs and drafting and implementing trade agreements.

While the donations to the influential members of these committees may not necessarily capture every dollar spent to lobby over trade issues, it is likely that the bulk of the money spent to directly influence lawmakers on trade would go to members of Congress who were most likely to have influence over the relevant policy matter, with the TPP being a key issue during this period. We also do not suggest that all of the money contributed to these committees was solely related to the TPP, or even trade more generally, as these committees certainly address many issues outside of the policy arena of trade. However, to the extent that the TPP-related issues that the firms lobbied for are within the purview of trade or have a tertiary relationship to it, it is not unreasonable to infer a relationship between the lobbying effort of the firm and the amount of money spent trying to influence trade policymakers during the TPP negotiations.

The last two columns of table 5.1 list the top 10 firms in terms of their total campaign contributions in 2006–2016. With over $7 million worth of donations, Comcast tops the list, followed by UPS, Aflac Incorporated, Boeing, Microsoft, Pfizer, Walmart, Morgan Stanley, Amgen Inc., and

Exxon Mobil. Interestingly, there is very little overlap between this list and the previous one on the number of lobbying reports; Comcast, Pfizer, and Walmart are the only firms that appear on both lists. This comparison may produce the impression that while firms can influence policies through either lobbying or donation, they seem to favor one strategy over the other. In reality, they do both, as the correlation between the two measures is 0.51.

The fact that a firm has disclosed having spent money lobbying for issues related to the TPP (and trade more broadly) does not, however, tell us anything about its stance toward the agreement—such information is not available in the lobbying reports. Therefore we adopted the following procedures to figure out whether the firms were lobbying for or against the TPP. First, we coded a firm as "clearly lobbying in favor of the TPP" if it was a member of the U.S. Coalition for TPP. In 2014 alone, members of the coalition spent at least $658 million on federal election activity, including $553.8 million on federal lobbying and $104.9 million on political campaigns.[11] A comparable amount has similarly been spent on influencing members of the House of Representatives. It was estimated that representatives who voted in favor of the TPP received approximately $230,000 more in campaign contributions over a two-year period from pro-TPP groups than those who voted against (Riestenberg and Germain 2015). Between January and March 2015, when fast-track authority for the TPP was being debated in the Senate, the Coalition donated an average of $17,678 to each of the 65 supporters, and the average Republican member received $19,673 from corporate TPP supporters (Gibson and Channing 2015). While it is difficult to prove cause and effect with respect to the campaign contributions and votes for the TPP, it is not irrational to assume a relationship between money spent on federal election activity and support for the passage of the bill.[12]

In total, 51 of the 110 "politically mobilized" Fortune 500 firms—i.e., firms that specifically mentioned "TPP" in their lobbying reports—were members of the Coalition. For the other 59 firms that were not members of the Coalition, we drew from a variety of sources, including the firms' websites, newspapers, political blogs, open letters to Congress signed by companies and associations, and many issue-specific websites to determine their stance. This yielded an additional 40 firms that were clearly in favor of the TPP.

We find explicit opposition to the TPP from only two firms, Altria and Phillip Morris, both in the tobacco industry. These firms opposed the TPP primarily because of the constraints that certain new rules in the proposed agreement would have imposed on their operations.[13] Given the rarity of explicit firm opposition to the TPP, and the fact that such opposition was driven by reasons unrelated to the firms' GVC linkages, we did not create a specific category for such firms in our coding scheme and dropped Altria and Phillip Morris from the analysis.

For the remaining 17 politically mobilized firms, we either were unable to find any direct evidence indicating a firm's support for or opposition to the TPP or were only able to find secondary sources indicating that the firm stood to benefit from the TPP. We coded these firms as "likely lobbying in favor of the TPP." Finally, we coded the remaining 390 firms that did not appear in any of the lobbying reports specifically mentioning the TPP as having taken "no action" on the issue. Using these classifications, we developed a measure of *TPP support scale*, an ordinal variable with three possible values: "clearly lobbying in favor of TPP" (3); "likely lobbying in favor of TPP" (2); and "no action" (1).

We can now relate these three measures of TPP lobbying support— number of lobbying reports, amount of donations, and TPP support scale—to the GVC positions of the firms using the industry-level measures developed in the previous section. Because the dependent variables were constructed from data over a period of 11 years, we take the average of industry-level GVC measures for the 2006–2011 period, with 2011 being the last year for which the TiVA data are available. In addition to the GVC measures, we also include in the models the period average of the following control variables to account for alternative explanations for corporate lobbying.

Employment. Because of their more complex and diverse interests, larger firms should have higher stakes in the policy process and greater financial resources for lobbying (e.g., Epstein 1969). Spurred by previous studies (e.g., Epstein 1969; Drope and Hansen 2006; Hansen 1990), we account for this possibility by using the logged value of the number of employees as a proxy for firm size.[14] Data for this variable are drawn from company financial information in the Compustat North America database.[15]

FDI. To address the possibility that internationally oriented firms may be more strongly inclined to support free trade—whether because protectionist policies increase the costs of internally transferred, internationally traded inputs or through fear of retaliation—we control for the industry's outward foreign direct investment (FDI) flows (e.g., Hillman and Ursprung

1993; Milner 1989). We use the logged value of industry-level outward FDI flows as the measure of FDI in our analysis, obtaining these data from the Bureau of Economic Analysis.[16]

Exports and *imports*. The model also includes the total values of an industry's exports and imports to TPP countries. According to standard trade theories, industries with higher levels of exports may be more inclined to support trade liberalization (e.g., Destler and Odell 1987; Milner 1989), whereas trade protection should appeal to those with higher levels of imports (e.g., Marks and McArthur 1990). Our theory, however, posits that when it comes to preferential trade liberalization, trade composition may matter more than trade volume, especially for Fortune 500 companies that tend to occupy higher positions on GVCs that span the globe.

Manufacturing industry. To control for the possibility that manufacturing and nonmanufacturing industries' trade-lobbying patterns may be differently affected by their GVC involvement, we include a dummy variable for manufacturing industry.

We estimate three models corresponding to each of the dependent variables. First, for the number of lobbying reports, we employ a negative binomial regression model, which is commonly used to model overdispersed count outcome variables, as in our case. Second, we use ordinary least squares (OLS) regression for donations, a continuous variable. To smooth out its skewed distribution, we take the natural log of the donations. Since these donations data capture money contributed to influence other trade issues in addition to the TPP, we restrict the analysis to the subsample of 110 politically mobilized firms. Finally, we use an ordered logistic regression model for TPP support measured on an ordinal scale. In all of these models, we use robust standard errors clustered at the two-digit ISIC code to account for unobserved heterogeneity across the industries.

The results of the analyses, shown in figure 5.3, provide strong support for both of our hypotheses—that firms having stronger GVC linkages with TPP countries are more likely to lobby in support of the agreement, while firms having higher GVC linkages with China are less inclined to do so. Focusing first on panel (a) of figure 5.3, we can see that GVC linkages to both TPP countries and China are strong predictors of the number of lobbying reports submitted by the firm. Using the estimates from the negative binomial model, we calculate the expected number of lobbying reports to be 1.5, holding all variables in the model at their mean (for continuous variables) or mode (for categorical variables). Put differently, for every additional unit increase in a

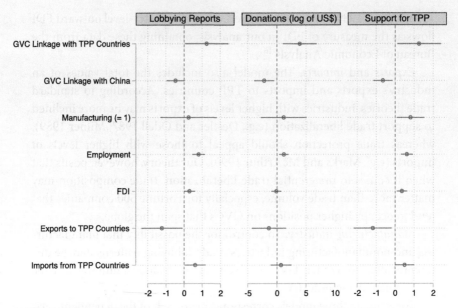

Fig. 5.3. Effect of GVC Linkages on Lobbying Reports, Political Donations, and Support for TPP

Source: Authors' own data.

Note: Results are from negative binomial, OLS, and ordered logistic regressions for lobbying reports, donations, and TPP support scale. Due to missing values in the control variables, the sample sizes for the three models are 304 for lobbying reports, 88 for donations, and 304 for TPP support. Full results are available in appendix 5.2.

firm's GVC linkages to TPP countries, the expected number of lobbying reports will more than double (an increase of 248 percent). Conversely, for every additional unit increase in a firm's GVC linkages to China, the expected number of lobbying reports will decrease by 38 percent.

Alternatively, we can use the estimates of the negative binomial model to calculate the predicted probabilities of the expected values of the dependent variable as a function of the GVC measures. We do this for the predicted probabilities that a firm did not submit any lobbying report regarding the TPP, which are graphically displayed in panels (a) and (b) of figure 5.4. For firms in industries with the lowest GVC linkages to TPP countries (e.g., coal mining), it is almost certain that they would not have bothered to lobby for the TPP at all. In contrast, for firms in industries with the highest GVC linkages to TPP countries (e.g., business services), more than half of them would have appeared in at least one lobbying report regarding the

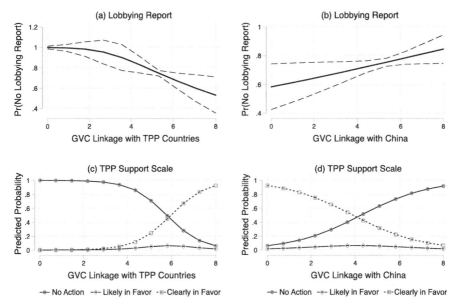

Fig. 5.4. Predicted Probabilities of Lobbying Report Submission and Level of TPP Support Scale
Source: Authors' own data.

TPP. The pattern is reversed for GVC linkages with China. The chance of a firm in one of the industries with the lowest GVC linkages to China (e.g., electric, gas, and sanitary services) not showing up in any lobbying report on the TPP is nearly three to two, which increases to over four to one if the firm belongs to one of the industries with the highest GVC linkages to China (e.g., engineering and management services).

Similarly, as can be seen in panel (b) of figure 5.3, among firms that submitted lobbying reports on the TPP, those with higher GVC linkages to TPP countries spent more in campaign contributions, while those with higher GVC linkages to China spent less. Since both spending and GVC measures are on the log scale, we can easily interpret the coefficients as the increase or decrease in the ratio of spending in response to changes in the ratio of two GVC linkage measures. For example, we would expect a 19 percent decrease in lobbying spending for any 10 percent increase in a firm's GVC linkages with China. Similarly, for any 10 percent increase in a firm's GVC linkages with TPP countries, the expected lobbying spending would increase by 45 percent.

Finally, panel (c) of figure 5.3 presents the results of the ordered logistic regression using the TPP support scale. Once again, the coefficient estimates for both of the GVC linkage measures are in the expected direction and statistically significant, and they can be interpreted as the change in the log odds of "clearly in favor" relative to "somewhat in favor" (or "somewhat in favor" over "no action") for a unit change in the GVC linkage of a firm with TPP countries or with China, respectively. Still, an easier way to assess the substantive effects is to calculate the predicted probabilities for each of the three outcomes as a function of the change in the GVC measures while holding everything else constant. The resulting graphs are displayed in panels (c) and (d) of figure 5.4, which show the contrasting effects of a firm's respective GVC linkages with TPP countries and China on the likelihood of a firm lobbying clearly in favor of the agreement versus taking no action. The lines for the predicted probabilities of the "likely in favor" outcome in both panels are almost flat and close to zero, partly because there are very few such observations in our data.

We now turn briefly to the control variables, most of which conform to the expectations of conventional theories of the political economy of lobbying. Most notably, we find strong evidence that larger firms, as measured by the number of employees, were more likely to have the capacity and willingness to submit lobbying reports and make campaign contributions regarding the TPP. There is also some evidence to suggest that firms in industries with a greater amount of FDI were more likely to support the TPP, though the coefficient estimate is insignificant in the model for donations. Finally, manufacturing firms did not seem to behave differently from those in services.

The effects of industry-level exports to and imports from TPP countries warrant further discussion. The coefficient estimates of exports are negative and statistically significant across all three models, while those of imports are positive and statistically significant in two of the three models. These results are opposite to what standard trade theories would predict—namely that exporters are more likely to engage in collective action and to lobby for trade liberalization, while importers are more likely to seek protection against foreign competition. This seeming contradiction can be resolved by the fact that the firms we examined are those most likely to have extensive production networks and to sit atop the GVCs. This means that unlike import-competing firms, which may worry about the influx of similar products, Fortune 500 companies rely on imports that are backward linked to their value chains; hence the TPP would have benefited them by reducing the costs of their inputs through lower tariffs.

On the export side, Fortune 500 companies may not be as sensitive to tariffs as ordinary export-oriented firms because the former have multiple production facilities across countries; hence they can more easily reallocate production along their horizontal production chains to circumvent capacity constraint, and they can use internal capital markets linked with their parent firms to mobilize additional funds in cases of liquidity constraint. Recent studies (Alfaro and Chen 2012; Manova et al. 2015) have shown that multinationals are more flexible in the face of external shocks and can react more swiftly than local exporters by exploiting their production and financial linkages. For example, in the case of antidumping tariffs on tires described in the case study earlier in this chapter, U.S. tire makers such as Goodyear simply shifted their exports from Chinese plants to plants in South Korea, Thailand, and Indonesia (Overy 2017). Furthermore, our results suggest that such firms may even prefer tariffs, as these can deter other competitors from entering the market but may not have the same effect on consumers, who may prefer the larger firms' products regardless of the tariffs due to their better quality and brand name. Overall, these results suggest that the main sources of trade preferences today may be going beyond traditional explanations that pit exporters against importers and instead may increasingly relate to the supplier-buyer relationships that characterize firms operating in today's ever-more-integrated global economy.

The Transition from TPP to CPTPP Negotiations

The above analysis focuses on the role of GVCs in shaping the pattern of corporate lobbying over the TPP, a proposed agreement that is now defunct following the United States' withdrawal in January 2017. In spite of this setback, the remaining 11 TPP members managed to revive the negotiations, signing the Comprehensive and Progressive Agreement for Trans-Pacific Partnership (CPTPP), also known as TPP 11 or TPP 2.0, in March 2018. As the third-largest free trade area in the world by GDP, the CPTPP incorporates most TPP provisions. The 22 suspended provisions were favored by the United States but did not enjoy the same support from other TPP members. They included, most notably, revisions to the investment and intellectual property chapters. By January 2019, the CPTPP had entered into force for seven countries—Australia, Canada, Japan, Mexico, New Zealand, Singapore, and Vietnam—and had yet to be ratified by Brunei, Chile, Malaysia, and Peru (Caporal and Lesh 2019).

The failure of the TPP raises questions about the degree to which our argument may explain the variation in the negotiation outcome. In our defense, we are not arguing whether or not firm lobbying can lead to the conclusion of trade agreements, as many other factors are involved in the process. Rather our argument and the supporting evidence suggest that while GVC-embedded firms in the United States failed to get the agreement in place through their lobbying activities, they did manage to influence the template of the proposed TPP agreement. Instead of simply addressing "at-the-border" trade barriers, the TPP broke new ground by incorporating provisions that deal with "behind-the-border" regulatory policies. These provisions bear importantly on the smooth functioning of the entire supply chain, such as disparate product standards, regulation of services, and policies regarding competition and trade facilitation, all of which were notably absent in previous PTAs ratified by the United States. The TPP additionally included chapters on e-commerce, sanitary and phytosanitary standards, and technical barriers to trade, all of which went far beyond the standards of the WTO and previous U.S. FTAs (Elliott 2017). These so-called gold-standard trade agreements for the 21st century therefore broadly reflected the success of GVC firms in obtaining their preferred outcomes prior to the Trump administration, when major institutional changes took place in U.S. trade politics.

The transition from TPP to CPTPP negotiations additionally raises questions about the relevance of our argument for CPTPP negotiations. With some voices in the United States calling for that country to rejoin the CPTPP (Bloomberg 2019), will American businesses start lobbying Washington toward that goal? Our argument suggests that GVC-linked firms should have incentives to do so, but there seems to be little movement thus far, probably because these firms have come to understand that their lobbying efforts will mostly likely be futile under the Trump administration. Nevertheless, recent anecdotal evidence suggests that U.S. businesses seem to be shifting their strategies to make the best of the CPTPP, and are doing so in a way that is consistent with our theoretical expectation about the correlation between GVC linkages and preferential trade liberalization.

Anticipating that the United States is unlikely to join the CPTPP, firms such as UPS and FedEx are now pivoting their unique role as service firms to capture the potential benefits of the CPTPP. For example, given the company's extensive GVC linkages with member countries of the CPTPP, UPS has actively promoted the new agreement on its website, emphasizing how the tariff reductions, streamlined customs clearance procedures, stronger trade rules, and "regional cumulation" provisions[17] under the CPTPP may enhance firms' ability to source parts and components from multiple countries and facilitate the diversification of its supplier base, therefore creating a favorable trade and investment environment. The company also has sought to attract more clients with advertising slogans such as "Take advantage of the CPTPP with UPS today" and "Start making the most of the CPTPP by shipping to Asia."[18] FedEx has made a similar pitch to increase awareness of the agreement among small- and medium-sized enterprises and to capitalize on the potential of the agreement for business expansion (Leong 2019; Reddington 2019).

More interestingly, U.S. firms have started to lobby foreign governments to join the CPTPP. In August 2019, a delegation from the US-ASEAN Business Council—the largest in 35 years, with 108 people from 46 American firms—met with the Thai Minister of Commerce in Bangkok and urged the Thai government to join the CPTPP. Among the U.S. delegation were representatives from Airbnb, Amazon, Apple, Chevron, Dow, ExxonMobil, FedEx, Ford, Harley-Davidson, and MSD, all multinational corporations with extensive supply chain networks in CPTPP member states. According to the president and chief executive of the US-ASEAN Business Council, joining the CPTPP would strengthen the Thai government's policies for "a modern and digital economy, e-commerce and foreign direct investment promotion," goals highly sought by GVC-linked firms (Arunmas 2019).

While the above examples are far from conclusive, they are largely in line with the expectation that firms with extensive GVC linkages to CPTPP countries should be favorably disposed toward the agreement and seek to capture the gains of further trade liberalization with CPTPP countries. The ongoing negotiations may provide opportunities for future studies to engage in a more detailed analysis of the role of GVCs in shaping the preferences and negotiation priorities of businesses in the United States or other CPTPP member countries.

Conclusion

This chapter yields a number of important findings. First, we show that GVCs reshape business preferences over PTAs by erasing the distinction between foreign- and domestic-made goods and by severing the link between the location in which final goods are produced and the country of origin of the value added that those goods embody. By reducing the costs of its main inputs and supplies and helping to ensure unimpeded access to essential supplies across national borders, a high level of foreign content in an industry's exports can increase its support for preferential trade liberalization.

Second, in addition to emphasizing how GVC integration with members of a potential trade agreement may increase businesses' propensity to support trade liberalization, we show that firms in industries with close GVC relations with non-PTA members tend to be less inclined to support the proposed agreement, possibly due to concerns about the costs of adjusting supply chain relationships in response to the agreement's tariff liberalization provisions. While our finding may need to be put into perspective, in that we focus on an excluded country that has emerged as a center of manufacturing activities in the world, it should nevertheless help to shed light on the potential consequences of PTA exclusion for industry trade preferences in an era of growing global supply chain integration.

Finally, what emerges from these results points to an important new cleavage in contemporary trade politics. Earlier explanations of industry support for trade liberalization emphasized an industry's dependence on production sharing, multinational production, or exports (e.g., Chase 2003; Milner 1989). The above findings help broaden our understanding of the political implications of value chain integration and international production segmentation. While the TPP was rendered dead on arrival by recent political developments within the United States, the politics behind the TPP and the heated debate around the agreement nonetheless provide valuable insights for evaluating both conventional and new theories about industry demand for preferential trade liberalization, and for better grasping what factors influence business support for modern PTAs.

CHAPTER 6

GVCs and the Formation of Preferential Trade Agreements

A Cross-National Analysis

In the preceding chapters, we have shown that firms and industries in both China and the United States actively involved in global value chains (GVCs) strongly support preferential trade liberalization *and* have channels to articulate their preferences to policymakers. If we accept the assumption that governments elsewhere also respond to increased pressure from GVC-embedded firms and industries for preferential trade liberalization, then we should expect GVC linkages to exert a positive effect on the formation of preferential trade agreements (PTAs).

> Hypothesis 6.1: *PTAs are more likely to be formed between a pair of countries if their domestic industries have strong backward and/or forward GVC linkages with each other.*

In addition to examining the impact of GVCs on PTA formation, we also analyze their effect on the depth of signed PTAs. The theoretical argument developed in chapter 1 would lead us to expect that firms with strong GVC linkages with foreign countries should be especially likely to favor rigorous trade and investment protection as well as liberalization terms that help increase the ease of conducting business transnationally. Our conjoint experiment of the preferences of Chinese executives regarding PTA provisions in chapter 4 further lent credence to this theoretical conjecture. Taking this argument to the country level, we expect that countries with strong GVC linkages with each other should be more likely to enter into deeper PTAs with stronger commitments in the areas of tariff and nontariff liberalization, investment protection and liberalization, and the harmonization of standards.

Hypothesis 6.2: *A pair of countries should be more likely to sign PTAs with stringent provisions if their domestic businesses have strong GVC ties in the form of either backward or forward GVC linkages with each other.*

In the remainder of this chapter, we adopt both qualitative and quantitative approaches to test the above hypotheses. First, we illustrate the logic of our theory with the recent PTA negotiations between the European Union (EU) and Asian countries such as South Korea. Using the "process-tracing" procedure, this case study seeks to illuminate the influence of GVCs on the firm preferences that underlie PTA negotiations. The case of EU-Asia PTA negotiations shows that as a result of the growth of backward GVC linkages with Asia, European firms dependent on supplies of intermediate products and other inputs from Asian countries (i.e., firms having backward linkages with Asian countries) have developed a strong interest in additional trade liberalization between the EU and Asia. These firms were further able to influence EU trade officials and shape the negotiation agenda through institutionalized lobbying channels within the EU decision-making process.

Next, we test the above propositions using data on PTA and GVC participation for the 62 countries included in the TiVA dataset between 1995 and 2011. Our empirical analyses based on these dyadic GVC measures reveal a positive and significant relationship between both backward and forward GVC linkages between a pair of countries and the likelihood that a PTA will be formed between them. These results sustain the inclusion of other variables that have been found to exert a strong effect on PTA formation. We further show that having higher backward and forward GVC linkages makes countries more likely to sign deeper PTAs that go beyond tariff liberalization.

Taken together, evidence from both the case study and the cross-national analysis provides strong support to our theoretical contentions, suggesting that by shaping domestic businesses' cost-benefit calculations of preferential trade liberalization and their subsequent lobbying strategy, the growing segmentation of trade and investment activities through GVCs may have emerged as an important driving force behind the creation and proliferation of modern PTAs.

Global Value Chains and the Negotiation of EU-Asia Trade Agreements

Since the mid-2000s, the European Union's trade policy has shifted from a multilateral to a bilateral approach. Such a shift was followed by the negotiation of preferential trade agreements between the EU and its key Asian trading partners, including the signing of a PTA with South Korea (EUKOR) in 2009 and with Singapore (EUSFTA) in 2018, as well as ongoing negotiations with India and other members of the Association of Southeast Asian Nations (ASEAN) (Eckhardt and Poletti 2016; Elsig 2007).

The initiation of negotiations for deep bilateral or regional trade agreements with Asia represented an integral part of the "Global Europe" strategy announced in 2006, designed to boost trade and investment and promote economic growth within the EU. In support of these objectives, the negotiators envisioned not only the simple elimination of trade barriers but also the reduction of nontariff barriers and the harmonization of standards, such as those relating to certification, intellectual property rights (IPRs), and regulatory transparency (European Commission 2006; Guerin et al. 2007).

What explains the flurry of PTA activities between the EU and Asia? In this section, we first provide a brief background on the aforementioned FTAs. We then look at a number of alternative explanations for the negotiation of EU-Asia FTAs before turning to our analysis of how firms and industries heavily embedded in GVCs played a critical role in pushing for the negotiation and conclusion of these agreements.

Background

The pace of FTA negotiations between the EU and Asian countries has accelerated since the late 2000s, with EUKOR being the first FTA that the EU has negotiated with an Asian country. Negotiated in 2009, EUKOR has been applied on a provisional basis since July 2011 and was formally ratified in December 2015.[1] Hailed by EU trade commissioner Karel De Gucht as the "most ambitious trade deal ever concluded by the EU" and "as representing a game-changer for our trade relations with Asia," the agreement promised to eliminate 98.7 percent of the tariffs between the EU and South Korea (Miller and Ramstad 2011). This was expected to lead to the creation of an additional $24.8 billion in new trade in goods and services for the EU and $16.7 billion for South Korea (Lee 2010).

Not only was EUKOR one of the largest FTAs for the EU, it also represented the most ambitious bilateral trade deal ever concluded by South Korea at the time. In particular, South Korea stood to benefit from the significant reduction in tariffs on imports of automobiles and auto parts from the EU. The agreement would also open South Korea's services sector by lifting barriers to the operation of EU services firms in the Korean market. Notably, besides tariff cuts, the agreement called for the reduction of nontariff barriers. For example, under EUKOR, European producers of consumer electronics and household appliances would no longer be required to undergo costly testing and certification procedures to export their products to South Korea. The government in Seoul also likely saw an opportunity in this FTA to push for greater market opening in those sectors that had been resistant to change and to cut back on cumbersome domestic regulations. For both sides, the agreement could additionally have served as a model for propelling the negotiation of future bilateral trade agreements when the WTO's Doha Round negotiations had all but failed (Miller and Ramstad 2011).

The negotiation of the EUSFTA followed on the heels of EUKOR.[2] This agreement, finalized in 2018, can be considered as a "second-best" solution to the ill-fated negotiations between the EU and ASEAN, which commenced in 2006 but reached a stalemate in 2009 (Alvstam 2017). It also represents the first FTA between the EU and an ASEAN country and would lead to the elimination of virtually all customs duties in many sectors; improve market access in sectors such as electronics, food products, and pharmaceuticals; and facilitate investment flows in both directions.[3] Importantly, the agreement could serve as a building block toward the negotiation of an EU-ASEAN FTA by more firmly anchoring the EU in the region. Recognizing the growing integration of the value chain in the region, the EUSFTA allows for the so-called rule of ASEAN cumulation, whereby products made by Singapore with parts, materials, and other supplies coming from other ASEAN countries would be considered as originating from Singapore for tariff purposes. In addition to enhancing Singapore's appeal for multinational corporations (MNCs), the agreement also helps to signal both parties' commitment to free trade at a time of rising protectionist sentiments in other parts of the world (Hussain 2018; Low 2018).

In addition to EUKOR and EUSFTA, the EU has also been engaged in FTA negotiations with India. Initiated in 2007, the Broad-based Trade and Investment Agreement (BTIA) with India is aimed at boosting bilateral trade and investment flows by enhancing European firms' access to one of the most populous markets in the world, opening the EU market further to Indian businesses, and establishing India as a major regional and global manufacturing center. Politically, the agreement would facilitate achieving the EU's goals of promoting regional economic cooperation and strengthening its role in global trade governance (Khorana 2015). However, negotiations for the agreement have been stalled since 2013 due to the two sides' diverging positions on a number of issues such as intellectual property rights, tariff reduction for automobiles and spirits, and the liberalization of services (Priya 2018).

Alternative Explanations for the Initiation of EU-Asia PTAs

The initiation of PTA negotiations between the EU and Asian countries presents a puzzling case from standard political economy perspectives that emphasize the inherent difficulties involved in trade liberalization between countries with different levels of economic development and factor endowments (Manger 2012), the role of European exporters in pushing for expanded market access in Asia, or the centralization of the trade policy-making process in the European Union that insulates trade officials from protectionist pressures and enhances their autonomy in shaping the EU trade policy agenda (Meunier 2005, 2007; Siles-Brügge 2011).

First, disparities in income levels and factor endowments between EU and Asian countries pose significant hurdles to trade liberalization because import-competing sectors in capital-abundant countries in the former are expected to mobilize for trade protection due to the substantial competitive pressure they would face from more cost-effective imports from countries in the latter that are abundantly endowed with labor. In addition, the relatively low income levels in Asian countries should have reduced their attractiveness as markets for European products. The geographical distance between Europe and Asia further diminishes the incentive for European exporters to push for preferential trade liberalization in order to capture economies of scale through regional production sharing (Chase 2003; Manger 2012).

Second, traditional theories of trade policy emphasizing the demand for trade protection or liberalization from domestic interest groups would predict import-competing groups in the EU to be opposed to trade agreements with Asian countries that involve significant trade liberalization in sectors such as light manufactured goods, electronics, and chemicals in which European producers face considerable competition (Francois et al. 2007; Sally 2007).[4] Similarly, exporters may not be so enthusiastic about some of the proposed agreements that would not generate significant gains for European exporters. As some studies (e.g., Sally 2007) suggest, preferential trade liberalization with India would be unlikely to substantially enhance European exporters' access to that country. For example, a trade and sustainability impact assessment of an EU-India FTA prepared for the European Commission shows that depending on its underlying level of trade liberalization, such an agreement would likely boost EU exports to India by somewhere between 0.26 percent and 0.39 percent, compared to predicted gains of 4.92 percent to 6.71 percent for India (*Phase 1: Global Analysis Report for the EU-India, 2008*). Furthermore, while EUKOR did promise to substantially enhance European businesses' access to the South Korean market, especially in sectors such as business services, machinery, pharmaceuticals, and chemicals, there also were expectations that the agreement may generate greater export gains for South Korean than for European firms, at least in the short term, mostly due to South Korea's small market and higher level of protection (Cherry 2018; European Parliament 2010).[5]

To be sure, European exporters, especially those in the services sector, did stand to benefit from the enhanced market access made possible by preferential trade liberalization with Asian countries and therefore supported the negotiation of such agreements (Alvstam 2017; Manger 2009).[6] They may also have hoped to offset the costs of trade diversion arising from the signing of PTAs with third parties such as the United States through such moves (Dür 2010). However, an explanation of the domestic demand for trade liberalization with Asia that focuses exclusively on the role of exporters would offer an incomplete picture, as it would neglect the support for preferential trade liberalization stemming from another group of players in the EU: importers that have developed a relatively high level of backward GVC linkages with the Asian market (Eckhardt and Poletti 2016).

In view of the weaknesses of society-centered approaches to explain EU's move toward the negotiations of PTAs with Asia, scholars have paid increasing attention to the role of the state in shaping the observed policy outcome, pointing to European trade officials as providing the key impetus for the negotiations. Such state-centered accounts have emphasized the importance of a number of factors in shaping the preferences of European trade officials, including, for example, growing frustration with the slow pace of the WTO's Doha Round negotiations, the liberal policy preferences of key bureaucratic actors in the EU and their ability to construct an economic discourse centered on the imperative of trade liberalization, or strategic considerations about enhancing the EU's influence in the Asian region (Elsig 2007; Garćia 2013; Siles-Brügge 2011). Elsig and Dupont (2012) further highlight the role of the EU Commission and the liberal-minded incoming EU commissioner in driving EUKOR negotiations, detailing how these actors have sought to garner support for launching the agreement from a broad segment of the EU business community so as to overcome resistance from the automobile industry and to address concerns about exporter discrimination.

While state-centered approaches shed light on the preferences and incentives of trade officials who influenced the launching and negotiation of the trade agreements, this does not mean that the preferences of domestic interest groups were completely irrelevant. What is missing from the above accounts is the role of rising GVC linkages between the EU and its Asian trading partners and how they have reshaped the preferences and incentives of European firms. In the following section, we show that as a result of the rapid growth of supply chain linkages, European importers of intermediate products from Asia have actively mobilized for preferential trade liberalization so as to reduce the costs of imports and burdens that may negatively impact on their operations, thereby maintaining unimpeded access to foreign markets and increasing the efficiency of production throughout the supply chain.

Growing Supply Chain Linkages between the EU and Asia and Implications for Firm Trade Preferences

The emergence of Asia as a key player in the international division of labor in a number of industries has increased the relevance of GVCs for the region. Importantly, while the region as a whole has become a more active participant in GVCs driven primarily by the rise of China, advanced economies (such as Europe, North America, and Japan) have increasingly shifted away from China as a major partner in production-sharing toward smaller and less-developed players in the region, a pattern especially pronounced in the more established sectors. This change has further coincided with an extensive process of delocalization as various production processes moved from newly industrialized countries toward less-advanced economies.

As a result of such developments, the backward GVC linkages of East and Southeast Asia with the rest of the world, and the developed economies in particular, have grown rapidly, from 10.2 percent in 1995 to 18.1 percent in 2011. Notably, while China's backward GVC linkages have remained stable, at about 32 percent, during this period, other countries such as Cambodia, South Korea, Malaysia, and Vietnam have seen relatively rapid growth in this figure. With respect to forward GVC linkages, the share of Asian value added in foreign exports has remained steady at about 16 percent between 1995 and 2011. However, there have been noticeable shifts in the forward GVC linkages of individual countries in the region, reflecting the growing importance of these countries as suppliers of intermediate inputs for production processes taking place elsewhere in the world. For example, while the increase in forward GVC linkages during this period was relatively modest for China, from 9.5 percent to 15.6 percent, it has been more significant for other Asian countries, by 2011 reaching 27.4 percent and 19.1 percent for the Philippines and India, respectively ("Trade and Economic Relations with Asia" 2016).

The growth of production networks in Asia has provided more opportunities for European firms, which have developed elaborate supply chain networks throughout the world by the late 2000s,[7] with the 28 member states of the EU (the so-called EU28) emerging as the most important source of foreign value added for many Asian countries. For example, it was estimated that Europe accounted for about one-fifth of the foreign value added embodied in Asian exports in 2011, compared to 13 percent for the United States. The share of European value added in exports reached 19.1 percent for Singapore, 13.5 percent for Malaysia, 15.7 percent for Hong Kong, and 17 percent for China. Compared to their backward GVC linkages with the EU, Asian countries' forward GVC linkages with the area were even more significant, with Asian value added accounting for about one-third of total EU exports in 2011, about 2.5 times the figure for the United States ("Trade and Economic Relations with Asia" 2016).

The rapid growth in GVC linkages between the EU and Asia has had an important effect on the trade policy preferences of EU businesses highly dependent on intermediate goods imported from Asia as part of an integrated global supply chain strategy. Notably, growing EU-Asia GVC integration took two different forms: producers (e.g., automakers) that have turned to outsourcing or offshoring their production through vertical foreign direct investment in Asia, in the process transforming themselves into importers from Asia, *and* retailers that were not directly involved in manufacturing activities but were instead engaged in the resale of finished goods imported from Asia to European consumers (Eckhardt 2013).

Regardless of the form that sourcing takes place—either directly in the foreign country or indirectly through foreign suppliers—European firms dependent on Asian imports were the primary beneficiaries of the reduction in tariff barriers through preferential trade liberalization. To the extent that PTAs aim to harmonize disparate national standards and ease the regulatory burdens faced by firms as they move goods across national borders, this should have further increased these businesses' incentive to lobby for preferential rather than multilateral trade liberalization (Kim 2015).

The Influence of GVC-Embedded Firms on EU Trade Strategy

Not only have European firms dependent on the supply of inexpensive products from Asian countries emerged as vocal proponents of PTAs with those countries, they also have the capacity to effectively organize to push for their preferred policy outcome. As previous studies (e.g., Eckhardt 2015; Eckhardt and Poletti 2016) have shown, many sectors in the EU with a high level of backward GVC linkages with Asia have seen a series of mergers and acquisitions since the late 1990s that led to a higher level of market concentration. The rise of a relatively small number of large firms eased the collective action problem, enhancing their ability to engage in coordinated action to lobby for preferential trade liberalization.

Even prior to the initiation of FTA negotiations with Asian countries, European firms dependent on imports from Asia had achieved some success in influencing the EU's main negotiation objectives as outlined in the Global Europe strategy. According to the document laying out the goals of Global Europe, "Europe needs to import to export," and "foreign barriers to the supply of inputs to European industries must be lifted to ensure their smooth operation" (European Commission 2006, 7).

During the process of PTA negotiations with various Asian countries, associations representing the interests of manufacturers and retailers were once again instrumental in shaping the negotiation agenda (Eurocommerce 2007). For example, in early 2007, Eurocommerce unambiguously expressed its support for moves to open trade negotiations with South Korea, India, and ASEAN countries, noting in particular the importance of the further reduction of tariff and nontariff barriers on imports from Asia and the harmonization and simplification of preferential rules of origin for the viability of member firms (Eurocommerce 2009, 2010, 2012).

Furthermore, the Foreign Trade Association (FTA-EU), another organization representing the interests of European firms keen on securing key input supplies from Asia, sought to drive home the potential benefits that preferential trade liberalization with Asia could deliver to their member states. In particular, the organization emphasized the importance of South Korea for the sourcing of textiles, electronics, and other consumer products, and India as a major supplier of lower-end products such as textiles, clothing, and footwear to the EU (FTA-EU 2007). It additionally favored the negotiation of a PTA with ASEAN countries, in particular Vietnam, to capitalize on the existing supply chain relationships (FTA-EU 2012). In the case of Vietnam, groups highly dependent on the supply of intermediate products from that country were particularly attracted to its downstream position in high-tech manufacturing industries and cheap labor supply in exerting their influence on the setting of the FTA negotiation agenda (Hoang and Sicurelli 2017).

Eckhardt and Poletti (2016) document in detail the lobbying activities of these groups, showing that both the FTA-EU and Eurocommerce had made very specific demands. For example, reflecting their interest in the supply of textiles, apparel, and footwear from India, both organizations strongly pushed for the dismantling of trade barriers in these sectors in the EU-India PTA negotiations. To secure the steady supply of inputs from Vietnam, an important sourcing country within ASEAN, they compiled a list of requests in the PTA negotiations with Vietnam, including the lifting of tariff barriers on industrial and agricultural products; the declassification of footwear, textiles, and clothing as sensitive sectors; the application of the Generalized System of Preferences' rules of origin for least developed countries to Vietnam; and the recognition of Vietnam as a market economy (Eckhardt and Poletti 2016).

These organizations were able to further influence the negotiation priorities and strategies of European Commission officials through existing channels of communication (European Business Organizations 2013). For example, as an organization representing the interests of European retailers and wholesalers, Eurocommerce worked closely with the European Commission and the European Parliament to press for its negotiation preferences. Even though it did not directly lobby EU member states, it did communicate its position to member governments—for example, through EU-wide meetings when representatives from most member states were present. Likewise, the FTA-EU was able to gain some influence in the decision-making process through the publication of a series of position papers and press releases (FTA-EU 2009, 2011), regular meetings with European Commission officials, and coordinated actions with Eurocommerce (Eckhardt and Poletti 2016).

Active lobbying by EU businesses dependent on the supply of inexpensive inputs from Asia led to the negotiation of agreements that reflected these preferences. For example, in EUKOR, the EU agreed to eliminate almost all import tariffs. It immediately phased out tariffs on sensitive products such as textiles and clothing and further agreed to phase out tariffs on high-value-added imports from South Korea such as medical equipment in eight years. The agreement additionally incorporated more rigorous provisions on the removal of certain nontariff barriers to trade such as safety standards. Furthermore, the demands of backward GVC-linked European firms have also been seriously considered by EU officials during the negotiation process. For instance, a former EU trade official was cited as saying that although many "Vietnamese companies can already export to Europe at lower tariff rates under our preference system for developing countries . . . more than half of Vietnam's exports are still subject to tariffs" (cited in Eckhardt and Poletti 2016). The Commission also expressed its support for proposals to lift barriers on a range of imports from Asia more broadly and to grant Vietnam market economy status.

Active lobbying by backward GVC-linked groups in the EU further allowed them to reach an accommodation with import-competing groups, which have taken more defensive positions during the negotiations (Sicurelli 2015). As an example, the EU managed to get South Korea to agree to cumulate rules of origin to simplify and harmonize divergent ROO requirements in return for the negotiation of stricter rules of origin in the textile sector, mostly to address the concerns of European textile producers that compete with Vietnamese imports, as represented by the European Apparel and Textile Organisation (EURATEX), about keeping these rules in place as a nontrade barrier against Vietnamese exports (EURATEX 2010). In the absence of strong lobbying by backward GVC-linked groups, import-competing groups bent on maintaining strict rules of origin in the textile sector could have prevailed in inserting such language in a larger number of FTAs with Asian countries, including the one with South Korea.

To be sure, traditional export-oriented industries and organizations representing the interests of exporters that aim to pursue expanded market access in Asia were also strong advocates of preferential trade liberalization. For example, during the EUKOR negotiations, export-oriented businesses in the services, chemicals, machinery, and electronics sectors actively lobbied for improved access to the South Korean market, in part to offset the competitive challenge posed by ongoing trade liberalization between South Korea and the United States (Erixon and Lee-Makiyama 2010). Similarly, during the EUSFTA negotiations, export industries in the automotive and energy sectors were forceful proponents of efforts to negotiate an agreement with a high level of reciprocal trade liberalization that could also set a "precedent" for future FTAs with ASEAN (European Commission 2010).

In pushing for FTAs with the Asian countries, EU negotiators may additionally have hoped to more closely connect member countries to the dynamic Asian economies, limit the trade diversion effects of PTAs between EU's trading partners and third countries such as the United States, and more effectively implement international trade regulations (Woolcock 2007). Still, the above analyses suggest that pressures from businesses dependent on Asian imports for an integrated supply chain, especially retailers and producers seeking to maintain a steady stream of supplies from Asia—also visibly influenced the EU's negotiation priorities as well as the terms of the final agreements.

GVC Linkage and PTA Formation

The case study of EU-Asia trade negotiations suggests that rising GVC linkages provided an important impetus to the formation of PTAs between the two parties. In the remainder of this chapter, we explore whether the same pattern can be found in a broader set of countries. The empirical analyses draw on two datasets we have used throughout the previous chapters, one on the backward and forward GVC linkages of the country pairs available from the Trade in Value Added (TiVA) database, and the other on the PTAs signed among these countries, the Design of Trade Agreements (DESTA) database. We describe each of these datasets and how we utilize them in our analyses in more detail below.

Country-Level GVC Measures

As in the last chapter, we rely on the TiVA database to generate our GVC measures. The 2016 version of TiVA, which is based on the OECD's Inter-Country Input-Output (ICIO) system, covers all 34 OECD countries and 28 non-OECD countries and economies: Argentina, Australia, Austria, Belgium, Brazil, Brunei Darussalam, Bulgaria, Cambodia, Canada, Chile, China, Colombia, Costa Rica, Croatia, Cyprus, Czech Republic, Denmark, Estonia, Finland, France, Germany, Greece, Hungary, Iceland, India, Indonesia, Ireland, Israel, Italy, Japan, Korea, Latvia, Lithuania, Luxembourg, Malaysia, Malta, Mexico, Morocco, Netherlands, New Zealand, Norway, Peru, Philippines, Poland, Portugal, Romania, Russian Federation, Saudi Arabia, Singapore, Slovak Republic, Slovenia, South Africa, Spain, Sweden, Switzerland, Taiwan, Thailand, Tunisia, Turkey, United Kingdom (U.K.), United States, and Vietnam.

The two TiVA measures most relevant for our purposes are the backward and forward GVC participation of these countries in each other's trade activities. Specifically, backward GVC participation of country i in country j is calculated as the value added embodied in the exports of country i to country j as a percentage of the total gross exports of country j. Forward GVC participation of country i in country j is calculated as the value added embodied in the exports of country i to country j as a percentage of the total gross exports of country i. Because the domestic and foreign value added are different for both countries, these indicators are different for the total value of source and exporting industries for each pair of countries in both directions (i.e., directed dyads). This is in contrast to trade statistics where country i's exports to country j is equivalent to country j's imports from country i for any two countries.

Figure 6.1 plots the average level of forward and backward GVC participation among the 62 countries over time. Several patterns are worth noting. First, consistent with the global trend in the rise of GVCs, both backward and forward GVC participation in our sample of countries increased steadily from 1995 to 2011. The only exception was 2008, when GVC participation dropped sharply before bouncing back again the following year. Second, average backward GVC participation is higher than forward GVC participation, but the gap has narrowed over time. Finally, more countries have become embedded in GVCs. In 1995, 24 percent of the 3,782 country

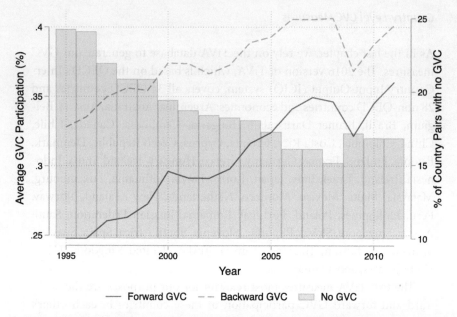

Fig. 6.1. GVC Participation of Sample Countries over Time, 1995–2011
Source: TiVA dataset, OECD.
Note: The solid and dashed lines represent the level of forward and backward GVC participation averaged over all 62 economies for each year, respectively. The bars represent the
proportion of country pairs that have no backward or forward GVC participation in each
year.

pairs had no forward or backward GVC participation. By 2011, this had
decreased to 16.8 percent.

While the average GVC participation among the 62 countries is low (0.3
percent forward and 0.37 percent backward), the distribution is skewed to
the right, with a number of countries strongly linked to their partners
through GVCs. In 2011, the top 10 country pairs with the highest level of
backward participation were: Russia to Bulgaria (13.2 percent), United
States to Ireland (13.2 percent), China to Cambodia (12 percent), United
States to Mexico (11.6 percent), United States to Costa Rica (10.9 percent),
Germany to Hungary (9.6 percent), United States to Canada (9.4 percent),
Germany to Czech Republic (9.3 percent), Russia to Slovak Republic (9.2
percent), and Germany to Luxembourg (9 percent). Almost all of these
cases involve the backward GVC participation of a larger economic entity
with its smaller neighbor. The top 10 dyads with the highest level of forward

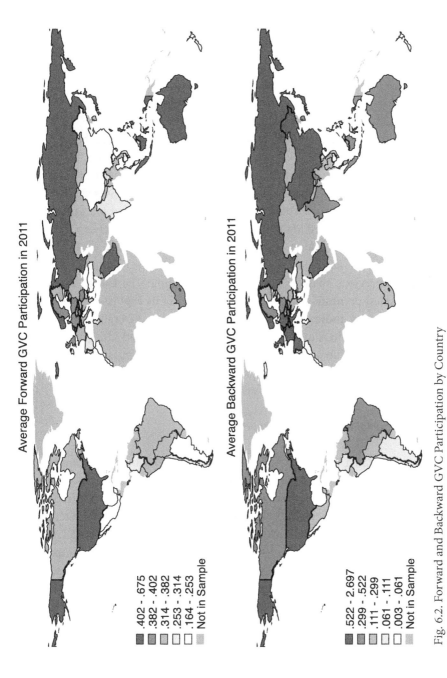

Fig. 6.2. Forward and Backward GVC Participation by Country

Source: TiVA dataset, OECD.

Note: This figure visualizes the forward and backward GVC participation of each of the 62 economies averaged over the other 61 trading partners in 2011.

participation in 2011 were: Taiwan to China (11.3 percent), Japan to China (10.4 percent), Chile to China (9.3 percent), Philippines to China (8.9 percent), Brunei to South Korea (8.7 percent), South Korea to China (8.4 percent), Norway to United Kingdom (8.4 percent), Colombia to United States (8 percent), Canada to United States (7.9 percent), and Australia to China (7.7 percent). In six of the 10 cases, the target country was China.

That China was much more likely to be backward linked in the GVCs of its trading partners can be made more apparent when we look at the average forward and backward GVC participation of every country with the rest of the countries. Figure 6.2 visualizes these measures for the last year of the data (2011) in quintiles, where darker colors represent higher average GVC participation. With few exceptions, most of the countries had one type of GVC participation ranked higher than the other relative to their peers. Furthermore, developing countries tended to have more backward GVC participation than forward. Here the contrast between the two countries covered in the previous chapters is particularly revealing. The United States had the highest domestic and foreign value added in its exports compared to other countries, indicated by the fact that both measures ranked in the top quintile. China, in contrast, had the highest foreign value added and the lowest domestic value added embodied in its exports, suggesting that in 2011 backward GVC participation played a more salient role in the country's trade patterns than forward GVC linkages.

The Formation of PTAs and Their Depth

We use the DESTA dataset to gather information on PTAs formed among the 62 countries between 1995 and 2011. As described in chapter 2, the DESTA dataset covers all agreements with the potential to liberalize trade, including bilateral agreements (e.g., the Australia-Chile FTA), plurilateral agreements (e.g., the North American Free Trade Agreement, or NAFTA), regional agreements (e.g., the European Community), accession agreements (e.g., the U.K.'s EU accession agreement signed in 1972), and accession agreements as a result of membership in a regional agreement (e.g., Romania signing the FTA with the EU and Mexico upon becoming a member of the EU). Since our theory is about how the GVC linkages between two countries affect the likelihood of them forming a PTA, we focus on bilateral agreements only, leaving out multilateral agreements and those arrangements where preferential market access is granted on a unilateral basis as in the case of accession agreements.

We extract from DESTA bilateral agreements signed among the 62 countries between 1995 and 2011, the period for which TiVA measures are available. This leads to a total of 84 PTAs, accounting for 4.4 percent of the dyadic country pairs in the sample (see appendix 6.1 for a list of these PTAs and their brief histories). Figure 6.3 illustrates the distribution of PTAs by country. The average number of bilateral PTAs signed by the sample countries is 2.7, with a standard deviation of 3.3. A total of 29 countries have signed no PTA with any of the other 61 countries, while the remaining 33 countries have signed at least one. Three countries—Chile, Japan, and Turkey—signed the largest number of PTAs (12). It is worth noting that the reason many of the European countries in our sample show up as signing no bilateral PTAs is because they are already members of plurilateral or regional agreements such as the EU.

Of course, not all of the PTAs are the same with respect to the scope and degree of liberalization. The "depth" of the PTAs can be measured by examining seven key provisions that can be included in PTAs (Dür et al. 2014). The first of these provisions captures whether the agreement foresees that all tariffs (with limited exceptions) should be reduced to zero (that is, whether the aim is to create a full free trade area). The other six provisions capture cooperation that goes beyond tariff reductions in areas such as services trade, investments, standards, public procurement, competition, and IPRs. Each of these areas is coded as "1" if the agreement contains any substantive provisions. A substantive provision, for example, is a national treatment clause in the services chapter. In contrast, a statement that the contracting parties desire to open their services markets does not count as a substantive provision. Thus the depth of an agreement can be operationalized as an additive index that ranges from zero to seven.

Figure 6.4 is a heat map that plots the PTAs signed by our sample countries. To improve the visualization, we only include the 33 countries that have signed at least one PTA during the period 1995–2011. For each country, the row and column are symmetrical, with the colored squares representing a PTA with the corresponding partner country in the column and row. Darker colors denote agreements that have more substantive provisions on tariff and nontariff liberalization. The average depth of the 84 PTAs is 3.9 with a standard deviation of 1.9. Three PTAs have the lowest rating of depth (1), and 9 have the highest rating of depth (7).

There are many variations between and within countries when it comes to the depth of their PTAs. This is evident when we engage in a closer exam-

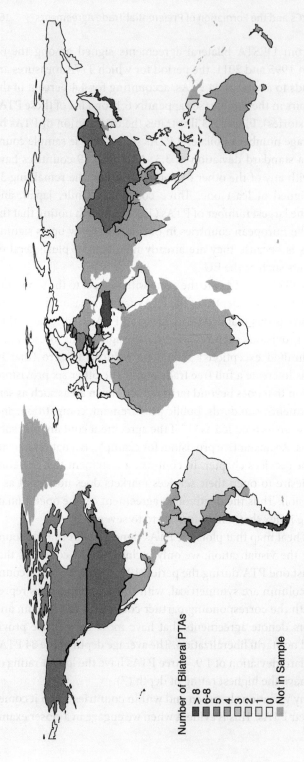

Fig. 6.3. Number of Bilateral PTAs by Country, 1995–2011

Source: TiVA dataset, OECD.

Note: This figure visualizes the number of bilateral FTAs signed by each of the 62 economies between 1995 and 2011.

Number of Bilateral PTAs

> 8
6-8
5
4
3
2
1
0
Not in Sample

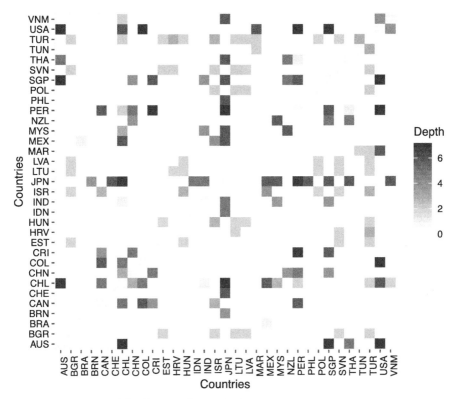

Fig. 6.4. PTA Depth by Country Pair, 1995–2011

Source: TiVA dataset, OECD.

Note: This heat map presents the depth of the bilateral PTAs signed between 33 economies between 1995 and 2011. Darker colors mean the agreements are deeper. The 29 economies that signed no bilateral FTAs in this period are not included in the figure.

ination of the three countries with the greatest number of PTAs. The majority of Japan's PTAs have depth indices equal to or greater than 6, the average being 5.8. In contrast, none of the 12 PTAs signed by Turkey has a depth index higher than 3. The depth indices for Chile's PTAs are almost evenly distributed, with an average of 4.1. It seems that developed countries tend to sign deeper PTAs with each other, whereas PTAs between developing countries tend to be shallower and do not go much further than tariff liberalization.

Research Design

Our main hypothesis suggests that two countries are more likely to form a PTA if domestic industries in the home country draw on a high level of foreign content in the exports of the partner country or if their domestic value added takes up a larger share of the exports of the home country, and vice versa (*Hypothesis 6.1*). We further expect that a pair of countries whose domestic industries have strong backward or forward GVC linkages will sign a PTA that not only contains strong tariff liberalization measures but also includes other provisions regarding services trade, investments, standards, competition, and IPR that facilitate trade and investment liberalization (*Hypothesis 6.2*).

To explore the question on PTA formation, we create a dichotomous variable (*PTA*) that equals "1" if country i and country j sign a bilateral PTA in year t, and "0" otherwise. We consider only the initial signing of an agreement, not subsequent years when an agreement is ratified. Since the backward and forward GVC participation measures are directional, we use the annual directed dyad as the unit of analysis. Each observation in the data is therefore a record of whether or not the two countries signed a PTA. The data is right censored in that once two countries sign a PTA, they are dropped from the dataset. It is also left censored because our GVC measures are not available before 1995. To isolate the effects of GVCs on PTA formation, we focus on the country pairs that had not entered into any trade agreements prior to 1995, dropping those dyads that either had signed an earlier PTA or were members to multilateral agreements.

This time-to-event data structure can then be estimated using the continuous-time survival model in the following equation:

$$\lambda_{ij}(t, x_{ij}(t)) = \lambda_0(t)\exp\{\beta x_{ij}(t)\} \tag{6.1}$$

where $x_{ij}(t)$ denotes the value of a vector of covariates for the non-directed dyad at year t, and $\lambda_0(t)$ is the baseline hazard function that describes the "risk" for the country pair signing a PTA with $x_{ij} = 0$.

Alternatively, we can model the likelihood of PTA signing by estimating the following logistic regression:

$$PTA_{ijt} = \beta_0 + \beta x_{ijt} + \varepsilon_{ijt} \tag{6.2}$$

where PTA_{ijt} is the log of the odds that countries i and j sign a PTA in year t.[8] As in the survival analysis, the observed value of PTA_{ijt} is coded as "1" in years when states sign a PTA but not in subsequent years when the agreement is in force.

In the case of PTA depth, we focused on the 84 PTAs only, by extracting from the previous dataset the dyads in the years those PTAs were signed. In doing so, we added back the dyads that had signed PTAs but were dropped in the models on PTA formation because of their membership in PTAs signed prior to 1995. Since the dependent variable of depth (*PTA depth*) is measured on a seven-point scale, we use ordinary least squares to estimate the following equation:

$$PTA\ Depth_{ij} = \beta_0 + \beta x_{ij} + \varepsilon_{ij} \tag{6.3}$$

In all of the above models, the key independent variables are the backward and forward and GVC participation of country i in country j, respectively. Since GVC integration is not the only driver for PTA formation, we include in the vector **x** a set of control variables that may affect the probability of PTA formation and depth. Specifically, these variables include the following:

Bilateral trade. Previous studies (e.g., Nye 1988; Yarbough and Yarbough 1992) suggest that more intensive trade linkages should increase the incentives for domestic groups that stand to benefit from such relations to lobby for the creation of PTAs in order to (*a*) forestall any negative developments in bilateral trade relations or (*b*) prevent the foreign government from engaging in opportunistic behavior that may negatively impinge on their commercial interests. We therefore include the total value of trade between the two countries in a given year. Data for this variable are taken from the International Monetary Fund's *Direction of Trade Statistics* (various years).[9]

GDP ratio. We also control for the effect that power disparities between two states may have on the establishment of PTAs, in the expectation that more powerful states should be more likely to possess greater bargaining power that will allow them to coerce smaller states into signing PTAs. We calculate *GDP ratio* by dividing the larger of the logarithms of the two countries' gross domestic product (GDP) by the smaller one. A positive relationship is expected between this variable and the main dependent variable.

GDP growth. We further expect fluctuations in economic growth to affect a country's incentives to form PTAs. On the one hand, it is reasonable to expect that countries experiencing economic growth should have stronger incentives to seek enhanced market access abroad through PTAs due to their larger export and import volumes. On the other hand, however, it is possible that states facing economic downturns may have particularly strong incentives to pursue PTA membership to enhance their growth potential through international trade integration (Mattli 1999). We take the average of the GDP growth rates of the two countries as the measure of this variable.

Regime type. Previous studies have identified political institutions, particularly a country's regime type, as another important factor that may exert some influence on the probability of PTA formation (Mansfield and Milner 2012a, 2012b; Mansfield, Milner, and Rosendorff 2002). For example, it has been argued that PTAs can serve an important informational role for political leaders by credibly signaling their desire to pursue economic policies conducive to long-term economic growth and therefore helping them to stay in power. Specifically, democratic leaders have to balance the need to provide protection to certain domestic interest groups whose support they may wish to win against the necessity of retaining the support of constituencies hurt by such protectionist policies. However, voters face an informational problem in that they cannot effectively distinguish between, on the one hand, adverse economic conditions resulting from economic shocks or other circumstances over which leaders have little control and, on the other hand, those caused by government rent seeking. This may increase democratic leaders' tendency to sign PTAs, so they can credibly demonstrate to the public that poor economic performance should be attributed to exogenous sources instead of the leaders' incompetent or extractive economic policies.

In the analysis, we measure each state's regime type using its POLITY score, available from the POLITY IV database (Marshall and Gurr 2014). The POLITY score consists of six component measures that capture key institutional differences between democracies and autocracies, including the competitiveness of the process for executive recruitment, the competitiveness of political participation, and the degree to which a country's chief executive's decision-making power is bounded by institutionalized rules and arrangements. These data have been used to create an 11-point index of a state's democratic characteristics (DEMOCRACY) and another one of its autocratic characteristics (AUTOCRACY) (Gurr et al. 1989; Jaggers and Gurr 1995). We measure a state's *Regime type* by subtracting its AUTOC-

RACY index from its DEMOCRACY index. The resulting measure is a continuous variable with values ranging from –10 for a highly autocratic state to +10 for a highly democratic one.

Alliance. In addition, political relations have been found to bear on states' propensity to form PTAs. Countries with similar political and military relations should be more likely to cooperate with each other on trade issues, and vice versa (Gowa 1994; Mansfield 1993). To address this possibility, we include in the analysis a variable for the alliance relationship between two states, measured as "1" if the two countries are members of a military alliance in a given year and "0" otherwise. Data for this variable are taken from the Correlates of War (COW) project.[10]

Distance and *Contiguity.* Previous research (e.g., Mansfield and Milner 2018) suggests that geographical proximity can increase the likelihood that a pair of countries will enter into a PTA. As geographical proximity helps to reduce transportation costs and other barriers to trade, states may be more likely to pursue PTAs with nearby partners in search of expanded market access. Consequently, this study draws on data from the French Centre d'Etudes Prospectives et d'Informations Internationales (CEPII)'s GeoDist database[11] to develop measures of geographical distance between two partner countries. Specifically, *Distance* is the logged value of the distance between the two capitals, and *Contiguity* is a dummy variable indicating whether the two countries are contiguous. We include both variables because it is possible for two countries to share a border and yet have distant capitals or to be in close geographical proximity but not share a border.

In addition to geographical distance, we also consider the possibility that cultural affinity and common colonial history (Mansfield et al. 2002; Mansfield and Reinhardt 2003) can increase the likelihood that a pair of countries will enter into a PTA. Specifically, *Language* is a dummy variable coded "1" if the two countries share a common official language and "0" otherwise. *Former colony* is also a dummy variable, indicating whether two countries have ever had a colonial link. The time-varying independent variables are all lagged by one year in the analysis.

Results

Table 6.1 presents the results of the analyses of the formation of PTAs as a function of GVC participation. Models 1–3 are estimated with Cox proportional hazard regression, and models 4–6 are estimated with logistic regression. In both cases, we use the backward and forward participation measures separately and then together. We also use robust standard errors clustered at the dyadic level to account for unmeasurable factors common to the country pairs.

We focus on the survival analysis first. In each model, a positive (negative) coefficient suggests that the effect of increasing that covariate is to increase (decrease) the likelihood that the countries in the dyad will sign a PTA. The positive and statistically significant coefficient estimates of both backward and forward GVC participation in the three models lend strong

Table 6.1. GVC Participation and PTA Formation

Dependent Variable: *PTA*	Model 1 Cox	Model 2 Cox	Model 3 Cox	Model 4 Logit	Model 5 Logit	Model 6 Logit
Backward GVC	0.0990**		0.107**	0.103*		0.104**
Participation	(0.049)		(0.0471)	(0.0497)*		(0.0466)
Forward GVC		0.331***	0.339***		0.367***	0.372***
Participation		(0.0879)	(0.0888)		(0.0907)	(0.0914)
Bilateral trade (billion $)	−0.0025	−0.00956*	−0.0125**	0.00154	−0.00576	−0.00848*
	(0.00317)	(0.00552)	(0.00587)	(0.00268)	(0.00477)	(0.00511)
GDP Ratio	0.000546	0.000695	0.000461	0.000206	0.000298	9.34e-05
	(0.00057)	(0.00051)	(0.00059)	(0.00057)	(0.00054)	(0.00062)
Average GDP Growth Rate	0.196***	0.189***	0.187***	0.185***	0.179***	0.178***
	(0.0489)	(0.0486)	(0.0489)	(0.0595)	(0.0598)	(0.0598)
Polity Score of Country 1	0.0197	0.0175	0.0196	0.0212	0.0218	0.0222
	(0.0187)	(0.0189)	(0.0187)	(0.0190)	(0.0189)	(0.0190)
Polity Score of Country 2	0.0174	0.0331*	0.0324*	0.0210	0.0347*	0.0347*
	(0.019)	(0.0194)	(0.0194)	(0.0190)	(0.0194)	(0.0194)
Military Alliance	0.938**	0.928**	0.910**	0.917**	0.883**	0.873**
	(0.443)	(0.438)	(0.439)	(0.426)	(0.417)	(0.418)
Contiguous	−0.264	−0.428	−0.503	−0.230	−0.474	−0.557
	(0.798)	(0.821)	(0.827)	(0.806)	(0.844)	(0.851)
Common Language	0.982**	0.989**	0.990**	0.947**	0.966**	0.949**
	(0.438)	(0.436)	(0.434)	(0.432)	(0.430)	(0.428)
Former Colony	−1.255	−1.188	−1.201	−1.395	−1.313	−1.309
	(1.074)	(1.074)	(1.07)	(1.088)	(1.084)	(1.080)
Distance	−0.121***	−0.119***	−0.114**	−0.121***	−0.117***	−0.112**
	(0.0463)	(0.046)	(0.0469)	(0.0452)	(0.0452)	(0.0460)
Constant				−6.028***	−6.179***	−6.235***
				(0.457)	(0.490)	(0.489)
Observations	34,101	34,101	34,101	34,101	34,101	34,101

Notes: Models 1–3 are estimated using Cox proportional hazard regression. Models 4–6 are estimated using logistic regression. Robust standard errors clustered at the dyadic level are included in parentheses; * $p < .1$, ** $p < 0.05$, *** $p < 0.01$.

support to *Hypothesis 6.1*. To interpret the substantive effects, we exponentiate the original coefficients to obtain the hazard ratios, also known as the relative risk. This procedure indicates that as a country's backward or forward GVC linkages to its partner country increase by one percent, while all other variables are held constant, the rate at which these two countries sign a PTA will increase by 40 percent or 11 percent, respectively.

Another way to examine these effects is to compare the survival functions with different values of the GVC measures. Figure 6.5 plots the survival functions with the maximum and minimum values of the backward and forward GVC participation measures using estimates from model 3 while holding the rest of the variables in the model at their mean. As before, we see significant differences in the two survival functions—in both cases, high GVC participation values increase the likelihood of PTA formation over time, whereas the likelihood that countries with no GVC linkage will form a PTA is almost zero. Furthermore, the results show that the substantive effect of forward GVC participation is much stronger. In 2011, the probability that countries with the maximum forward GVC participation in their partner countries would form a PTA was 0.48, while the same probability for countries with the maximum backward GVC participation was 0.08.

The logistic regressions in models 4–6 yield similar results. The coefficient estimates for backward and forward GVC are all positive and statistically significant, with the substantive effects of forward GVC participation being much larger. For instance, if the United States had raised its forward GVC participation with Malaysia to that of Germany in 2011, which is roughly equivalent to a one standard deviation increase, the odds of it signing a PTA with Malaysia would have increased by 45 percent, holding other variables constant. A similar increase in the odds would have required the United States to raise its backward GVC participation with Malaysia to that of Canada in 2011, which is roughly equivalent to over five times the standard deviation of backward GVC participation.

Moving on to the control variables in the model, we first look at those variables that are statistically significant. Consistent with conventional wisdom, countries that have military defense pacts and share the same official language are more likely to sign a PTA, while those far away from each other are less likely to do so. In addition, countries that have experienced positive economic growth rates are also more likely to enter into PTAs.

However, there is relatively little support for the hypothesis that the more powerful player should be more likely to take advantage of its bar-

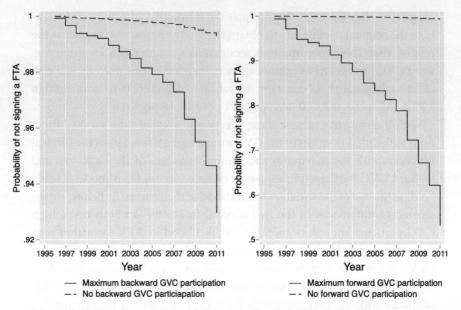

Fig. 6.5. Survival Functions of PTA Formation with Varying Levels of Forward and Backward GVC Participation

Note: The cumulative hazard graphs are calculated using estimates from model 3, with the rest of the variables in the model held at their mean.

gaining power to force the smaller player into a preferential arrangement (Gruber 2000), as the variable measuring the bilateral power imbalance is statistically insignificant. In addition, there is no evidence to suggest that colonial relationships, regime type, or shared borders promote the creation of PTAs.

Interestingly, the coefficient estimates of bilateral trade are negative and achieve statistical significance in models 3 and 6 only. This is in contrast to existing studies (e.g., Mansfield and Milner 2018) that find bilateral trade to have a positive effect on PTA formation. This suggests that, at least for countries that have not previously signed bilateral free trade agreements, GVC connection is a much more important factor than trade in their decision to sign a PTA with each other. This also echoes the finding in chapter 5 suggesting that traditional theories of trade may not be sufficient to explain preferential trade liberalization.

We now turn to the analysis of PTA depth. Our hypothesis suggests that a pair of countries whose domestic industries have strong backward or forward GVC linkages are more likely to sign deep PTAs, which not only contain ambitious tariff liberalization measures but also include other provisions regarding services trade, investments, standards, competition, and IPRs that facilitate trade and investment liberalization. Table 6.2 presents the results from ordinary least squares regressions using Equation 6.3. Once again, we use the backward and forward participation measures first separately and then together. Note that the sample sizes are much smaller because the unit of analysis is the dyadic-year pair when a PTA is signed.

The results are broadly consistent with our expectation about the role of GVC linkages in shaping the depth of PTAs. The backward and forward GVC measures are positive and statistically significant at the $p < 0.1$ level in

Table 6.2. GVC Participation and PTA Depth

Dependent Variable: *PTA depth*	Model 7 Depth	Model 8 Depth	Model 9 Depth
Backward GVC Participation	0.130*		0.184**
	(0.071)		(0.080)
Forward GVC Participation		0.191*	0.247**
		(0.108)	(0.114)
Bilateral Trade (billion $)	0.080***	0.082***	0.067***
	(0.015)	(0.014)	(0.015)
GDP Ratio	0.007*	0.007*	0.006*
	(0.004)	(0.004)	(0.004)
Average GDP Growth Rate	−0.086	−0.103	−0.096
	(0.083)	(0.084)	(0.085)
Polity Score of Country 1	0.024	0.029	0.022
	(0.032)	(0.031)	(0.031)
Polity Score of Country 2	0.036	0.040	0.054
	(0.032)	(0.033)	(0.033)
Military Alliance	1.032*	0.928	0.939
	(0.596)	(0.598)	(0.592)
Contiguous	−1.488**	−1.523**	−1.639***
	(0.625)	(0.599)	(0.556)
Common Language	0.927	1.018*	1.030*
	(0.579)	(0.582)	(0.580)
Former Colony	0.537	0.579	0.605*
	(0.387)	(0.374)	(0.347)
Distance	0.087**	0.080*	0.081*
	(0.0410)	(0.0418)	(0.0419)
Constant	2.451***	2.487***	2.358***
	(0.897)	(0.884)	(0.881)
Observations	148	148	148
R-squared	0.486	0.489	0.497

Notes: Models 7–9 are estimated using OLS regression. Robust standard errors clustered at the dyadic level are included in parentheses; * $p < .1$, ** $p < 0.05$, *** $p < 0.01$.

models 7 and 8, and at the $p < 0.05$ level in model 9. Using the estimates in model 9, we can say that for countries that have signed a PTA, a one unit increase in backward and forward participation will lead to respective ncreases of 0.25 and 0.18 in the depth of the PTA if the rest of the variables are held constant.

Turning to the effects of the control variables, we see that bilateral trade volume and GDP ratio exert strong positive effects on PTA depth. These results suggest that states that trade more with each other are more likely to sign deep PTAs. Further, while greater power disparity may not enhance a bigger player's ability to get a smaller player to sign a PTA, it does increase the likelihood that the two parties will sign a deep PTA once an agreement is reached. In addition, there is some evidence that military alliance, language affinity, and colonial links facilitate the formation of deep agreements. Somewhat counterintuitively, geographical contiguity and distance affect PTA depth in the opposite direction of what was expected. In this set of models, GDP growth rate and regime type are broadly insignificant.

Conclusion

This chapter assesses the implications of growing GVC integration for the formation of PTAs. Empirical analyses yield findings that are consistent with the main theoretical propositions, suggesting that a pair of countries are more likely to form PTAs when their domestic industries have strong GVC linkages with one another. Furthermore, this pattern is most pronounced when home-country industries have strong forward GVC linkages to those in the foreign country. It is possible that firms with forward GVC participation may be more likely to have investment, in addition to trade relations, with partner countries and may therefore have even stronger incentives to seek preferential trade liberalization compared to firms with extensive backward linkages with their suppliers and/or subsidiaries through cross-border trade activities. Our analyses additionally yield evidence suggesting that countries with a large proportion of industries that are heavily dependent on GVCs should be more likely to push for the signing of PTAs that have deeper provisions with regard to tariff and nontariff barrier reduction or to investment protection and liberalization that promise particularly rigorous safeguards for their interests. This result is consistent with the finding in chapter 4 regarding the role of GVCs in shaping firm preferences for PTA design.

Overall, the above findings lend strong support to the proposition that growing PTA integration may increase the pressure on governments to sign PTAs that will reduce tariff and nontariff barriers to trade as well as other behind-the-border barriers that impede business operations. As such, these results reinforce the findings in previous chapters and point to the emergence of a potentially new cleavage in trade politics that pits GVC-embedded industries against those without such linkages. Since industries that are primarily import-competing may also need to import inputs or other intermediate products for their production, and may even export some of their products to foreign consumers indirectly through GVC-linked exporters, this means that the distinction between export-oriented and import-competing industries emphasized in the existing literature (Destler and Odell 1987; Milner 1997) may no longer be as clear-cut in the GVC era. By highlighting the powerful incentives that GVCs have generated for firms highly embedded in such relationships to pursue preferential trade liberalization, and how their lobbying activities have in turn affected PTA formation, this chapter therefore contributes to a growing body of literature on the sources of these agreements (e.g., Chase 2003; Gilligan 1997a; Grossman and Helpman 1995; Krishna 1998; Manger 2009; Mansfield and Milner 2012a; Milner 1997).

CHAPTER 7
Conclusion

The proliferation of preferential trade agreements (PTAs) has been a salient feature of the world economy in recent decades, a trend that has not shown any signs of slowing down. As trade liberalization at the multilateral level has stalled, with the Doha Round entering its 18th year, more free trade agreements (FTAs) have been formed or are currently being negotiated. In July 2018, at the height of the trade war between the United States and China, Japan and the European Union (EU) signed an FTA. The deal, which would remove most EU tariffs on Japanese automobiles and auto parts and Japanese duties on European products such as cheese and wines, would lead to the world's largest open economic area between the two economies that together account for a third of global gross domestic product (GDP) (White 2018).

Further attesting to the commitment of countries to preferential trade liberalization is the Comprehensive and Progressive Agreement for Trans-Pacific Partnership (CPTPP), a revised version of the Trans-Pacific Partnership (TPP), which was signed by the remaining 11 countries led by Japan on March 8, 2018, after President Trump pulled the United States out of the TPP shortly after assuming the presidency in January 2017. The agreement, which retains about two-thirds of the provisions in the TPP draft at the time the United States left the negotiating process, entered into force on December 30, 2018, after it was ratified by six of its member countries—Australia, Canada, Japan, Mexico, New Zealand, and Singapore. With coverage of around 16 percent of global economic output and 500 million people, the CPTPP has attracted other countries, such as Thailand, which are now engaged in talks to join the pact (Arunmas 2018).

The embracing of PTAs as an alternative to multilateral trade liberalization under the World Trade Organization (WTO) parallels another notable development: the rise of the dynamic network structure of the global economy, whereby countries increasingly are connected, specialize, and grow in a set of complicated relationships captured by global value chains (GVCs). Due to the rapid growth of GVCs, the share of domestic value added in global GDP has declined steadily from 85 percent in 1995 to around 80 percent in 2014, while GVC trade has accounted for between 60 and 67 percent of global trade in value-added terms since 2008 (World Bank 2017).

The parallel development of both of the above trends prompted us to consider the potential linkages between them. In this book, we have combined the insights from existing scholarship on GVCs and the political economy of trade liberalization to develop a theory that explains how GVC integration has reshaped the domestic political cleavages over trade policy. We hypothesized and found substantial evidence that the rise of GVCs have incentivized firms embedded in such relationships to push for the signing of PTAs, in particular PTAs with rigorous provisions about trade and investment liberalization. This in turn increased the likelihood that a PTA will be formed between a pair of countries with strong GVC linkages.

In this concluding chapter, we briefly summarize our main findings and discuss their theoretical and empirical contributions. We additionally consider the policy implications of our analysis and identify directions for future research.

Findings

We set out analyzing the effect of GVCs on PTAs by focusing on their implications for firms' trade preferences. Evidence from our fieldwork and survey analysis of the trade policy preferences of firms in China presented in chapters 3 and 4 show that firms with either extensive backward or forward GVC linkages with PTA partner country(s) are more likely to take advantage of such agreements, become repeat users, and support the further expansion of China's FTA network. These findings are consistent with our theoretical proposition that firms are more likely to support preferential trade liberalization with countries with which they have substantial GVC linkages (*Proposition 1.1*). A firm's GVC position additionally influences its preferences for the depth of PTA provisions, with GVC-embedded firms demonstrating more favorable attitudes toward deep PTAs that set higher standards on issues such as intellectual property rights, investor protection, and dispute settlement procedures (*Proposition 1.3*).

In chapter 5, we additionally considered whether GVC-linked firms are more likely to act on their perceived interests and utilize institutionalized channels of interest representation to lobby for preferential trade liberalization through an analysis of the politics surrounding TPP negotiations. We tested our propositions with a combination of qualitative and quantitative methods, including a most likely case design that compares and contrasts the preferences of firms in two industries *and* statistical analysis of the pattern of corporate lobbying and campaign contributions for the TPP by the Fortune 500 companies in the United States. Empirical findings strongly support our argument that firms in industries with strong GVC linkages with TPP countries were more likely to lobby in favor of the TPP and to make campaign finance contributions to elected officials to influence votes on TPP-related issues. This is in contrast to firms in industries with strong GVC linkages to China, which turned out to have been far less active in their lobbying and donation activities, suggesting that firms are less likely to support a PTA that excludes a country with which they have strong GVC linkages, due to the substantial adjustment costs associated with PTA-induced trade and investment diversion (*Proposition 1.2*).

In chapter 6, we shifted our analytical focus from the firm to the country level to consider the macro-level effect of GVCs on the pattern of PTA formation between countries as a function of their varying degrees of GVC linkages. Using a case study of the EU-Asia FTA negotiations, we first highlighted how European firms dependent on the supply of cheap intermediate products and inputs from Asia drove the process and outcome of EU's free trade negotiations with South Korea and other Asian countries. Extending this insight to analysis of the cross-national pattern of PTA formation, we found that two countries with strong backward or forward GVC linkages are both more likely to enter into a PTA with each other (*Proposition 1.4*) and sign PTAs with deep provisions (*Proposition 1.3*), findings that are consistent with those from our firm-level analyses.

Taken together, these results illuminate the powerful role of GVCs in reshaping the domestic politics behind the negotiation of contemporary preferential trade agreements, suggesting that the growing fragmentation of production processes across countries have generated new incentives for domestic businesses embedded in GVCs to push for more and deeper agreements that address their evolving needs and interests. In other words, the rise of GVCs, by accentuating the importance of developing appropriate rules and mechanisms for dealing with the complex issues associated with their spread, may have exerted a profound impact on the changing governance structures and institutions of the global economy.

Theoretical Contributions

Theoretically, this book brings together the literature on both GVCs and PTAs. As we discussed in chapter 2, most existing scholarship on the nexus between the two (e.g., Johnson and Noguera 2014; Laget et al. 2018; Noguera 2012; Osgano et al. 2016) tends to focus on the effect of PTAs and their heterogeneity in promoting value-added trade. While a growing number of studies in both economics and political science have directed attention to the role of production network trade in fostering deep trade agreements (Damuri 2012; Kim 2013; Orefice and Rocha 2014; UNCTAD 2011) or in affecting firm trade preferences (Kim et al. 2019; Osgood 2017, 2018), few studies have made an attempt to connect the two. Our book fills this gap in the literature by clarifying the causal pathways through which the rise of GVCs affects firm preferences and lobbying behavior, and subsequently the formation of PTAs and the depth of their provisions.

In doing so, this book contributes to a growing body of literature on the formation of PTAs, which is increasingly shifting away from an analytical focus on macro-level factors such as country size (Krugman 1991) or regime type (Mansfield et al. 2002; Mansfield and Milner 2012) to its micro-foundations (Baccini 2019). Aided by newly available data on the lobbying activities of firms and industries and the design of PTAs, this strand of research (Chase 2008; Kim 2013; Manger 2009) highlights the importance of the offshoring of production by multinational corporations (MNCs) as a major driver of the proliferation of preferential trade agreements. The main theoretical insights from these studies resemble our argument in that they too highlight the role of PTAs in facilitating the movement of parts and components across national borders. Nevertheless, we go beyond these studies' emphasis on ownership concerns to develop a more general framework for understanding the complexities of the trade and investment activities that connect firms together in an increasingly integrated global economy. Further, while we follow Blanchard et al. (2017) in adopting a value-added approach, we depart from them by emphasizing the role of GVCs in shaping firm and industry interests and preferences, rather than governments' incentives to impose trade protection.

In addition to focusing on the impact of GVCs on the preferences of firms embedded in such relationships, this book also explored the flip side of the coin—the impact of GVCs on firms' attitudes toward a PTA that excludes countries with which they have substantial GVC linkages. Our finding that producers with significant supply chain linkages with PTA-excluded countries were less enthusiastic about such agreements broadens the existing theoretical discussions of the trade diversion and investment discrimination that PTAs generate for nonsignatories (Baccini and Dür 2015; Blanchard 2015; Fernández and Portes 1998; Haftel 2004; Mansfield 1998; Mattli 1999) by pointing to the disruptions such agreements may cause to firms' cross-border business activities.

Our findings also have implications for understanding the trade preferences of firms in manufacturing versus nonmanufacturing industries such as retail and services, for which the logic of production fragmentation seems less immediately apparent. It should be noted that our argument about the role of GVCs in affecting trade preferences should extend to these nonmanufacturing industries. For example, services not only can be considered the glue holding supply chains together but also constitute part of many production and sales processes and have been incorporated into supply chain production as traded inputs. As manufacturing firms increasingly purchase, produce, and export services, we are witnessing a gradual movement toward the "servicification of manufacturing," whereby services inputs are used in the manufacturing process, a phenomenon that is increasingly blurring the distinction between trade in manufacturing and services. The fragmentation of services production into services inputs is also giving rise to services networks or services value chains. Recent statistics on trade in value added capture the servicification of both manufacturing and services networks, as the figures take into account the contribution of domestic and foreign services content in goods and services (Lanz and Maurer 2015; Low 2013). Our case study of the lobbying and campaign contributions behavior of two major Fortune 500 firms in the transportation and warehousing industries, UPS and FedEx, lends some support to the above conjecture, suggesting that a similar logic driven by GVCs may be at work in both manufacturing and nonmanufacturing industries.

Overall, by bridging the gap between the scholarship on GVCs and PTAs, this book highlights the evolving cleavages in contemporary trade politics. Previous studies of the domestic politics of trade policy (e.g., Milner 1989; Odell and Willett 1990) generally posit that export-oriented interests and MNCs are more likely to support free trade, whereas import-competing interests tend to be more protectionist. While our findings suggest that such a divide continues to be relevant, it may also be increasingly necessary to take into consideration the role of businesses heavily dependent on GVCs—for example, import users of foreign intermediate products and inputs—to understand the coalitional politics behind trade policymaking. In highlighting the policy preferences of GVC-embedded firms, this book thus helps enrich our understanding of the political implications of international production segmentation and value-chain integration.

Empirical Contributions

Empirically, this book makes several contributions to the study of the political economy of PTAs. First, adopting both quantitative and qualitative approaches to disentangle the effects of GVCs on preferential trade liberalization has allowed us to paint a rich picture of their linkages. In addition to drawing on data from fieldwork and using the "process-tracing" procedure to highlight the incentives that GVCs generate for firms embedded in such relationships, we also used survey experiments to map the trade preferences of firms with different GVC positions. We supplemented this firm-level analysis with quantitative analyses of the lobbying behavior of industries, using a small-N approach as well as the cross-national pattern of PTA formation through a large-N design. Using multiple methods to tackle our key analytical questions increases the book's empirical richness and our confidence in the validity of our findings.

Second, as mentioned in chapter 4, the commonly employed GVC measures in existing empirical work rely on either global or regional input-output tables to capture the GVC positions of industries. With a few exceptions (e.g., Ahmad et al. 2013; Gangnes et al. 2014; Kim et al. 2019; Manova et al. 2015), there have been relatively few systematic attempts to measure the GVC positions of individual firms. The survey-based measures of firms' backward and forward GVC linkages developed in chapter 4 provide another alternative to such a measure that has afforded us with the opportunity to more directly assess the effect of a firm's GVC position on its attitudes toward preferential trade liberalization. Researchers in the future can use our template as a basis in developing their own firm-level GVC measures.

Last, our findings have important implications for understanding trade politics in both the United States and China, the world's two largest economies. Despite growing scholarly interest in corporate influence over preferential trade liberalization, empirical evidence on lobbying activities over the formation of PTAs surprisingly remains somewhat sparse (Baccini 2019). Notable exceptions include Chase's study of lobbying over the North American Free Trade Agreement (NAFTA) (2003, 2005) and Osgood's more recent articles (2017, 2018) on the influence of vertical foreign direct investment (FDI) and input sourcing on lobbying over preferential trade liberalization. Our study of the pattern of corporate lobbying over the TPP in the United States enriches this literature by shedding light on lobbying activities over what could have been the world's largest trade agreement if negotiations had succeeded.

In addition to advancing our understanding of lobbying patterns in the United States, this book helps to illuminate firm trade preferences in China. Previous studies (e.g., Kennedy 2005; Zeng 2007) have shown that despite continued central control over the decision-making process in many areas, the trade policymaking process in China has become more porous, with societal actors playing an increasingly important role in shaping policy outcomes. Given the growing influence of Chinese businesses in foreign economic policymaking (Kennedy 2008; Li 2013), a clearer delineation of their preferences and interests in the context of rising GVCs should enrich our knowledge of how these firms' agendas are formed and how they filter into the decision-making process. The Chinese firms' preferences and political influence described in this book may also partly help to explain why Chinese President Xi Jinping has repeatedly made public statements that are in favor of free trade and position him as a defender of globalization and an open international trading system (Elliott and Wearden 2017; Yan 2018). Given the importance of sustained economic growth for regime legitimacy, even authoritarian leaders may be compelled to respond to domestic businesses' demands for trade liberalization.

Caveats

Several caveats are in order before we proceed. First, our argument emphasizes the role of GVCs in shaping firms' preferences for preferential trade liberalization. We have not considered the possibility that firms may be able to "vote with their feet." It is certainly the case that firms can relocate intermediate goods production to third countries, as seen by the decision of some U.S. firms to move their operations from China to Southeast Asian countries such as Vietnam to get around tariffs in the ongoing trade war. However, we argue that this seems to represent a suboptimal strategy for GVC firms. For one thing, not all firms possess the option of relocating production without incurring substantial costs. Firms with "sunk costs" in the local market, or that are more highly dependent on the economies of scale or specialized resources offered by the host country, simply may not be able to effectively pursue such an exit strategy. In addition, even if firms can achieve their preferred outcome without a formal PTA, this still may not represent the optimal or most efficient outcome. For example, there are now reports about firms that moved to Vietnam and other Southeast Asian countries regretting their decisions, as these new locales cannot match China in terms of labor quality, infrastructure, cost, and policy environment, at least in the short run (*Forbes* 2019). Furthermore, if firms move to a third country that does not have a PTA with the home country, they will still lose the benefit of reciprocal market liberalization available through a PTA.

A second caveat is that our focus in this book is primarily on firm preferences instead of policy outcomes. Of course, it is possible that, despite their interest in further trade liberalization, GVC-embedded firms may fail to obtain their preferred outcome, as the ill-fated TPP negotiations amply demonstrate. Indeed, a large body of literature (e.g., Baccini and Urpelainen 2014; Betz 2017; Lechner and Wüthrich 2018; Mansfield and Milner 2012, 2018) has emphasized how both domestic and international factors such as institutions, leadership preferences, and the ambition of the proposed PTA may influence how negotiations play out and the possibility of reaching a final agreement. A full discussion of these other domestic and international factors that may influence the success or failure of a prospective PTA, while valuable for illuminating the processes leading to the final policy outcome, is nevertheless beyond the scope of this book.

Third, in focusing on bilateral PTAs, this book has not considered other international economic agreements, such as bilateral investment treaties (BITs) and multilateral or regional PTAs (the only exception being the TPP). This is because despite their general similarities, there are also some important differences among different types of international economic agreements. BITs, for example, focus primarily on investment protection, which means that firms would support BITs only if they are involved in investment activities. This could limit the ability to analyze the preferences of firms that are integrated into GVCs only or primarily through trade activities. At the same time, the negotiation of multilateral and regional PTAs involves more than two countries, going beyond our theory of how GVC linkages between two countries affect the likelihood of them forming a PTA. Furthermore, examining multilateral and regional PTAs would require the use of GVC measures across all member countries, which, to the best of our knowledge, are not yet available. We therefore have focused on bilateral agreements only, leaving out multilateral agreements and those agreements where preferential market access is granted on a unilateral basis, as in the case of accession agreements. Nevertheless, we expect our argument to apply to other types of international economic agreements, as GVCs should similarly give rise to incentives for open international economic flows and rigorous standards that facilitate business transactions across the entire supply chain.

Policy Implications

An important practical lesson to be drawn from our findings for many ongoing PTA negotiations is that growing GVC linkages may create new domestic constituencies in favor of preferential trade liberalization. These new constituencies may offset the rise of protectionist forces around the world. This can be illustrated with the automobile industry during the recent saga of the NAFTA renegotiation.

When the Trump administration threatened to withdraw from NAFTA in 2017, the U.S. automotive industry, whose competitiveness depends heavily on its integrated NAFTA supply chain, vociferously opposed the move. Auto trade associations representing major automakers such as General Motors, Toyota Motor Corp., Volkswagen AG, Hyundai Motor Co., and Ford Motor Co. formed part of a coalition called "Driving American Jobs," launching an advertising campaign to convince government officials and voters that NAFTA has played a pivotal role in boosting U.S. auto production and jobs. The Motor and Equipment Manufacturers Association and the American International Automobile Dealers Association were particularly vocal in this effort, proclaiming that "we're winning with NAFTA" and that ending NAFTA would jeopardize jobs in the U.S. auto sector, as the agreement governs $1.2 trillion in annual trade of automobiles among the three countries (Shepardson 2017).

Notably, the auto industry emphasized the challenges involved in rebuilding a U.S. supplier base and cautioned that the loss of markets on both sides of the border would suppress production capacity, leading to substantial price increases and job losses (Einstein 2017). Representatives of the Original Equipment Suppliers Association, a Michigan-based trade group representing about 500 automotive suppliers in North America, pointed out that a typical "American-made" vehicle contains more than 2,000 parts, increasing to over 10,000 parts when all the nuts and bolts are taken into consideration. Since these components are sourced from across the globe, and U.S. auto parts are also used in vehicles manufactured in foreign countries such as Mexico, ending NAFTA would disrupt the supply chain and increase the overall cost of production for automakers (Margolis 2018). The transportation and logistics industry, in particular trucking and freight rail companies, joined automakers in the fight to preserve NAFTA. The American Trucking Association, for instance, urged administration officials to take note of the tremendous benefits of NAFTA to both the trucking industry and the U.S. economy, as "cross-border trade supports over 46,000 U.S. trucking jobs, including 31,000 U.S. truck drivers, and generates $6.5 billion in revenue" (Eisenstein 2017).

When the Trump administration decided to renegotiate the terms of NAFTA, the auto industry once again was concerned, this time regarding a proposed change to the rules governing automobiles' country of origin, which would significantly increase the share of local content sourced from NAFTA countries from 62.5 percent to 85 percent, with a total of at least 50 percent of the total content originating from the United States (Bainwol and Hamberger 2017). Many U.S. automakers were nervous because, due to their extensive supply chain linkages across the globe, it would be difficult for them to meet the higher local content requirement without "assembling more core components—powertrains, engines, and transmissions—in North America" in order to avoid paying an additional 25 percent tax (Margolit 2018). The alternative of relocating production was not appealing either, as it would potentially drive up the cost of the supply chain in North America, reduce the efficiency and competitiveness of the U.S. auto industry, and lead to the exit of some production, such as that of smaller vehicles with thin profit margins (McGregor 2018).

When details of the newly negotiated United States-Mexico-Canada Agreement (USMCA), also dubbed NAFTA 2.0, was announced in early October 2018, the auto industry breathed a collective sigh of relief as it would no longer face the threat of a hefty 25 percent tariff on imports of automobiles and auto parts into the United States. Under the USMCA, imports of passenger vehicles will have to be built with at least 75 percent of parts made in North America, as opposed to the originally proposed 85 percent (Kulisch 2018). That the behind-the-scenes details of the renegotiations have not yet surfaced would have rendered any assessment of the role of the auto industry in the USMCA highly preliminary.[1] Nevertheless, given what we saw in chapter 5, it is perhaps not too far-fetched to say that the auto industry probably played a major role in steering the agreement away from a worst-case scenario that would have resulted in substantial disruption to the auto market in the United States and beyond.

As a further illustration of the role of GVCs in influencing the dynamics of ongoing FTA negotiations, Canada has recently been actively pursuing regional trade liberalization. In addition to embracing the Comprehensive Economic and Trade Agreement (CETA) with the European Union, Ottawa has pivoted toward Asia in an effort to promote closer economic cooperation with the region. Currently, formal exploratory discussions are under way toward the negotiation of a free trade agreement between Canada and the Association of Southeast Asian Nations (ASEAN), or the Canada-ASEAN FTA. In addition, it is also exploring the possibility of establishing an FTA with India. A likely motivation behind these moves is to reorient the GVCs of Canadian firms to Asia. For example, a major trade deal with ASEAN would help connect Canadian producers to global supply chain hubs centered around China, increase their ability to tap into the opportunities opened up by China's Belt and Road Initiative, and pave the way for Canada to eventually join the Regional Comprehensive Economic Partnership (RCEP) when it comes to fruition. In the event that domestic ratification processes for the USCMA fall through, these arrangements may become more than fallback plans as they could enhance the attractiveness of Canada for American firms as they seek preferential market access to ASEAN and the Asian region as a whole (Capri 2017).

The importance of GVCs in resisting protectionism is also reflected in the ongoing trade war between the United States and China. A survey of 430 American companies with substantial operations in China that the American Chamber of Commerce in China conducted between August and September of 2018 suggests that 60 percent of these companies have already felt the negative impact from the $50 billion in tariffs that Washington and Beijing each imposed on the other's products. However, 64 percent of the respondents indicated they had no intention of relocating production to third countries, and only 6 percent reported having plans to do so. In light of the rising trade tensions between the two countries, the president of the U.S.-China Business Council, Allen Craig, reportedly warned that trade conflicts would "increase input costs for U.S. manufacturers and spur supply chain disruptions in the U.S. and Asia," and he urged trade negotiators to resolve the dispute through diplomatic negotiations rather than punitive tariffs (Hoyoma and Harada 2018).

The above examples suggest that the pro-free-trade coalition comprised of export-oriented industries and MNCs may have been reinforced by the rise of business actors interested in maintaining unimpeded access to either intermediate inputs and supplies or upstream producers through preferential trade liberalization. While the resulting proliferation of PTAs may lead to the further fragmentation of the global trading system into smaller trading blocks, the emergence of new pro-free-trade interests may nevertheless help cushion against the protectionist backslide and sustain the momentum toward trade liberalization in the long term.

Additionally, while there is some evidence that companies are starting to reevaluate their strategic supplier relationships and adjust supply chains in the midst of tariff wars, it is also unlikely that the complex supplier-buyer relationships linking numerous companies across the globe can easily be unraveled. For example, it would be nearly impossible for Apple to purchase all iPhone components in the United States, even if it planned to do so. The same goes for other products, such as automobiles (Vitasek 2017).

As large companies with complex global supply chains may have invested millions, even billions of dollars, to build supplier relationships that span the globe, it will likely take both time and resources for firms to change suppliers, restructure strategic supplier agreements, or move operations back to home or third countries. The complex processes that companies will need to go through before any actual changes are made may therefore also shield them from changes in the political environment and at the same time offer a glimmer of hope for the prospect of future trade liberalization amidst the rising protectionism and economic nationalism sweeping across the world today.

Directions for Future Research

Despite the book's theoretical and empirical contributions, we would be remiss not to acknowledge its limitations. In this section, we identify areas of our study that can be further improved, which may also help inform fruitful avenues for future research in GVCs and PTAs.

GVC Trade in Intermediate versus Finished Products

In analyzing the implications of GVCs for trade politics, this project adopted a general model for capturing the complexity and diversity of GVCs, setting aside the potential distinction between GVC trade in intermediate versus finished products. Such a distinction is starting to receive some attention in the scholarly literature. Baccini et al. (2018), for example, suggest that the reduction of tariffs on intermediate goods in the PTA context should take place at a faster pace than that on final goods. This is because firms dependent on importing intermediate goods for their production and exports should have stronger incentives to push for lower tariffs in order to reduce the cost of production, as seen in the efforts by the European industries with extensive backward GVC linkages with Asian countries to lobby for the liberalization of import tariffs on the goods needed for their production processes in chapter 6. Similarly, Gulotty and Li (2020) examine Chinese firms' anticipatory responses to China's exclusion from TPP negotiations, finding that compared to final goods producers dependent on TPP member country markets, who stand to lose from exclusion, intermediate goods producers with supply chain linkages to TPP countries were instead favorably disposed to the TPP due to their greater ability to capitalize on expanded market opportunities in downstream industries.

The dynamics of trade liberalization in finished goods may be somewhat different from that in intermediate products. Baccini et al. (2016), for example, suggest that the liberalization of finished goods should encounter stronger opposition from domestic interest groups than that of intermediate goods. Competitive producers of finished goods may either oppose liberalization or be indifferent if they engage in exports and therefore are mainly concerned about foreign market access rather than domestic tariff liberalization. This should be further reinforced by strong opposition to liberalization from import-competing interests. Overall, therefore, domestic reactions to the liberalization of finished products should tend to be negative, and domestic cleavages over trade liberalization among producers of finished goods should be less prominent.

Despite such theoretical conjectures, relatively little empirical evidence has been marshalled to illuminate the preferences and incentives of domestic interest groups when it comes to the liberalization of finished products. Future studies could more specifically analyze the distinctions between intermediate and final goods and the implications of these differences for firm preferences, look for potential cross-country variation, or examine how the incentives generated by each type of GVC trade for domestic manufacturers are filtered through the institutional context to shape policy outcomes.

The Impact of GVCs on the Dynamics of Trade Liberalization in Service Industries

Our study yields some preliminary evidence suggesting that GVCs may influence the trade policy preferences of firms in manufacturing as well as in service industries. However, more research could be conducted to ascertain the impact of GVCs on the dynamics of trade liberalization in service industries. The role of services in the expansion of global trade is increasingly being recognized, as global production networks cannot function effectively in the absence of efficient network infrastructures such as transport, logistics, communication, and other complementary services, including finance.

The participation of service industries in GVCs can take several forms. Service firms may choose to source their inputs internationally, in which case services would constitute the end stage of a GVC. Services may also function as links between different stages of the production chain or represent critical inputs in various stages of goods and services production that may be developed through either arm's-length market-based transactions or in-house (Heuser and Mattoo 2017). When the value added by services in goods manufacturing (i.e., the servicification of manufacturing) is taken into account, services constitute an even larger share of global trade than what traditional statistics present, amounting to 55 percent of OECD countries' total exports and 42 percent of China's (OECD 2015).

Given the growing importance of services trade, recent research has increasingly drawn attention to the coalitional politics of services trade liberalization (Chase 2008; Weymouth 2017). For example, it has been suggested that while workers' support for services trade liberalization seems to vary according to their skill or education level (Chase 2008), the higher level of skill intensity in tradeable services compared to manufacturing or nontradable services sectors also implies that workers in a country abundantly endowed with skilled labor should be more likely to benefit from and therefore support services trade liberalization. This should in turn lead us to expect support for trade openness in services to be stronger among tradable services than among manufacturing industries in such a country (Jensen 2011; Jensen et al. 2017). Furthermore, since it is firms rather than industries that are involved in international trade, the "new new" trade theory has increasingly drawn our attention to firm heterogeneity, showing that only the largest and most productive firms engage in international trading activities (Antràs and Helpman 2004; Bernard et al. 2007; Melitz 2003), a pattern that extends to the services sector (Breinlich and Criscuolo 2011). In other words, services trade liberalization will be most likely to draw support from the large and productive firms within tradable services industries.

While the above arguments focus on the coalitional politics behind services trade liberalization in general instead of GVC trade in particular, they should have implications for understanding support for trade liberalization among GVC-embedded firms in the services sector. In particular, it would be worth examining whether the dynamics mentioned above also characterize GVC trade in services. It would also be interesting to explore whether the distinctive nature of services trade along with a firm's GVC position shapes trade policy preferences. For example, services firms may be more sensitive to behind-the-border regulatory measures, such as restrictions on foreign ownership and regulatory requirements, than border measures, such as tariffs (Heuser and Mattoo 2017). This may in turn affect services' firms' preference for PTA provisions, as they seek to reduce barriers to GVC expansion. In addition, it has been suggested that large importers, such as retailers highly dependent on the supply of foreign goods and materials, should have strong interests in the liberalization of not only goods but also services (Weymouth 2017). Future studies could more systematically analyze the impact of GVCs on corporate support for trade liberalization in manufacturing versus services sectors and, more specifically, identify the pathways through which GVC integration shapes the trade preferences of firms in tradable services.

The Broader Distributional Consequences of GVCs

In analyzing the impact of GVCs on the politics of preferential trade liberalization, this study has focused mainly on support for PTAs from GVC-embedded firms. Relatively little attention has been directed to opposition arising from firms that are not part of GVCs. Intuitively, domestic producers of intermediate goods and less productive producers of finished goods should have incentives to oppose trade liberalization in intermediates due to concerns about direct competition in the case of the former, or indirect competition in the case of the latter, because of the competitive advantage that PTAs confer upon their direct competitors (Baccini et al. 2016). Furthermore, as discussed earlier, domestic producers of finished products should also be more likely to oppose preferential trade liberalization. While the above conjectures are clearly plausible, more direct evidence regarding the preferences and behaviors of these firms could lend further credence to these claims.

Our analysis of the pattern of corporate support for the TPP also suggests that support for preferential trade liberalization may be specific rather than principled. For example, the significant support that firms having strong GVC linkages with TPP countries provided for the proposed agreement contrasts sharply with the lukewarm reactions from firms having strong GVC linkages with China, the excluded country. This finding points to PTA exclusion as a potential source of opposition to the negotiation of such agreements. Overall, our research highlights support for PTAs from GVC-embedded firms without examining in detail the sources of domestic opposition to trade liberalization. Future research could be conducted to more specifically assess the policy preferences of actors that are outside of GVCs as well as their influence on policy outcomes.

In addition, our focus on the implications of GVCs for business support for preferential trade liberalization does not permit us to consider the implications of GVCs for different factors of production, specifically capital and labor. However, there is preliminary evidence that GVCs may differently affect productivity and income growth for these different factors and therefore may have broader distributional consequences for capital- and labor-intensive firms in GVCs.

For example, through an analysis of income distribution in the information communication technology industry in the United States and

China between 1995 and 2009, Dollar (2017) shows that GVC participation disproportionately benefited high-skilled rather than low- or medium-skilled workers in the United States, as compensation for the latter either was flat or increased at a significantly slower pace than for the former. The pattern is somewhat similar in China. While labor's share of productivity growth decreased from more than 40 percent to about 30 percent, capital's share rose from less than 69 percent to almost 70 percent during the same period. In other words, capital—including both domestic private owners of capital and MNCs involved in GVCs—has been able to capture much of the gains from the country's growing GVC integration. While labor as a whole saw significant wage increases, high-skilled labor experienced the largest increase, at almost double the rate, followed by medium- and low-skilled workers at 80 percent and 50 percent, respectively.

The above statistics point to GVCs as an important factor in explaining the contrasting responses to globalization in developing versus developed countries. While globalization is being received positively in developing countries, it is encountering growing resistance in advanced economies. Future studies could further explore the broader domestic distributional implications of the expansion of GVCs and identify the pathways through which GVCs affect the income and therefore the political positions of different domestic interest groups.

GVCs, Preferential versus Multilateral Trade Liberalization, and PTA Partner Choice

The relative merits of regional versus multilateral trade liberalization have received considerable scholarly attention. In traditional trade models, where there is no cross-border production and where tariffs represent the only trade policy instruments, preferential trade liberalization is considered less effective than multilateral trade liberalization in promoting world welfare, even though it may still generate both economic and noneconomic gains for individual countries.[2]

In the presence of GVCs, however, the above logic may no longer hold, as the fragmentation of production across national borders generates "new forms of international policy spillovers and time-consistency problems" (Ruta 2017: 181) that call for deeper integration arrangements. Economic and noneconomic considerations may still motivate countries to form

PTAs, but considerations about the potential increases in efficiency deriving from the reduced heterogeneity of member countries' policy preferences that comes with preferential trade liberalization may dominate interests in capturing greater economies of scale through an expanded market, which in turn may generate strong incentives for firms and businesses to pursue deep trade agreements. By allowing countries to engage in more effective policy coordination than what would have been possible at the global level, PTAs may therefore complement rather than substitute for multilateral trade liberalization (WTO 2011).

Though this book deals mainly with the effect of GVCs on preferential trade liberalization, we do examine the question of preferential versus multilateral trade liberalization in chapter 4. In particular, our survey of Chinese executives shows that while firms with strong forward or backward GVC linkages are more likely to support the former, there is no evidence that GVC linkages of either form increase a firm's support for the latter. These results offer micro-level evidence that GVCs may enhance firms' incentives to pursue efficient forms of deep integration, such as those made possible by PTAs rather than multilateral trade liberalization. Of course, the evidence drawn from the case of China is far from conclusive, and future studies should more systematically examine how the fragmentation of global production influences support for multilateral versus preferential trade liberalization.

A related question that merits some attention is the role of GVCs in influencing PTA partner choice. Our finding that support for PTAs correlates with the level of GVC integration with the partner country in question hints at the possible linkages between the two variables. Indeed, recent scholarship has devoted some attention to the role of GVC complementarity in influencing PTA partner choice. Cheng et al. (2016) address this question by examining the effect of variations in China's GVC linkages on its FTA partner choice. Borrowing insights from the so-called smile curve, which depicts the various stages of the GVC from upstream to downstream activities on the horizontal axis and the value added derived from each of these stages on the vertical axis, the authors suggest that vertical PTAs may be formed as countries seek to exploit complementarities in member countries' comparative advantage and the vertical division of labor along the supply chain. Our argument that GVC firms may provide the key impetus for trade liberalization may therefore have direct implications for PTA partner choice and priorities.

The Need for Better GVC Measures

More systematic examination of the above questions would also hinge on the development of new GVC measures that better capture the complexities associated with the fragmentation of production across national borders. For example, industry-level GVC data from the TiVA dataset are available for only 63 economies, while the World Input-Ouput Database covers only 43 countries. GVC data for a larger number of countries and economies would allow us to better assess the external validity of our empirical results. The development of firm-level GVC measures would also be extremely valuable, enabling us to more specifically analyze the impact of GVCs on firm preferences and behavior.

Furthermore, future research could benefit from more fine-grained GVC data that disaggregate the different factor contents embodied in various products, such as land, labor, and capital, as they cross national borders within a unified framework. For example, Wang et al. (2017a) propose a production activity decomposition framework that distinguishes between embedded factor content that is used solely for domestic production activities and that is related to GVC activities. This method allows the authors to decompose production activities based on either backward or forward GVC linkages and then to build a pair of GVC participation indices that allow for more comprehensive coverage of international production-sharing activities and a clearer distinction between participation in simple and complex GVC activities. Wang et al. (2017b) further classify production activities into four types based on whether the generated value added is absorbed within the border, crosses the border only once for either consumption or production, or crosses borders multiple times. This approach yields GVC measures at the country-sector level that more effectively capture the average production length and the relative "upstreamness" of production activities.

Johnson (2017) similarly argues for the need to more fully capture the range of activities incorporated under GVCs by capitalizing on the convergence between the macro-approach to measuring GVCs, which utilizes national input-output tables derived from bilateral trade data in the construction of global input-output tables, and the micro-approach, which provides a detailed account of firms' sourcing decisions and the organization of production networks by multinational companies. Los and Timmer (2018) further develop a unified framework for measuring exports of value added. In addition to taking account of earlier measures of value-added exports, such as the measure of value added that is consumed abroad (Johnson and Noguera 2012) and of value added in exports (Los et al. 2016), this approach goes further by proposing a third measure of the value added that is used abroad in the final stage of production.

Overall, the development of these novel GVC measures should facilitate scholarly analysis of their political implications and provide exciting opportunities for more fully unravelling the complex changes brought about by the fragmentation of global production at both domestic and international levels.

The Role of PTAs in Promoting GVC Participation

Last but not least, our research has focused on the implications of GVCs for trade preferences without also considering the potential for reverse causality, that is, the possibility that the formation of PTAs may in turn facilitate GVC participation. As mentioned in chapter 2, recent studies (e.g., Gonzalez 2012; Johnson and Noguera 2012; Noguera 2012) have increasingly drawn attention to the role of PTAs, including deep PTAs, in stimulating value-added trade. Future studies that combine these two lines of inquiry may thus paint a more complete picture of the evolving relationship between the two.

The case of the ongoing negotiations between China and ASEAN over an upgraded FTA provides a good indication of the possible reciprocal relations between PTA formation and the expansion of GVCs. Since China's entry into the WTO in 2001, the Chinese leadership has come to view participation in FTAs at either the bilateral or the regional level as a useful supplement to multilateral trade liberalization in its pursuit of expanded market access abroad. In 2000, China proposed the establishment of a free trade area with ASEAN in an effort to promote regional trade integration. The proposal was endorsed by ASEAN leaders in 2001, and a framework agreement was signed in November 2002. Under the agreement, ASEAN countries agreed to reduce the average tariff rate on Chinese goods from 12.8 percent to 0.6 percent starting January 1, 2010, while China committed to cutting its average tariff rate on imports from ASEAN from 9.8 percent to 0.1 percent ("Backgrounder: Upgraded Version of ASEAN-China FTA" 2015). The agreement reduced tariffs on nearly 8,000 product categories, or 90 percent of the total imported goods, to zero (Devonshire-Ellis 2014).

Since taking effect in 2010, the ASEAN-China Free Trade Area (ACFTA) has emerged as the third-largest free trade area in terms of gross domestic product and the largest in terms of population, with an internal market size of 1.7 billion people (Whalley and Li 2014). The substantial trade liberalization brought about by the agreement has since led the trade volume between China and ASEAN to grow at an average annual rate of more than 20 percent, rising from $54.8 billion in 2002 to $480.4 billion in 2014. As a result, China has become ASEAN's biggest trading partner and ASEAN China's third largest ("China, ASEAN Seals Deal to Upgrade Bilateral FTA" 2015; "Backgrounder: Upgraded Version of ASEAN-China FTA" 2015).

In addition to the expansion of overall trade, GVC linkages between China and ASEAN countries have deepened since ACFTA took effect as both domestic and multinational firms based in China increasingly incorporated ASEAN countries into their regional supply chains. The decision by Foxconn Technology Group, a Taiwanese electronics manufacturer and major supplier of Apple's iPhones and iPads, to gradually relocate low-end manufacturing from China to Indonesia provides a good example of this logic. In 2014, Foxconn announced its plan to diversify its production chain and invest $10 billion in Indonesia over the subsequent five years. While considerations of Indonesia's large labor market, low costs, and modest manufacturing skills likely influenced the decision, the shift also seems to have been motivated by a desire to take advantage of the FTA between China and ASEAN in order to manufacture products at lower wages and export them to China duty free ("China Set to Lose Foxconn to Indonesia" 2014).

In the electronics sector, too, there are growing signs of firms relocating technology and intermediate-input manufacturing from China to Southeast Asian countries to capitalize on deepening regional trade integration and shifting market fundamentals, with countries such as Vietnam emerging as one of the world's most attractive outsourcing locations due to the liberalization reforms undertaken by the government ("Where in the World?" 2015). The above pattern can similarly be observed in the garments and textiles sector. For instance, H&M, a Swedish retailer, shifted its sweater production from China to a Chinese-run factory in the outer Yangong region in Myanmar in 2015, reportedly to tap into the region's low-cost potential, reinforced by the reduction of trade and investment barriers made possible by ACFTA ("A Tightening Grip" 2015).

Overall, while China remains a global center of manufacturing and assembly, some final assembly activities in labor-intensive industries have started to relocate to other low-cost countries, with ASEAN countries' factor endowments and level of development playing an important role in shaping the nature and type of partnerships with China. Aggregate statistics further confirm the trend toward the regionalization of economic activity taking place in Southeast Asia in which China is increasingly playing an indispensable role. In terms of backward GVC linkages, ASEAN countries were gradually shifting away from countries or regions that have traditionally provided most of their foreign value added such as EU and NAFTA countries toward sourcing from either within the region or from China. For example, the share of Chinese inputs in ASEAN's total exports has experienced a steady increase, from 1 percent in 1990 to 2 percent in 2000, and then to 5 percent in 2013 ("Global Value Chains in ASEAN" 2017). With regard to forward GVC linkages, there has also been a notable increase in the share of value added originating from ASEAN in the exports of other countries, including China, with ASEAN's forward GVC linkages with China increasing from 0 percent in 1990 to 3 percent by 2013 (Yamaguchi 2018).

This expansion of GVCs between China and ASEAN countries paved the foundation for the renegotiation of the ACFTA. While there is as of yet no direct evidence that pressure from domestic businesses constituted the main driving force behind the initiative, official statements and policy documents offer some preliminary evidence that considerations about promoting further trade and investment liberalization in response to the rapidly changing landscape of the regional economy underlay the calculations of both parties. For example, in an interview with *China Daily*, an expert at the Cambodia Institute for Strategic Studies commented that the upgraded ACFTA would provide valuable opportunities for businesses in Cambodia, in particular small and medium enterprises, to increase their participation in regional supply chains, especially in areas such as agriculture and the agro-industry (Xue and Sovan 2016). At a meeting between China and ASEAN leaders held in Brunei in October 2013, Chinese Premier Li Keqiang reiterated the importance of an upgraded version of ACFTA for fostering trade and investment relations with ASEAN, emphasizing the need to strengthen regional production networks and supply chains by simplifying rules of origin, eliminating nontariff barriers to trade, and boosting the export capacity of the region's less-developed economies ("Upgrading China-ASEAN FTA Version to Boost Greater Trade, Investment Ties" 2013). In an interview with China's Xinhua News Agency, the Chinese ambassador to ASEAN similarly emphasized the importance of the agreement for forging closer trade and investment relations between the two sides and promoting the negotiation of the RCEP, in an effort to "optimize the production networks and value chains in the region and help Asia become a 'world factory' in the world value chains" ("Upgrading China-ASEAN FTA to Expand Cooperation" 2016).

While far from conclusive, such official rhetoric points to the possibility that the signing of FTAs may promote the expansion of production networks, thereby generating incentives for the negotiation of even deeper agreements to address the interests of GVC-enmeshed businesses in further trade and investment liberalization. In other words, there appears to be a feedback loop between GVC participation and the formation of PTAs, with the two reinforcing each other. It is possible for countries to sign PTAs with the goal of promoting GVC participation, but it is doubtful that governments will be able to successfully pursue the initiative in the absence of business support. As we show in the example of the China-ASEAN FTA renegotiation, the increased GVC integration that arose after the original agreement—which may or may not have been the government's initial goal—has given firms incentives to push for *further* liberalization through deeper PTAs. Future studies could engage in more systematic analysis of the conditions under which PTAs facilitate GVC integration, and the possible reciprocal interactions between GVCs and PTA formation.

APPENDIXES

Appendix 2.1. Overview of China's Bilateral and Regional FTA Activities

a. FTAs Concluded

Country or Region	Agreement	Date of entry into force
Brunei Darussalam	ASEAN-China (G)	1-Jan-05
Myanmar	ASEAN-China (G)	1-Jan-05
Cambodia	ASEAN-China (G)	1-Jan-05
Indonesia	ASEAN-China (G)	1-Jan-05
Lao People's Democratic Republic	ASEAN-China (G)	1-Jan-05
Malaysia	ASEAN-China (G)	1-Jan-05
Philippines	ASEAN-China (G)	1-Jan-05
Singapore	ASEAN-China (G)	1-Jan-05
Viet Nam	ASEAN-China (G)	1-Jan-05
Thailand	ASEAN-China (G)	1-Jan-05
Brunei Darussalam	ASEAN-China (S)	1-Jul-07
Myanmar	ASEAN-China (S)	1-Jul-07
Cambodia	ASEAN-China (S)	1-Jul-07
Indonesia	ASEAN-China (S)	1-Jul-07
Lao People's Democratic Republic	ASEAN-China (S)	1-Jul-07
Malaysia	ASEAN-China (S)	1-Jul-07
Philippines	ASEAN-China (S)	1-Jul-07
Singapore	ASEAN-China (S)	1-Jul-07
Viet Nam	ASEAN-China (S)	1-Jul-07
Thailand	ASEAN-China (S)	1-Jul-07
Bangladesh	APTA (G)	1-Jan-02
India	APTA (G)	1-Jan-02
Korea, Republic of	APTA (G)	1-Jan-02
Lao People's Democratic Republic	APTA (G)	1-Jan-02
Sri Lanka	APTA (G)	1-Jan-02
Chile	Chile-China (G)	20-Jun-07
Chile	Chile-China (S)	18-Nov-10
Costa Rica	China-Costa Rica (G&S)	1-Aug-11
Hong Kong	China-Hong Kong (G&S)	29-Jun-03
Macao	China-Macao, China (G&S)	17-Oct-03
New Zealand	China-New Zealand (G&S)	1-Oct-08
Singapore	China-Singapore (G&S)	1-Jan-09
Iceland	Iceland-China (G&S)	1-Jul-14
Pakistan	Pakistan-China (G)	1-Jul-07
Pakistan	Pakistan-China (S)	10-Oct-09
Peru	Peru-China (G&S)	1-Mar-10
Switzerland	Switzerland-China (G&S)	1-Jul-14
Taiwan	ECFA(G&S)	12-Sep-10
Australia	China-Australia (G&S)	20-Dec-15
Korea	China-ROK (G&S)	20-Dec-15

Country or Region	Agreement	Date of entry into force
Maldives	China-Maldives (G&S)	8-Dec-17
Georgia	China-Georgia (G&S)	1-Jan-18

b. FTAs under Negotiation

Regional Comprehensive Economic Partnership (RCEP)
China-GCC (Gulf Cooperation Council) FTA
China-Norway FTA
China-Japan-Korea FTA
China-Israel FTA
China-ASEAN FTA Upgrade Negotiations
China-Sri Lanka FTA
China-Pakistan FTA second phase
China-Singapore upgrade FTA
China-New Zealand upgrade FTA
China-Mauritius FTA
China-Moldova FTA

c. FTAs under Consideration

China-Colombia FTA Joint Feasibility Study
China-Fiji FTA Joint Feasibility Study
China-Nepal FTA Joint Feasibility Study
China-Papua New Guinea FTA Joint Feasibility Study
China-Canada FTA Joint Feasibility Study
China-Bengal FTA Joint Feasibility Study
China-Mongol FTA Joint Feasibility Study
China-Panama FTA Joint Feasibility Study
China-Palestine FTA Joint Feasibility Study
China-Peru Upgrade FTA Joint Feasibility Study
China-Switzerland Upgrade FTA Joint Feasibility Study

Source: Chinese Ministry of Commerce, *China FTA Network*, available at http://fta.mofcom.gov.cn/english/fta_qianshu.shtml (accessed June 4, 2018).

Note: (G) denotes goods and (S) services.

APPENDIX   201

Appendix 3.1. Background Information on China's FTAs with Australia and South Korea

China-Australia FTA (ChAFTA)

Since the establishment of diplomatic relations between China and Australia in 1972, bilateral trade has grown rapidly. According to China Customs statistics, the volume of trade between China and Australia reached $20.39 billion in 2004, a year-on-year increase of 50.3 percent, more than 230 times the volume in the year diplomatic relations were established (*China Statistical Yearbook* 2005).

In October 2003, during President Hu Jintao's visit to Australia, the two countries signed the Trade and Economic Framework, announcing that the two sides would work for balanced and comprehensive trade and investment facilitation through economic and trade cooperation. Since then, the two governments have conducted a series of joint free trade agreement (FTA) feasibility studies, concluding that the proposed ChAFTA should "create more bilateral trade, investment, [and] a larger market to promote productivity via greater competition and economies of scale, add momentum to regional and multilateral trade liberalization efforts, and provide a framework for closer economic cooperation" (Embassy of the People's Republic of China in Australia 2005).

In March 2005, Australian Trade Minister Mark Vail and Chinese Minister of Commerce Bo Xilai jointly announced the two sides had reached a consensus that "under a possible FTA negotiation, products across all sectors would be negotiable, including liberalization and facilitation of goods and services and the issue of investment flows, with a view to achieving a balanced outcome through a single undertaking" (Embassy of the People's Republic of China in Australia 2005). A month later on April 18, 2005, talks on the FTA officially commenced. According to the free trade feasibility study report by the two sides, if China and Australia achieved the establishment of a free trade zone in 2006, the annual gross domestic product (GDP) growth rate of the two countries would increase by 0.04 percentage points over the next 10 years, and Australian exports to China would increase by 14.8 percent. Chinese exports to Australia would increase by an additional 7.3 percent (Embassy of The People's Republic of China in Australia 2005).

However, the negotiations did not go as smoothly as expected. Australia hoped for better market access conditions for its agricultural products and service industries to enter the Chinese market, while China wished to have its investments in Australia treated the same as those from the United States and New Zealand—that is, any investments below AUD100 million would not be subject to review by the investment review board. Neither request sat too well with the other party. Another sticking point was the agreement's proposed memorandum on temporary workers, which alarmed the Australian public as well as labor organizations such as the Australian Council of Trade Unions, who feared an influx of cheap Chinese labor (Armstrong 2017). The negotiation process was further complicated by changes in government in Australia, coming to an almost complete halt when the Labor Party took over in 2007, only to gain momentum again in 2013 when the Liberal Party won the election (Hua 2015).

Despite the bumpy road, after 21 rounds of intense negotiations that spanned over a decade, Australian Minister for Trade and Investment Andrew Robb and Chinese Minister of Commerce Gao Hucheng signed a Declaration of Intent on November 17, 2014, formalizing the conclusion of the ChAFTA negotiations. At the time of the signing, bilateral trade had reached $136.9 billion, 16 times that in 2000 (Ministry of Commerce of The People's Republic of China 2015). A year later, on December 20, 2015, ChAFTA entered into force.

China-South Korea FTA (China-ROK FTA)

China and South Korea (ROK) have been important trading partners. During the first two decades since the countries established diplomatic relations in 1992, bilateral trade maintained an impressive growth rate of more than 20 percent per year, reaching $79.35 billion in 2004, when China overtook the United States to become South Korea's largest trading partner for the first time. Hoping for more substantial economic gains amidst the changing landscape of East Asian regionalism, Chinese President Hu Jintao and ROK President Roh Moo-Hyun declared the launch of an unofficial feasibility study on the China-ROK FTA in November of that year.

Like ChAFTA, the road to the China-ROK FTA was far from smooth sailing. While Beijing was keen on pushing forward the FTA talks, South Korea was more reluctant, fearing that low-priced agricultural products from China would flood the domestic market. In fact, when South Korea adopted its national roadmap for FTA policies, the FTA with China was relegated to being a long-term target, in favor of FTAs with traditional trading partners such as the United States, Japan, and the European Union (Cheong 2016).

It was not until after the global financial crisis in October 2009, when Chinese Minister of Commerce Chen Deming and South Korean Minister for Trade Kim Jong-hoon signed an agreement to increase economic cooperation between the two countries, that Seoul began to consider serious talks with Beijing about the FTA. Still the feasibility study took an astonishing eight years to complete, during which time the two countries conducted unofficial joint studies with research institutes; then a trilateral study with academics, industry, and the government; and finally a joint evaluation report by trade authorities of the two countries.

Official negotiations began in May 2012, and the first stage was completed in September 2015, when a preliminary agreement was reached on the tariff schedules for three types of goods: "regular," "sensitive," and "highly sensitive." The last category contained around 1,200 tariff lines, or 10 percent of the 12,000 or so goods traded between the two countries. Not surprisingly, these "highly sensitive" products were the main reasons that the negotiations dragged on for the next couple of years. Among them, the biggest sticking point was agriculture (especially rice and related products) for South Korea and industrial products (especially automobiles and auto parts) for China.

Eventually, after 14 rounds of negotiations, a compromise was reached as negotiators in both countries yielded to the demands of domestic lobbies seeking to maintain protection for key farm and industrial products. Specifically, the agricultural liberalization ratio for South Korea in the FTA was 40 percent by import values and 70 percent by tariff lines (compared to 89 percent and 78 percent in South Korea's first 10 FTAs). Meanwhile, China's liberalization ratio of manufacturing products was agreed to be 85 percent, the lowest in China's signed FTAs at the time (Cheong 2016).

On November 9, 2014, Chinese President Xi Jinping and South Korean President Park Geun-hye declared the substantial settlement of the FTA during a summit in Beijing, reaching a final conclusion on all essential points. At the time the FTA was signed, bilateral trade had reached $235.4 billion, making China the ROK's top import source and top export destination. On December 20, 2015, the China-ROK FTA finally entered into force.

Summary

Like many of China's other FTAs, the ChAFTA and the China-ROK FTA were seen by Beijing as vital to achieving its political and strategic interests in the global context, especially in the face of challenges posed by the TPP (Pan 2014). This was evident in the way China announced the conclusion of the negotiations with both Australia and South Korea around the time of the 2014 Asia-Pacific Economic Cooperation Leaders' Summit in Beijing, where President Barack Obama, Japanese Prime Minister Shinzo Abe, and leaders from the 10 other countries negotiating the TPP were also meeting.

Such strategic and noneconomic considerations in China's FTA diplomacy have often led negotiators to rush into agreements with low levels of obligations (Bergsten, Freeman, Lardy, and Mitchell 2008). While similar criticisms have been leveled against ChAFTA and the China-ROK FTA (e.g., Schott et al. 2015; Tienhaara and Van Harten 2015), and while there are certainly areas that leave much to be desired (e.g., agriculture and government procurement), a closer examination of the agreements reveals high levels of commitment in several traditional areas as well as deep integration in areas such as financial services, the environment, and e-commerce.

Appendix 3.2. List of Interviews Cited in Chapter 3

ID	City	Province	Main Product (Firm) / Government Position (Official)
JS01	Nantong	Jiangsu	Carpets
JS07	Zhenjiang	Jiangsu	Insecticides, fungicides, and herbicides
JS10	Huaian	Jiangsu	Tire
JS13	Suzhou	Jiangsu	Home appliances
JS14	n.a.	Jiangsu	Deputy Director, Municipal Customs Division
JS15	n.a.	Jiangsu	Director, Legal Division, provincial CCPIT
JS23	n.a.	Jiangsu	Deputy Director, municipal AQSIQ
JS27	Suzhou	Jiangsu	Semiconductors
JS33	Suzhou	Jiangsu	Deputy Director, Municipal Bureau of Commerce
JS40	Wuxi	Jiangsu	Biomedical materials
GD01	Maoming	Guangdong	Fish gelatin
GD04	Panyu	Guangdong	Jewelry
GD09	Dongguan	Guangdong	Elastic materials
GD10	Guangzhou	Guangdong	Textile imports and exports
GD11	n.a.	Guangdong	Director, local CCPIT office
GD12	n.a.	Guangdong	Director, local customs office
GD13	n.a.	Guangdong	Secretary General, Provincial Industrial Association for Light Industry
ZJ09	Tongxiang	Zhejiang	Apparel
ZJ10	Tongxiang	Zhejiang	Fiberglass woven roving
ZJ11	Tongxiang	Zhejiang	Processed wool
ZJ12	Yuyao	Zhejiang	Plastics materials
ZJ17	Wenzhou	Zhejiang	Electronic component
ZJ18	n.a.	Zhejiang	Director, Research Institute of the Municipal Bureau of Commerce
ZJ19	n.a.	Zhejiang	Director, local customs office
ZJ20	Hangzhou	Zhejiang	Import of skincare products
ZJ21	n.a.	Zhejiang	Deputy Director, municipal AQSIQ
SD01	Rizhao	Shandong	Yarn
SD02	Qingdao	Shandong	Trading firm
SD05	Zibo	Shandong	Chief, Inspection Division, municipal AQSIQ
SD07	Zibo	Shandong	Ceramic fiber
SD10	Rizhao	Shandong	Auto parts
SD12	Weifang	Shandong	Textile products
SD13	n.a.	Shandong	Director, Office of International Trade Policies, Municipal Bureau of Commerce
BJ01	n.a.	Beijing	Senior official, CCPIT
BJ02	n.a.	Beijing	Scholar, China Institute of Contemporary International Relations

Note: Only interviews cited in the chapter are listed here. City names are not shown for government officials to ensure the interviewees' anonymity.

Appendix 4.1. Control Variables Used in the Survey Analysis

We include a number of control variables that may influence firm trade preferences in our survey analysis of Chinese executives. These variables are the following:

Age. We include a firm's age, measured as the number of years that have elapsed since the firm was first established, into the analysis out of expectation that firms with a longer history of operation may have more experience with the international market that will increase their likelihood of having a favorable attitude toward international trade.

Ownership type. Previous studies (e.g., Blanchard and Matschke 2015; Milner 1989) suggest that multinational corporations may be more likely to favor trade liberalization due to the costs that protectionism may impose on their intra-firm trade. It is therefore possible that foreign-invested enterprises (FIEs) and joint ventures (JVs) may be more likely to support preferential trade liberalization than state-owned or collective enterprises. To account for this possibility, we include a dummy variable for a firm's ownership type that equals "1" if a firm is a state-owned enterprise (SOE) and "0" otherwise.

Employees and *sales.* We additionally consider a couple of firm characteristics that may influence trade preferences. Previous studies (e.g., Melitz 2003; Thacker 2000) suggest that firm size may play an important role in shaping firm trade policy preferences, with larger firms more likely to possess competitive advantages in international markets due to their greater ability to take advantage of economies of scale or oligopolistic competition. We therefore develop two variables, *employees* and *sales*, to capture firm size.

Employees. We asked a simple question of how many employees the company employs across all locations. *Employees* is a categorical variable with five possible values: "0–10 employees" (1), "11–50 employees" (2), "51–200 employees" (3), "201–500 employees" (4), and "more than 500 employees" (5).

Sales. We use the volume of the firm's sales (in RMB) in the past year as another measure of firm size. We code *sales* based on the following coding scheme: "less than 5 million" (1); "5–10 million" (2); "10–15 million" (3); "15–20 million" (4); "20–40 million" (5); "40–80 million" (6); "80–200 million" (7); and "200 million and more" (8).

Productivity. The role of productivity in shaping firm trade preferences has also received some attention in the literature. Theories of firm heterogeneity and trade (e.g. Melitz 2003; Bernard et al. 2007; Eaton, Kortum, and Kramarz 2011) suggest that trade liberalization should raise average industry productivity through the reallocation of resources within the industry, leading highly productive firms to expand to enter the export market, less productive firms to produce only for the domestic market, and the least productive firms to exit the market. This logic should lead us to expect that more productive firms should be more favorably disposed toward free trade, whereas less productive ones should be in favor of protection. Recent empirical studies (e.g., Kim 2017; Plouffe 2017) have yielded some evidence in support of this conjecture. We rely on firm self-assessment of their productivity relative to that of other companies in the same industry in coding this variable. Specifically, *productivity* is a categorical variable ranging from "1" to "5," indicating "significantly less productive," "somewhat less productive," "about the same," "somewhat more productive," and "significantly more productive," respectively.

Political connections. It is possible that in China's transitional economy, politically connected firms may be in a better position to secure financial and other resources from the government that will allow them to overcome the constraints in exporting to international markets. We therefore measure a firm's political connections with the following question in the survey: "Is your firm's CEO a member of the National People's Congress?" As a robustness check, we also measure political connections based on the following survey question: "Does your firm's board of directors contain members of the NPC?" Regression results using this alternative measure of political connections are very similar.

Substitutability. Previous studies (e.g., Anderson 1979; Deardorff 1998) have found that the degree of substitutability between domestic and imported varieties of goods may be another factor influencing firm trade preferences. As trade protection has a strong effect on trade flows when products are highly substitutable, firms faced with greater product substitutability should be more likely to support trade liberalization. To measure the firm's product substitutability, we asked respondents the following question: "How easy would it be to substitute your products with similar products produced by other manufacturers in the same industry?" Reponses to this question were coded on a "1" to "4" scale, with "1"–"4" indicating "not easy at all," "not easy," "somewhat easy," and "very easy," respectively.

FDI. Finally, we include a dummy variable for whether a firm owns a facility or has investment in another country into the analysis to address the possible influence of multinational production on the firm's trade preferences.

Appendix 4.2. Summary Statistics of the Survey Sample

Variable	Obs	Mean	Std. Dev.	Min	Max
Free Trade	559	4.33	0.69	1	5
Trade Agreement	554	4.14	0.72	1	5
WTO	557	4.17	0.70	2	5
PTA	557	4.14	0.76	1	5
Multinational	569	0.44	0.50	0	1
Exporter	569	0.29	0.45	0	1
Importer	569	0.06	0.23	0	1
Domestic firm	569	0.21	0.41	0	1
Forward GVC Linkages	416	17.50	18.96	0	100
Backward GVC Linkages	253	7.89	7.51	0	70.31
Firm Age	566	19.95	14.43	1	125
Private	569	0.60	0.49	0	1
Foreign	569	0.14	0.35	0	1
Collective	569	0.02	0.13	0	1
Joint Venture.	569	0.07	0.25	0	1
Employees	569	3.89	0.98	1	5
Sales	560	5.78	1.91	1	8
Political Connections	569	0.35	0.48	0	1
Productivity	565	3.74	0.92	1	5
Substitutability	560	2.68	0.71	1	4
FDI	569	0.31	0.46	0	1

Appendix 4.3. Regression Results for Figure 4.4

Variable	(1)	(2)	(3)	(4)
Trader	0.496***	0.192*	0.187**	0.231**
	(5.47)	(1.88)	(2.05)	(2.47)
Exporter	0.343***	0.150	0.223**	0.200**
	(3.62)	(1.50)	(2.45)	(2.15)
Importer	0.171	0.00126	0.174	−0.370*
	(1.24)	(0.01)	(1.32)	(1.92)
Firm Age	0.003	0.003*	−0.003	−0.005**
	(1.56)	(1.67)	(0.92)	(1.99)
Private	0.0796	0.0965	0.0425	−0.105
	(0.98)	(1.05)	(0.43)	(1.07)
Foreign	−0.0436	0.0693	−0.138	−0.156
	(0.43)	(0.65)	(1.24)	(1.37)
Collective	0.163	0.150	−0.099	0.224
	(0.85)	(0.56)	(0.47)	(1.14)
Joint Venture	−0.0002	0.125	0.226*	0.088
	(0.00)	(0.95)	(1.67)	(0.70)
Employees	−0.049	0.043	0.066	0.041
	(1.00)	(0.97)	(1.49)	(0.84)
Sales	−0.011	−0.014	−0.016	0.025
	(0.51)	(0.66)	(0.76)	(1.10)
Connections	0.073	0.008	0.089	0.050
	(1.12)	(0.11)	(1.31)	(0.71)
Productivity	0.092**	0.139***	0.034	0.047
	(2.58)	(3.73)	(0.95)	(1.17)
Substitutability	0.028	−0.036	−0.014	−0.025
	(0.72)	(0.82)	(0.33)	(0.54)
FDI	0.023	0.020	0.150**	−0.149*
	(0.33)	(0.25)	(2.03)	(1.78)
Constant	3.707***	3.362***	3.735***	3.791***
	(15.51)	(13.17)	(14.49)	(13.90)
N	541	535	537	538

Notes: The dependent variables are (1) free trade; (2) trade agreements; (3) WTO; and (4) PTA; OLS regression with robust standard errors in parentheses; * $p < .1$, ** $p < 0.05$, *** $p < 0.01$.

Appendix 4.4. Regression Results for Figure 4.5(a)

Variable	(1)	(2)	(3)	(4)
Forward GVC Linkage	0.003	0.005*	0.002	0.007**
	(0.91)	(1.87)	(0.56)	(2.48)
Firm Age	0.002	0.0006	−0.005	−0.006
	(0.40)	(0.13)	(0.90)	(1.21)
Private	0.0184	−0.142	−0.0910	−0.269
	(0.11)	(0.94)	(0.53)	(1.62)
Foreign	−0.452*	−0.0783	−0.313	−0.214
	(1.74)	(0.39)	(1.49)	(1.14)
Collective	−0.0384	−0.320	−0.867**	−0.0749
	(0.11)	(1.32)	(2.46)	(0.22)
Joint Venture	−0.392	−0.498	−0.00104	−0.320
	(1.53)	(1.25)	(0.00)	(1.03)
Employees	−0.061	0.025	0.131	0.00005
	(0.58)	(0.33)	(1.49)	(0.00)
Sales	−0.007	−0.060	0.025	0.035
	(0.15)	(1.55)	(0.57)	(0.87)
Connections	0.0921	−0.120	−0.193	0.0427
	(0.74)	(0.93)	(1.43)	(0.35)
Productivity	0.104	0.209***	0.071	0.007
	(1.44)	(2.79)	(1.03)	(0.11)
Substitutability	−0.051	−0.024	−0.198**	−0.009
	(0.59)	(0.29)	(2.30)	(0.12)
FDI	0.014	−0.025	−0.088	−0.085
	(0.08)	(0.18)	(0.61)	(0.59)
Constant	4.309***	3.803***	4.106***	4.242***
	(7.63)	(7.06)	(7.06)	(8.14)
N	159	156	155	157

Notes: The dependent variables are (1) free trade; (2) trade agreements; (3) WTO; and (4) PTA; OLS regression with robust standard errors in parentheses; * $p < .1$, ** $p < 0.05$, *** $p < 0.01$.

Appendix 4.5. Regression Results for Figure 4.5(c)

Variable	(1)	(2)	(3)	(4)
GVC Embeddedness	0.011**	0.010*	0.004	0.003
	(2.53)	(1.84)	(0.58)	(0.33)
Firm Age	0.002	0.004	−0.006	−0.008**
	(0.51)	(1.31)	(1.19)	(2.47)
Private	0.196	0.113	−0.301	−0.314
	(1.44)	(0.62)	(1.57)	(1.62)
Foreign	0.062	0.088	−0.406*	−0.438**
	(0.35)	(0.40)	(1.75)	(2.13)
Collective	0.403	0.163	−0.411*	−0.0553
	(1.36)	(0.43)	(1.76)	(0.17)
Joint Venture	0.406**	0.237	0.093	0.059
	(2.05)	(1.16)	(0.40)	(0.28)
Employees	0.030	−0.121	0.024	0.058
	(0.33)	(1.18)	(0.22)	(0.50)
Sales	−0.044	0.009	0.021	0.015
	(1.07)	(0.20)	(0.43)	(0.31)
Connections	−0.101	0.220	0.136	0.0505
	(0.89)	(1.53)	(0.90)	(0.33)
Productivity	0.097	0.080	−0.011	0.017
	(1.38)	(0.88)	(0.12)	(0.18)
Substitutability	0.122	−0.110	−0.018	−0.073
	(1.48)	(1.19)	(0.17)	(0.83)
FDI	−0.027	0.02472	0.268*	0.029
	(0.23)	(0.20)	(1.90)	(0.23)
Constant	3.743***	4.314***	4.211***	4.397***
	(7.60)	(6.59)	(6.73)	(6.48)
N	124	123	124	122

Notes: The dependent variables are (1) free trade; (2) trade agreements; (3) WTO; and (4) PTA; OLS regression with robust standard errors in parentheses; * $p < .1$, ** $p < 0.05$, *** $p < 0.01$.

Appendix 4.6. Regression Results for Figure 4.6

Variable	(1) prefer	(2) prefer	(3) prefer	(4) prefer
Tariff				
Zero tariff	0.0677***	0.0246	0.179***	0.0640
	(0.0205)	(0.0325)	(0.0539)	(0.0836)
No change	−0.118***	−0.155***	−0.311***	−0.401***
	(0.0187)	(0.0362)	(0.0495)	(0.0947)
Investor Protection				
High Standard	0.0534***	−0.0121	0.141***	−0.0315
	(0.0181)	(0.0327)	(0.0481)	(0.0846)
None	−0.061***	−0.0998***	−0.162***	−0.260***
	(0.018)	(0.035)	(0.048)	(0.090)
IP Protection				
Strict	0.0949***	0.0981***	0.250***	0.256***
	(0.0184)	(0.0346)	(0.0486)	(0.0897)
None	−0.0953***	−0.0533	−0.251***	−0.138
	(0.0193)	(0.0328)	(0.0510)	(0.0847)
Trade Remedy				
Conditional use	−0.0349*	−0.0125	−0.0913*	−0.0322
	(0.0198)	(0.0335)	(0.0522)	(0.0865)
Unrestricted use	−0.0874***	−0.0857**	−0.232***	−0.224**
	(0.0190)	(0.0374)	(0.0505)	(0.0967)
Time to Liberalization				
1 years	−0.0331*	0.00154	−0.0891*	0.00342
	(0.0191)	(0.0352)	(0.0508)	(0.0916)
5 years	−0.0114	0.00696	−0.0317	0.0195
	(0.0188)	(0.0355)	(0.0497)	(0.0923)
Dispute Resolution				
Some condition	−0.0295	−0.0485	−0.0773	−0.129
	(0.0185)	(0.0338)	(0.0490)	(0.0877)
Strict conditions	−0.104***	−0.0498	−0.276***	−0.131
	(0.0193)	(0.0365)	(0.0514)	(0.0946)
Controls				
Firm Age	−4.94e−05	0.000178	−0.000128	0.000369
	(0.000145)	(0.000363)	(0.000382)	(0.000950)
Private	0.0116*	−0.0211**	0.0294*	−0.0548**
	(0.00660)	(0.00940)	(0.0174)	(0.0245)
Foreign	0.00923	−0.0198	0.0225	−0.0497
	(0.00739)	(0.0233)	(0.0195)	(0.0600)
Collective	−0.00406	−0.0182	−0.0156	−0.0464
	(0.0207)	(0.0388)	(0.0553)	(0.101)
Joint Venture	0.0118	−0.0103	0.0294	−0.0261
	(0.00851)	(0.0129)	(0.0231)	(0.0327)
Employees	0.00278	−0.00781*	0.00681	−0.0208*
	(0.00302)	(0.00467)	(0.00799)	(0.0123)
Sales	−0.00127	0.00227	−0.00326	0.00648
	(0.00159)	(0.00242)	(0.00421)	(0.00631)

Variable	(1) prefer	(2) prefer	(3) prefer	(4) prefer
Connections	0.000752	0.0108	0.00133	0.0287
	(0.00473)	(0.00864)	(0.0125)	(0.0225)
Productivity	0.00221	0.00865**	0.00692	0.0227**
	(0.00264)	(0.00418)	(0.00697)	(0.0109)
Substitutability	−0.00326	−0.000406	−0.00896	0.000744
	(0.00328)	(0.00535)	(0.00870)	(0.0139)
FDI	−0.00327	−0.000734	−0.00620	−0.000486
	(0.00505)	(0.00934)	(0.0133)	(0.0242)
Constant	0.610***	0.626***	0.291***	0.323**
	(0.0330)	(0.0539)	(0.0869)	(0.139)
Observations	3,974	1,354	3,974	1,354
R-squared	0.070	0.054		

Notes: Models (1) and (2) are based on linear probability regression with the binary choice as the dependent variable; Models (3) and (4) are based on probit regression; robust standard errors clustered on the firm in parentheses; * $p < .1$, ** $p < 0.05$, *** $p < 0.01$.

Appendix 4.7. Survey Questionnaire

Q1. In which industry are you currently employed?

- Agriculture, Hunting, Forestry and Fishing (1)
- Mining and Quarrying (2)
- Food, Beverages and Tobacco (3)
- Textiles and Textile Products (4)
- Leather, Leather and Footwear (5)
- Wood and Products of Wood and Cork (6)
- Pulp, Paper, Paper, Printing and Publishing (7)
- Coke, Refined Petroleum and Nuclear Fuel (8)
- Chemicals and Chemical Products (9)
- Rubber and Plastics (10)
- Other Non-Metallic Mineral (11)
- Basic Metals and Fabricated Metal (12)
- Machinery, Nec (13)
- Electrical and Optical Equipment (14)
- Transport Equipment (15)
- Manufacturing, Nec; Recycling (16)
- Electricity, Gas and Water Supply (17)
- Construction (18)
- Sale, Maintenance and Repair of Motor Vehicles and Motorcycles; Retail Sale of Fuel (19)
- Wholesale Trade and Commission Trade, Except of Motor Vehicles and Motorcycles (20)
- Retail Trade, Except of Motor Vehicles and Motorcycles; Repair of Household Goods (21)
- Hotels and Restaurants (22)
- Inland Transport (23)
- Water Transport (24)
- Air Transport (25)
- Other Supporting and Auxiliary Transport Activities; Activities of Travel Agencies (26)
- Post and Telecommunications (27)
- Financial Intermediation (28)
- Real Estate Activities (29)

- Renting of Machinery and Equipment and Other Business Activities (30)
- Public Admin and Defense; Compulsory Social Security (31)
- Education (32)
- Health and Social Work (33)
- Other Community, Social and Personal Services (34)
- Private Households with Employed Persons (35)

Q2. In which province is your company located?

- Beijing (1)
- Tianjin (2)
- Hebei (3)
- Shanxi (4)
- Inner Mongolia (5)
- Liaoning (6)
- Jilin (7)
- Heilongjiang (8)
- Shanghai (9)
- Jiangsu (10)
- Zhejiang (11)
- Anhui (12)
- Fujian (13)
- Jiangxi (14)
- Shandong (15)
- Henan (16)
- Hubei (17)
- Hunan (18)
- Guangdong (19)
- Guangxi (20)
- Inner Mongolia (21)
- Hainan (22)
- Chongqing (23)
- Sichuan (24)
- Guizhou (25)
- Yunnan (26)
- Tibet (27)

- Shaanxi (28)
- Gansu (29)
- Qinghai (30)
- Ningxia (31)
- Xinjiang (32)
- Hong Kong (33)
- Macao (34)
- Other (35)

Q3. In what year was your company founded? _____

Q4. What is your company's registration type?

- SOE (1)
- Private (2)
- Foreign-invested (3)
- Collective (4)
- Joint Venture (5)

Q5. How long have you worked at this company?

- 0–6 Months (1)
- 7–12 Months (2)
- 13–24 Months (3)
- More than 24 Months (4)

Q6. What products does your company make? (List up to three)

- Product 1 (1)
- Product 2 (2)
- Product 3 (3)

Q7. Is your company doing better compared to last year?

- Yes (1)
- No (2)
- About the same (3)
- Don't know (4)

Q8. How many employees does this company employ across all locations?

- 0–10 Employees (1)
- 11–50 Employees (2)
- 51–200 Employees (3)
- 201–500 Employees (4)
- More than 500 Employees (5)
- Don't know (6)

Q9. What was your company's total sales volume last year?

- less than 5 million RMB (1)
- 5–10 million RMB (2)
- 10–15 million RMB (3)
- 15–20 million RMB (4)
- 20–40 million RMB (5)
- 40–80 million RMB (6)
- 80–200 million RMB (7)
- Over 200 million RMB (8)
- Don't know (9)

Q10. Is the owner or CEO of your company a member of the national/provincial/municipal People's Congress?

- Yes (1)
- No (2)
- Don't know (3)

Q11. Is any member of the board of your company a member of the national/provincial/municipal People's Congress?

- Yes (1)
- No (2)
- Don't know (3)
- Our company does not have a board (4)

Q12. How productive is your company compared to other companies in the same industry?

- Significantly less productive (1)
- Somewhat less productive (2)
- About the same (3)
- Somewhat more productive (4)
- Significantly more productive (5)
- Don't know (6)

Q13. How easy would it be to substitute your products with similar products produced by other manufacturers in the same industry?

- Not easy at all (1)
- Not easy (2)
- Somewhat easy (3)
- Very easy (4)
- Don't know (5)

Q14. What's your company's main source of competition?

- Similar products produced by foreign invested enterprises (1)
- Similar imported products (2)
- Hard to say (3)

Q15. Has your company sold goods abroad (exported) in the last year?

- Yes (1)
- No (2)
- I don't know (3)

Display This Question:

If (Q15) Has your company sold goods abroad (exported) in the last year?
Yes Is Selected

Q16. Approximately what percentage of your company's sales are to customers abroad?
_____ share of exports in total sales volume (%)

Display This Question:

If (Q15) Has your company sold goods abroad (exported) in the last year?
  Yes Is Selected

Q17. Approximately what percentage of your company's exports are intermediate products or raw materials?

_____ share of intermediate products or raw materials in total exports (%)

Display This Question:

If (Q15) Has your company sold goods abroad (exported) in the last year?
  Yes Is Selected

Q18. Please rank the importance of each of the following regions for your
exports: 1 = "least important"; 10 = "very important."

- _____ Africa (1)
- _____ Central Asia (2)
- _____ East Asia and Pacific (3)
- _____ South Asia (4)
- _____ Europe (5)
- _____ North America (6)
- _____ Latin America & Caribbean (7)
- _____ Middle East (8)

Display This Question:

If (Q15) Has your company sold goods abroad (exported) in the last year?
  Yes Is Selected

Q19. Has your company exported to the following country(s)? (You can
choose more than one)

- Australia (1)
- United States (2)
- Japan (3)
- Russia (4)
- Germany (5)

- Canada (6)
- Mexico (7)
- Brazil (8)
- Vietnam (9)
- South Korea (10)
- Indonesia (11)
- Other (please specify) (12) _____

Q20. Has your company purchased goods from abroad (imported) in the last year?

- Yes (1)
- No (2)
- Don't know (3)

Display This Question:

If (Q20) Has your company purchased goods from abroad (imported) in the last year? Yes Is Selected

Q21. Approximately what percentage of your final products comes from imported parts and components or other inputs?
_____ % of imported products in final products (1)

Display This Question:

If (Q20) Has your company purchased goods from abroad (imported) in the last year? Yes Is Selected

Q22. On a scale of 1–10, please rank the importance of each of the following regions as suppliers of your imports: 1 = "least important"; 10 = "very important."

- _____ Africa (1)
- _____ Central Asia (2)
- _____ East Asia and Pacific (3)
- _____ South Asia (4)
- _____ Europe (5)
- _____ North America (6)

- _____ Latin America & Caribbean (7)
- _____ Middle East (8)

Display This Question:

If (Q20) Has your company purchased goods from abroad (imported) in the last year? Yes Is Selected

Q23. Has your company imported from the following country(s)? (You can choose more than one)

- Australia (1)
- United States (2)
- Japan (3)
- Russia (4)
- Germany (5)
- Canada (6)
- Mexico (7)
- Brazil (8)
- Vietnam (9)
- South Korea (10)
- Indonesia (11)
- Other (please specify) (12) _____

Q24. Overall, which of the following is more important to your industry: export or import?

- export (1)
- import (2)
- don't know (3)

Q25. Does your company own a facility or has investment in another country?

- Yes (1)
- No (2)

Display This Question:

If (Q25) Does your company own a facility or has investment in another country? Yes Is Selected

Q26. On a scale of 1 to 10, how would you rank the importance of foreign investment or production for your company's business: 1 = "least important"; 10 = "very important."

_____ Importance of foreign investment (1)

Display This Question:

If (Q25) Does your company own a facility or has investment in another country? Yes Is Selected

Q27. Please rank the importance of each of the following regions for your foreign investment: 1 = "least important"; 10 = "very important."

- _____ Africa (1)
- _____ Central Asia (2)
- _____ East Asia and Pacific (3)
- _____ South Asia (4)
- _____ Europe (5)
- _____ North America (6)
- _____ Latin America & Caribbean (7)
- _____ Middle East (8)

Q28. Do you agree or disagree with the following statement? "International trade is good for my business."

- Strongly Disagree (1)
- Disagree (2)
- Neither Agree nor Disagree (3)
- Agree (4)
- Strongly Agree (5)
- Don't know (6)

Q29. Do you agree or disagree with the following statement? "Trade agreements are good for my business."

- Strongly Disagree (1)
- Disagree (2)
- Neither Agree nor Disagree (3)
- Agree (4)
- Strongly Agree (5)
- Don't know (6)

Q30. Do you agree or disagree with the following statement? "The World Trade Organization is good for my business."

- Strongly Disagree (1)
- Disagree (2)
- Neither Agree nor Disagree (3)
- Agree (4)
- Strongly Agree (5)
- Don't know (6)

Q31. Do you agree or disagree with the following statement? "Regional trade agreements such as the China-ASEAN FTA are good for my business."

- Strongly Disagree (1)
- Disagree (2)
- Neither Agree nor Disagree (3)
- Agree (4)
- Strongly Agree (5)
- Don't know (6)

Q32. Do you agree or disagree with the following statement? "Bilateral free trade agreements such as the China-South Korea FTA are good for my business."

- Strongly Disagree (1)
- Disagree (2)
- Neither Agree nor Disagree (3)
- Agree (4)
- Strongly Agree (5)
- Don't know (6)

Q33. Do you agree or disagree with the following statement? "Compared to regional trade agreements, multilateral trade liberalization under the World Trade Organization (WTO) is better for the expansion of our business."

- Strongly Disagree (1)
- Disagree (2)
- Neither Agree nor Disagree (3)
- Agree (4)
- Strongly Agree (5)
- Don't know (6)

Q34. Suppose that the Chinese government will sign a preferential trade agreement with (a) the countries with which your company has the most business OR (b) some of its largest trading partners. We will show you five sets of PTA design, each with a pair of proposals with comparable attributes such as the level of tariff reduction, dispute settlement mechanism, intellectual property rights protection, and so on. Please carefully compare the attributes in each pair before making your selection.

Attributes	FTA design A	FTA design B
Level of tariff reductions on your company's major products		
Investor protection		
Intellectual property rights protection		
Trade remedies (antidumping and countervailing duties, etc.)		
Time frame for the liberalization of tariff and other trade barriers		
Dispute settlement mechanism		

Q35. In comparison, which FTA design do you prefer?

- FTA design A (1)
- FTA design B (2)

Appendix 5.1. Fortune 500 Companies and Their GVC Linkages

Here is a list of the industry and the names of the Fortune 500 companies in each industry in descending order by their annual sales.

Weak GVC linkages with both China and TPP countries:

Electric, Gas, & Sanitary Services: Energy Transfer Equity, L.P., Exelon Corporation, Duke Energy Corporation, The Southern Company, The AES Corporation, PG&E Corporation, American Electric Power Company, Inc., NextEra Energy, Inc., FirstEnergy Corp., ONEOK, Inc., Kinder Morgan, Inc., Waste Management, Inc., Dominion Resources, Inc., Edison International, Consolidated Edison, Inc., PPL Corporation, Entergy Corporation, NRG Energy, Inc., Xcel Energy Inc., Sempra Energy, Public Service Enterprise Group Incorporated, DTE Energy Company, Republic Services, Inc., CenterPoint Energy, Inc., Northeast Utilities, UGI Corporation, Ameren Corporation, CMS Energy Corporation, Targa Resources Corp., Calpine Corporation, Energy Future Holdings Corp., NiSource Inc., Integrys Energy Group, Inc., Spectra Energy Corp

Eating & Drinking Places: McDonald's Corporation, Starbucks Corporation, Aramark Holdings Corporation, Yum! Brands, Inc., Darden Restaurants, Inc.

Hotels & Other Lodging Places: Marriott International, Inc., Hilton Worldwide Holdings, Inc., Starwood Hotels & Resorts Worldwide, Inc., Wynn Resorts

Amusement & Recreation Services: Las Vegas Sands Corp., MGM Resorts International, Caesars Entertainment Corporation, Live Nation Entertainment, Inc.

Strong GVC linkages with China but weak GVC linkages with TPP countries:

Metal, Mining: Cliffs Natural Resources Inc., Freeport-McMoRan Copper & Gold, Inc., Newmont Mining Corporation

Coal Mining: CONSOL Energy Inc., Peabody Energy Corporation

Oil & Gas Extraction: Noble Energy, Inc., ConocoPhillips, Enterprise Products Partners L.P., Chesapeake Energy Corporation, Baker Hughes Incorporated, Apache Corporation, Marathon Oil Corporation, EOG Resources, Inc., Occidental Petroleum Corporation, Halliburton Company, Devon Energy Corporation, Anadarko Petroleum Corporation

Food & Kindred Products: ConAgra Foods, Inc., The J. M. Smucker Company, Tyson Foods, Inc., Mondelez International, Inc., Campbell Soup Company, H. J. Heinz Company, Leucadia National Corporation, The Coca-Cola Company, The Hershey Company, Hormel Foods Corporation, Ingredion Incorporated, PepsiCo, General Mills, Inc., Dr Pepper Snapple Group, Inc., Coca-Cola Enterprises, Inc., Land O'Lakes, Inc., Kellogg Company, Archer Daniels Midland, Dean Foods Company, Kraft Foods Group, Inc., Smithfield Foods, Inc.

Tobacco Products: Lorillard, Inc., Reynolds American Inc., Altria Group, Inc., Philip Morris International, Inc.

Paper & Allied Products: Rock-Tenn Company, Sealed Air Corporation, 3M Company, MeadWestvaco Corporation, International Paper Company, Kimberly-Clark Corporation, Avery Dennison Corporation, Bemis Company, Inc., R.R. Donnelley & Sons Company, Gannett Co., Inc.

Rubber Products: The Goodyear Tire & Rubber Company.

Miscellaneous Plastics Products: Jarden Corporation.

Primary Metal Industries: General Cable Corporation, Steel Dynamics, Inc., Nucor Corporation, United States Steel Corporation, AK Steel Holding Corporation, Alcoa, Inc.

Fabricated Metal Products: Crown Holdings, Inc., Ball Corporation, Masco Corporation, Parker-Hannifin Corporation

Others: Domtar Corporation, US Foods, Inc., Con-way, Inc.

Strong GVC linkages with TPP countries but weak GVC linkages with China:

General Building Contractors: Lennar Corporation, D. R. Horton, Inc., PulteGroup, Inc.

Heavy Construction, Except Building: KBR, Inc., Jacobs Engineering Group, Inc., Fluor Corporation, Peter Kiewit Sons', Inc.

Special Trade Contractors: Quanta Services, Inc., EMCOR Group, Inc.

Stone, Clay, & Glass Products: Owens-Illinois, Inc., Owens Corning

Transportation by Trucking: J.B. Hunt Transport Services, Inc.

Transportation & Warehousing: United Parcel Service, FedEx Corporation.

Transportation by Air: American Airlines Group, Inc., United Continental Holdings, Inc., Southwest Airlines Co., JetBlue Airways Corporation, Alaska Air Group, Inc., Delta Air Lines, Inc.

Communications: CC Media Holdings, Inc., CenturyLink, Inc., Windstream Holdings, Inc., Twenty-First Century Fox, Inc., CBS Corporation, Comcast, Viacom, Inc., DIRECTV, The Walt Disney Company, Cablevision Systems Corporation, AT&T, Level 3 Communications, Inc., Time Warner, Inc., DISH Network Corporation, Charter Communications, Inc., Time Warner Cable, Inc., NII Holdings, Inc., Verizon Communications, Discovery Communications, Inc.

Building Materials & Gardening Supplies: Home Depot, Tractor Supply Company, Lowe's Companies

Depository Institutions: BB&T Corporation, SunTrust Banks, Inc., Wells Fargo, Regions Financial Corporation, The Bank of New York Mellon Corporation, Fifth Third Bancorp, The Western Union Company, U.S. Bancorp, Visa Inc., State Street Corporation, The PNC Financial Services Group, Inc., Bank of America, TIAA-CREF, MasterCard Incorporated

Nondepository Institutions: State Farm Insurance Cos., Discover Financial Services, Citigroup, Capital One Financial Corporation, Fannie Mae, Freddie Mac, Deere & Company, American Financial Group Inc., SLM Corporation, American Express Company

Security & Commodity Brokers: J. P. Morgan Chase & Co., Morgan Stanley, INTL FCStone Inc., The Charles Schwab Corporation, BlackRock, Inc., Oaktree Capital Group, LLC, Principal Financial Group, Inc., The Blackstone Group L.P., Ameriprise Financial, Inc., Pacific Life, Spectrum Group International, Inc., KKR & Co. L.P., Franklin Resources, Inc., The Goldman Sachs Group, Inc., The Jones Financial Companies, L.L.L.P.

Insurance Carriers: Liberty Mutual Holding Company, Inc. Loews Corporation: Reinsurance Group of America, Incorporated, American Family Ins. Group, Lincoln National Corporation, Humana, Inc., New York Life Insurance Company, MetLife, Health Net, Inc., American International Group, Genworth Financial, Inc., Alleghany Corporation, WellPoint, WellCare Health Plans, Inc., The Hartford Financial Services Group, Inc., Unum Group, Prudential Financial, Inc., W.R. Berkley Corporation, CIGNA Corporation, Assurant, Inc., Auto-Owners Insurance Group, Aetna, Inc., Centene Corporation, The Chubb Corporation, Massachusetts Mutual Life Insurance Company, UnitedHealth Group, Fidelity National Financial, Inc., Molina Healthcare, Inc., Aflac Incorporated, The Allstate Corporation, Old Republic International Corporation, The Progressive Corporation, Erie Insurance

Group, United Services Automobile Association, Nationwide Mutual Insurance Co., Mutual of Omaha Insurance Company, Guardian Life Ins. Co. of America, Thrivent Financial for Lutherans, Marsh & McLennan Companies, Inc., Northwestern Mutual Life Insurance Company, Inc.

Real Estate: CBRE Group, Inc., Realogy Holdings Corp., Wyndham Worldwide Corporation

Holding & Other Investment Offices: Host Hotels & Resorts, Inc., Simon Property Group, Inc.

Business Services: Fidelity National Information Services, Inc., Booz Allen Hamilton Holding Corp., eBay, Inc., Kelly Services, Inc., The Priceline Group, Inc., Computer Sciences Corporation, Facebook, Inc., Oracle Corporation, Leidos Holdings, Inc., The Interpublic Group of Companies, Inc., Quintiles Transnational Holdings, Inc., United Rentals, Inc., Google, Xerox Corporation, International Business Machines, McGraw Hill Financial, Inc., Microsoft, Ally Financial, Inc., First Data Corporation, The Travelers Companies, Inc., Avis Budget Group, Inc., ManpowerGroup, Inc., Symantec Corporation, Automatic Data Processing, Inc., Cognizant Technology Solutions Corporation, Omnicom Group, Inc.

Auto Repair, Services, & Parking: Hertz Global Holdings, Inc., Ryder System, Inc.

Health Services: Universal Health Services, Inc., Kindred Healthcare, Inc., Community Health Systems, Inc., Tenet Healthcare Corporation, Quest Diagnostics Incorporated, Laboratory Corporation of America Holdings, Vanguard Health Systems, Inc., DaVita HealthCare Partners Inc., HCA Holdings, Inc.

Non-Classifiable Establishments: Berkshire Hathaway, General Electric, Seaboard Corporation

Strong GVC linkages with both China and TPP countries:

Textile Mill Products: Mohawk Industries, Inc.

Apparel & Other Textile Products: V.F. Corporation, PVH Corp., Ralph Lauren Corporation

Lumber & Wood Products: Weyerhaeuser Company

Furniture & Fixtures: Johnson Controls, Inc., Lear Corporation

Chemical & Allied Products: Abbott Laboratories, Baxter International, Inc., Dow Chemical, Procter & Gamble, Pfizer, FMC Technologies,

Inc., Praxair, Inc., Celanese Corporation, The Mosaic Company, Celgene Corporation, Ashland, Inc., CF Industries Holdings, Inc., E. I. du Pont de Nemours and Company, Huntsman Corporation, PPG Industries, Inc., Allergan, Inc., Eli Lilly and Company, Air Products & Chemicals, Inc., Biogen Idec, Inc., Ecolab, Inc., The Estelle Lauder Companies, Inc., Bristol-Myers Squibb Company, Merck & Co., Inc., Avon Products, Inc., Colgate-Palmolive Company, Eastman Chemical Company, Amgen, Inc., Gilead Sciences, Inc., The Clorox Company, AbbVie, Inc., Johnson & Johnson, The Sherwin-Williams Company, Mylan, Inc.

Petroleum & Coal Products: Hess Corporation, Marathon Petroleum, Exxon Mobil, Tesoro Corporation, Western Refining, Inc., Calumet Specialty Products Partners, L.P., Chevron, PBF Energy, Inc., HollyFrontier Corporation, Phillips 66, Murphy Oil Corporation, Valero Energy

Leather & Leather Products: Coach, Inc.

Industrial Machinery & Equipment: NetApp, Inc., NCR Corporation, SanDisk Corporation, EMC Corporation, AGCO Corporation, Illinois Tool Works, Inc., National Oilwell Varco, Inc., Caterpillar, Western Digital Corporation, Terex Corporation, Applied Materials, Inc., Cisco Systems, Inc., Cummins, Inc., Apple, Cameron International Corporation, Stanley Black & Decker, Inc., Joy Global, Inc., Hewlett-Packard, First American Financial Corporation, Dover Corporation

Electronic & Other Electric Equipment: Micron Technology, Inc., Whirlpool Corporation, Sanmina, Qualcomm Incorporated, Harris Corporation, Advanced Micro Devices, Inc., Intel Corporation, Broadcom Corporation, Motorola Solutions, Inc., Jabil Circuit, Inc., Harbinger Group, Inc., Corning Incorporated, Texas Instruments Incorporated, Rockwell Automation, Inc., Emerson Electric Co.

Transportation Equipment: Dana Holding Corporation, Oshkosh Corporation, United Technologies, TRW Automotive Holdings Corp., Visteon Corporation, General Motors, Navistar International Corporation, PACCAR, Inc., Icahn Enterprises L.P., Textron, Inc., Precision Castparts Corp., Huntington Ingalls Industries, Inc., Ford Motor, BorgWarner, Inc., Boeing, Autoliv, Inc., Lockheed Martin Corporation, Harley-Davidson, Inc., Tenneco, Inc., The Williams Companies, Inc., General Dynamics Corporation

Instruments & Related Products: Medtronic, Inc., Stryker Corporation, St.

Jude Medical, Inc., Agilent Technologies, Inc., Raytheon Company, Northrop Grumman Corporation, Boston Scientific Corporation, Danaher Corporation, Thermo Fisher Scientific, Inc., Honeywell International, Inc., Becton, Dickinson and Company

Miscellaneous Manufacturing Industries: Mattel, Inc., Newell Rubbermaid, Inc.

Railroad Transportation: Norfolk Southern Corporation, CSX Corporation, Union Pacific Corporation

Pipelines, Except Natural Gas: Buckeye Partners, L.P.

Wholesale Trade—Durable Goods: Limited, Owens & Minor, Inc., Anixter International, Inc., Genuine Parts Company, Insight Enterprises, Inc., LKQ Corporation, HD Supply Holdings, Inc., Synnex Corporation, Arrow Electronics, Inc., WESCO International, Inc., Avnet, Inc., W. W. Grainger, Inc., Tech Data Corporation, Ingram Micro, Inc., Airgas, Inc., Henry Schein, Inc., United Stationers, Inc., Reliance Steel & Aluminum Co., Graybar Electric Company, Inc., MRC Global, Inc., Commercial Metals Company, CDW Corporation

Wholesale Trade—Nondurable Goods: Plains GP Holdings, L.P., Core-Mark Holding Company, Inc., World Fuel Services Corporation, McKesson, United Natural Foods, Inc., Global Partners LP, Cardinal Health, The Andersons, Inc., AmerisourceBergen, Sysco Corporation, CHS, Inc.

General Merchandise Stores: J. C. Penney Company, Inc., Wal-Mart Stores, Family Dollar Stores, Inc., Sears Holdings Corporation, Kohl's Corporation, Dollar General Corporation, Macy's, Inc., Big Lots, Inc., Target, Dillard's, Inc., Dollar Tree, Inc., Costco Wholesale

Food Stores: Supervalu, Inc., Safeway, Inc., Kroger, Publix Super Markets, Inc., Whole Foods Market, Inc.

Automotive Dealers & Service Stations: Murphy USA, Inc., AutoNation, Inc., Asbury Automotive Group, Inc., Advance Auto Parts, Inc., CST Brands, Inc., O'Reilly Automotive, Inc., TravelCenters of America LLC, Susser Holdings Corporation, Group 1 Automotive, Inc., Casey's General Stores, Inc., The Pantry, Inc., CarMax, Inc., Penske Automotive Group, Inc., AutoZone, Inc., Sonic Automotive, Inc.

Apparel & Accessory Stores: Nike, Inc., The Gap, Inc., Foot Locker, Inc., The TJX Companies, Inc., Nordstrom, Inc., L Brands, Inc., Ross Stores, Inc.

Furniture & Home Furnishings Stores: Best Buy Co., Inc., Bed Bath & Beyond, Inc., GameStop Corp.

Miscellaneous Retail: Dick's Sporting Goods, Inc., Express Scripts Holding, Walgreen Co., Rite Aid Corporation, Office Depot, Inc., Barnes & Noble, Inc., Amazon.com, Liberty Interactive Corporation, Staples, Inc., PetSmart, Inc., Omnicare, Inc., Toys "R" Us, Inc., CVS Caremark

Engineering & Management Services: URS Corporation, AECOM Technology Corporation, CH2M HILL Companies, Ltd., L-3 Communications Holdings, Inc.

Appendix 5.2. Full Estimation Results for Figure 5.3

Variable	Model (1) Lobbying Report	Model (2) Donations	Model (3) TPP Support
GVC Linkage with TPP Countries	1.249**	3.910**	1.261**
	(0.611)	(1.409)	(0.582)
GVC Linkage with China	−0.476*	−2.185**	−0.646**
	(0.254)	(0.813)	(0.260)
Manufacturing (= 1)	0.249	1.156	0.813**
	(0.786)	(1.895)	(0.372)
Employment	0.802***	1.176***	0.618***
	(0.176)	(0.378)	(0.158)
FDI	0.293*	−0.118	0.354**
	(0.160)	(0.401)	(0.140)
Exports to TPP Countries	−1.230**	−1.390	−1.178**
	(0.574)	(1.410)	(0.510)
Imports from TPP Countries	0.611**	0.684	0.504**
	(0.293)	(0.857)	(0.257)
Constant cut1			4.870***
			(1.531)
Constant cut2			5.115***
			(1.534)
Constant	−4.270**		
	(2.020)		
Ln(alpha)	2.273***		
	(0.219)		
Observations	304	88	304

Note: Results are from negative binomial, OLS, and ordered logistic regressions for Models (1), (2), and (3), respectively. Robust standard errors in parentheses. *** $p < 0.01$, ** $p < 0.05$, * $p < 0.1$

Appendix 6.1. List of PTAs Used in the Analysis

1. **Israel-Turkey Free Trade Agreement**
   Date of Signature: March 14, 1996
   Areas of Deep Liberalization: standards and services
   Depth_index: 3
   Depth_rasch: 0.62

2. **Latvia-Slovenia Free Trade Agreement**
   Date of Signature: April 22, 1996
   Areas of Deep Liberalization: standards
   Depth_index: 2
   Depth_rasch: 0.42

3. **Lithuania-Poland Free Trade Agreement**
   Date of Signature: June 27, 1996
   Areas of Deep Liberalization: standards
   Depth_index: 2
   Depth_rasch: 0.56

4. **Canada-Israel Free Trade Agreement (CIFTA)**
   Date of Signature: July 31, 1996
   Areas of Deep Liberalization: standards and competition
   Depth_index: 3
   Depth_rasch: 0.35

5. **Lithuania-Slovenia Free Trade Agreement**
   Date of Signature: October 4, 1996
   Areas of Deep Liberalization: standards
   Depth_index: 2
   Depth_rasch: 0.74

6. **Estonia-Slovenia Free Trade Agreement**
   Date of Signature: November 26, 1996
   Areas of Deep Liberalization: standards
   Depth_index: 2
   Depth_rasch: 0.69

7. **Canada-Chile Free Trade Agreement (CCFTA)**
   Date of Signature: December 5, 1996
   Areas of Deep Liberalization: standards, investments, services and
      competition
   Depth_index: 5
   Depth_rasch: 1.42

8. **Bulgaria-Slovenia Free Trade Agreement**
   Date of Signature: 1996
   Areas of Deep Liberalization: standards
   Depth_index: 2
   Depth_rasch: 0.26

9. **Latvia-Poland Free Trade Agreement**
   Date of Signature: January 1, 1997
   Areas of Deep Liberalization: standards
   Depth_index: 2
   Depth_rasch: 0.86

10. **Estonia-Turkey Free Trade Agreement**
    Date of Signature: March 6, 1997
    Areas of Deep Liberalization: standards
    Depth_index: 2
    Depth_rasch: 0.42

11. **Lithuania-Turkey Free Trade Agreement**
    Date of Signature: June 11, 1997 (Lithuanian source) / February 6,
       1997 (Turkish source)
    Areas of Deep Liberalization: standards
    Depth_index: 2
    Depth_rasch: 0.42

12. **Israel-Poland Free Trade Agreement**
    Date of Signature: July 21, 1997
    Areas of Deep Liberalization: standards
    Depth_index: 2
    Depth_rasch: 0.42

13. **Hungary-Turkey Free Trade Agreement**
    Date of Signature: August 1, 1997
    Areas of Deep Liberalization: standards
    Depth_index: 2
    Depth_rasch: 0.10

14. **Croatia-Slovenia Free Trade Agreement**
    Date of Signature: December 12, 1997
    Areas of Deep Liberalization: standards
    Depth_index: 2
    Depth_rasch: 0.89

15. **Hungary-Israel Free Trade Agreement**
    Date of Signature: 1997 (exact date missing)
    Areas of Deep Liberalization: standards and procurement
    Depth_index: 3
    Depth_rasch: 0.42

16. **Chile-Mexico Free Trade Agreement**
    Date of Signature: April 17, 1998
    Second Areas of Deep Liberalization: standards, investments, services,
        competition and intellectual property rights
    Depth_index: 6
    Depth_rasch: 1.69

17. **Slovenia-Turkey Free Trade Agreement**
    Date of Signature: May 5, 1998
    Areas of Deep Liberalization: standards
    Depth_index: 2
    Depth_rasch: 0.27

18. **Latvia-Turkey Free Trade Agreement**
    Date of Signature: June 16, 1998
    Areas of Deep Liberalization: standards
    Depth_index: 2
    Depth_rasch: 0.10

19. **Israel-Slovenia Free Trade Agreement**
    Date of Signature: September 1, 1998
    Areas of Deep Liberalization: standards
    Depth_index: 2
    Depth_rasch: 0.27

20. **Estonia-Hungary Free Trade Agreement**
    Date of Signature: November 4, 1998
    Areas of Deep Liberalization: standards
    Depth_index: 2
    Depth_rasch: 0.35

21. **Bulgaria-Turkey Free Trade Agreement**
    Date of Signature: November 7, 1998
    Areas of Deep Liberalization: standards
    Depth_index: 2
    Depth_rasch: 0.56

22. **Hungary-Lithuania Free Trade Agreement**
    Date of Signature: November 13, 1998
    Areas of Deep Liberalization: standards
    Depth_index: 2
    Depth_rasch: 0.27

23. **Morocco-Tunisia Free Trade Agreement**
    Date of Signature: March 16, 1999
    Areas of Deep Liberalization: standards
    Depth_index: 2
    Depth_rasch: −0.53

24. **Hungary-Latvia Free Trade Agreement**
    Date of Signature: June 10, 1999
    Areas of Deep Liberalization: standards
    Depth_index: 2
    Depth_rasch: 0.19

25. **Poland-Turkey Free Trade Agreement**
    Date of Signature: October 4, 1999
    Areas of Deep Liberalization: standards
    Depth_index: 2
    Depth_rasch: 0.56

26. **Israel-Mexico Free Trade Agreement**
    Date of Signature: March 6, 2000
    Areas of Deep Liberalization: standards, procurement and competition
    Depth_index: 4
    Depth_rasch: 0.62

27. **United States-Vietnam Agreement on Trade Relations**
    Date of Signature: July 13, 2000
    Areas of Deep Liberalization: standards, investments, services and intellectual property rights
    Depth_index: 4
    Depth_rasch: 1.53

28. **New Zealand-Singapore Closer Economic Partnership (ANZSCEP)**
    Date of Signature: November 14, 2000
    Areas of Deep Liberalization: standards, investments, services and procurement
    Depth_index: 5
    Depth_rasch: 1.37

29. **Canada-Costa Rica Free Trade Agreement (CCRFTA)**
    Date of Signature: April 23, 2001
    Areas of Deep Liberalization: standards, investments and competition
    Depth_index: 4
    Depth_rasch: 1.07

30. **Bulgaria-Lithuania Free Trade Agreement**
    Date of Signature: May 8, 2001
    Areas of Deep Liberalization: standards
    Depth_index: 2
    Depth_rasch: 0.42

31. **Bulgaria Israel Free Trade Agreement**
   Date of Signature: June 8, 2001
   Areas of Deep Liberalization: standards
   Depth_index: 2
   Depth_rasch: 0.42

32. **Bulgaria-Estonia Free Trade Agreement**
   Date of Signature: December 11, 2001
   Areas of Deep Liberalization: standards
   Depth_index: 2
   Depth_rasch: 0.74

33. **Japan-Singapore Economic Partnership Agreement (JSEPA)**
   Date of Signature: January 13, 2002
   Areas of Deep Liberalization: standards, investments, services, procurement and competition
   Depth_index: 6
   Depth_rasch: 1.22

34. **Croatia-Turkey Free Trade Agreement**
   Date of Signature: March 13, 2002
   Areas of Deep Liberalization: standards and procurement
   Depth_index: 3
   Depth_rasch: 0.69

35. **Brazil-Mexico Economic Complementation Agreement**
   Date of Signature: July 3, 2002
   Areas of Deep Liberalization: standards
   Depth_index: 1
   Depth_rasch: 0.27

36. **Bulgaria-Latvia Free Trade Agreement**
   Date of Signature: October 16, 2002
   Areas of Deep Liberalization: standards
   Depth_index: 2
   Depth_rasch: 0.49

37. **Croatia-Lithuania Free Trade Agreement**
   Date of Signature: October 24, 2002
   Areas of Deep Liberalization: standards
   Depth_index: 2
   Depth_rasch: 0.56

38. **US-Singapore Free Trade Agreement**
   Date of Signature: May 6, 2003
   Areas of Deep Liberalization: standards, investments, services, procure-
      ment, competition and intellectual property rights
   Depth_index: 7
   Depth_rasch: 1.81

39. **US-Chile Free Trade Agreement (USCFTA)**
   Date of Signature: June 6, 2003
   Areas of Deep Liberalization: standards, investments, services, procure-
      ment and intellectual property rights
   Depth_index: 6
   Depth_rasch: 1.81

40. **Singapore-Australia Free Trade Agreement (SAFTA)**
   Date of Signature: July 28, 2003
   Areas of Deep Liberalization: standards, investments, services, procure-
      ment, competition and intellectual property rights
   Depth_index: 7
   Depth_rasch: 1.69

41. **Morocco-Turkey Free Trade Agreement**
   Date of Signature: April 7, 2004
   Areas of Deep Liberalization: standards
   Depth_index: 2
   Depth_rasch: 0.62

42. **Australia-United States Free Trade Agreement (AUSFTA)**
   Date of Signature: May 18, 2004
   Areas of Deep Liberalization: standards, investments, services, procure-
      ment, competition and intellectual property rights
   Depth_index: 7
   Depth_rasch: 2.01

43. **Morocco-US Free Trade Agreement (USMFTA)**
    Date of Signature: June 15, 2004
    Areas of Deep Liberalization: standards, investments, services, procure-
      ment and intellectual property rights
    Depth_index: 6
    Depth_rasch: 2.01

44. **Australia-Thailand Free Trade Agreement (TAFTA)**
    Date of Signature: July 5, 2004
    Areas of Deep Liberalization: standards, investments, services and
      competition
    Depth_index: 5
    Depth_rasch: 1.42

45. **Japan-Mexico Economic Partnership Agreement**
    Date of Signature: September 17, 2004,
    Areas of Deep Liberalization: standards, investments, services, procure-
      ment and competition
    Depth_index: 6
    Depth_rasch: 1.58

46. **Tunisia-Turkey Free Trade Agreement**
    Date of Signature: November 25, 2004
    Areas of Deep Liberalization: standards and competition
    Depth_index: 3
    Depth_rasch: 0.62

47. **New Zealand-Thailand Closer Economic Partnership Agreement**
    Date of Signature: April 19, 2005
    Areas of Deep Liberalization: standards, investments, competition and
      intellectual property rights
    Depth_index: 5
    Depth_rasch: 1.17

48. **India-Singapore Comprehensive Economic Cooperation
    Agreement**
    Date of Signature: June 29, 2005
    Areas of Deep Liberalization: standards, investments and services

Depth_index: 4
Depth_rasch: 1.17

49. **China-Chile Free Trade Agreement**
Date of Signature: November 18, 2005
Areas of Deep Liberalization: standards and intellectual property rights
Depth_index: 3
Depth_rasch: 0.27

50. **Peru-Thailand Free Trade Agreement**
Date of Signature: November 19, 2005
Areas of Deep Liberalization: standards
Depth_index: 1
Depth_rasch: −0.37

51. **Japan-Malaysia Economic Partnership Agreement (JMEPA)**
Date of Signature: December 13, 2005
Areas of Deep Liberalization: standards, investments, services, competition and intellectual property rights
Depth_index: 6
Depth_rasch: 1.58

52. **Chile-India Preferential Trade Agreement**
Date of Signature: March 8, 2006
Areas of Deep Liberalization: standards
Depth_index: 1
Depth_rasch: 0.10

53. **Peru-US Trade Promotion Agreement (PTPA)**
Date of Signature: April 12, 2006
Areas of Deep Liberalization: standards, investments, services, procurement, competition and intellectual property rights
Depth_index: 7
Depth_rasch: 2.17

54. **Chile-Peru Free Trade Agreement**
Date of Signature: August 22, 2006
Areas of Deep Liberalization: standards, investments, services and competition

Depth_index: 5
Depth_rasch: 1.32

55. Japan-Philippines Economic Partnership Agreement (JPEPA)
Date of Signature: September 9, 2006
Areas of Deep Liberalization: standards, investments, services, competition and intellectual property rights
Depth_index: 6
Depth_rasch: 1.42

56. Colombia-US Trade Promotion Agreement
Date of Signature: November 22, 2006
Areas of Deep Liberalization: standards, investments, services, procurement, competition and intellectual property rights
Depth_index: 7
Depth_rasch: 2.17

57. Chile-Colombia Free Trade Agreement
Date of Signature: November 27, 2006
Areas of Deep Liberalization: standards, investments, services and procurement
Depth_index: 5
Depth_rasch: 1.42

58. Japan-Chile Economic Partnership Agreement
Date of Signature: March 27, 2007
Areas of Deep Liberalization: standards, investments, services, procurement, competition and intellectual property rights
Depth_index: 7
Depth_rasch: 1.58

59. Japan-Thailand Economic Partnership Agreement (JTEPA)
Date of Signature: April 3, 2007
Areas of Deep Liberalization: standards, investments, services, competition and intellectual property rights
Depth_index: 6
Depth_rasch: 1.58

60. **Japan-Brunei Economic Partnership Agreement (JBEPA or BJEPA)**
    Date of Signature: June 18, 2007
    Areas of Deep Liberalization: standards, investments and services
    Depth_index: 4
    Depth_rasch: 1.22

61. **Indonesia-Japan Economic Partnership Agreement (IJEPA)**
    Date of Signature: August 20, 2007
    Areas of Deep Liberalization: investments, services, competition and
        intellectual property rights
    Depth_index: 5
    Depth_rasch: 1.42

62. **China-New Zealand Free Trade Agreement**
    Date of Signature: April 7, 2008
    Areas of Deep Liberalization: standards, investments, services
    Depth_index: 4
    Depth_rasch: 1.22

63. **Canada-Peru Free Trade Agreement (CPFTA)**
    Date of Signature: May 29, 2008
    Areas of Deep Liberalization: standards, investments, services, procure-
        ment and competition
    Depth_index: 6
    Depth_rasch: 1.64

64. **Peru-Singapore Free Trade Agreement (PeSFTA)**
    Date of Signature: May 29, 2008
    Areas of Deep Liberalization: standards, investments, services, procure-
        ment and competition
    Depth_index: 6
    Depth_rasch: 1.58

65. **Australia-Chile Free Trade Agreement (ACl-FTA)**
    Date of Signature: July 30, 2008
    Areas of Deep Liberalization: standards, investments, services, procure-
        ment, competition and intellectual property rights
    Depth_index: 7
    Depth_rasch: 1.94

66. **China-Singapore Free Trade Agreement (CSFTA)**
    Date of Signature: October 23, 2008
    Areas of Deep Liberalization: standards, investments and services
    Depth_index: 4
    Depth_rasch: 1.22

67. **Canada-Colombia Free Trade Agreement**
    Date of Signature: November 21, 2008
    Areas of Deep Liberalization: standards, investments, services, procurement and competition
    Depth_index: 6
    Depth_rasch: 1.69

68. **Japan-Vietnam Economic Partnership Agreement (JVEPA)**
    Date of Signature: December 25, 2008
    Areas of Deep Liberalization: standards, investments, services, competition and intellectual property rights
    Depth_index: 6
    Depth_rasch: 1.64

69. **Japan-Switzerland Free Trade and Economic Partnership Agreement (JSFTEPA)**
    Date of Signature: February 19, 2009
    Areas of Deep Liberalization: standards, investments, services, competition and intellectual property rights
    Depth_index: 6
    Depth_rasch: 2.17

70. **China-Peru Free Trade Agreement**
    Date of Signature: April 28, 2009
    Areas of Deep Liberalization: standards, investments, services and intellectual property rights
    Depth_index: 5
    Depth_rasch: 1.48

71. **Chile-Turkey Free Trade Agreement**
    Date of Signature: July 14, 2009
    Areas of Deep Liberalization: standards

Depth_index: 2
Depth_rasch: 0.42

72. **Malaysia-New Zealand Free Trade Agreement (MNZFTA)**
Date of Signature: October 26, 2009
Areas of Deep Liberalization: standards, investments, services, competition and intellectual property rights
Depth_index: 6
Depth_rasch: 1.64

73. **Costa Rica-Singapore Free Trade Agreement (SCRFTA)**
Date of Signature: April 6, 2010
Areas of Deep Liberalization: standards, investments, services, procurement and competition
Depth_index: 6
Depth_rasch: 1.53

74. **China-Costa Rica Free Trade Agreement**
Date of Signature: April 8, 2010
Areas of Deep Liberalization: standards, investments, services and intellectual property rights
Depth_index: 5
Depth_rasch: 1.12

75. **Chile-Malaysia Free Trade Agreement**
Date of Signature: November 13, 2010
Areas of Deep Liberalization: standards and investments
Depth_index: 3
Depth_rasch: 0.49

76. **Japan-India Economic Partnership Agreement**
Date of Signature: February 16, 2011
Areas of Deep Liberalization: standards, investments, services and competition
Depth_index: 5
Depth_rasch: 1.32

77. **India-Malaysia Comprehensive Economic Cooperation Agreement (MICECA)**
    Date of Signature: February 18, 2011
    Areas of Deep Liberalization: standards, investments and services
    Depth_index: 4
    Depth_rasch: 1.09

78. **Costa Rica-Peru Free Trade Agreement**
    Date of Signature: May 22, 2011
    Areas of Deep Liberalization: standards, investments, services, procurement, competition and intellectual property rights
    Depth_index: 7
    Depth_rasch: 1.94

79. **Japan-Peru Economic Partnership Agreement**
    Date of Signature: May 31, 2011
    Areas of Deep Liberalization: standards, investments, services, procurement, competition and intellectual property rights
    Depth_index: 7
    Depth_rasch: 1.93

80. **Vietnam-Chile Free Trade Agreement (VCFTA)**
    Date of Signature: November 12, 2011
    Areas of Deep Liberalization: standards
    Depth_index: 2
    Depth_rasch: 0.17

Appendix 6.2. Summary Statistics of the Estimation Sample for the Analysis of the Impact of GVCs on PTA Formation

Variable	N	Mean	SD	Min	Max
Backward GVC Participation	62,942	0.37	0.98	0	20.67
Forward GVC Participation	62,942	0.3	0.65	0	13.04
PTA Formation	62,942	0	0.05	0	1
PTA Depth	160	3.9	1.94	1	7
Bilateral Trade (billion $)	59,160	4.34	19.46	0	598.06
GDP Ratio	58,226	31.11	122.4	1	2,913.06
Average GDP Growth Rate	57,688	3.63	2.86	−14.77	12.8
Polity Score of Country 1	59,835	7.12	5.11	−10	10
Polity Score of Country 2	59,819	7.12	5.1	−10	10
Military Alliance	62,942	0.1	0.3	0	1
Contiguous	60,868	0.03	0.18	0	1
Common Language	60,868	0.07	0.25	0	1
Former Colony	60,868	0.03	0.16	0	1
Distance	60,868	7.15	4.97	0.06	19.81

Source: authors' own data.

NOTES

Chapter 1

1. In this book, $ denotes U.S. dollar unless otherwise specified (e.g. AUD for Australian dollar).

2. We use the term GVCs to describe these enduring changes in the structure of global trade and investment activities. It should be noted, however, that other terms have been used in the literature to denote the same phenomenon, including global commodity chains (Bair 2009; Gereffi 1994), global production networks (Borrus et al. 2003; Curran 2015; Henderson et al. 2002; Yeung and Coe 2015), and international supply chains (Escaith et al. 2010). For studies that adopt the term GVC, see, for example, Gereffi et al. (2005); Humphrey and Schmitz (2002); Ponte and Sturgeon (2014); Ravenhill (2014); Sturgeon et al. (2013). See also chapter 2 for a brief introduction to the history of the GVC research program.

3. https://www.wto.org/english/tratop_e/region_e/region_e.htm (accessed August 25, 2017).

4. We discuss the different forms of PTAs in detail in chapter 2. For ease of presentation, we use the terms PTAs, FTAs, and regional trade agreements (RTAs) interchangeably throughout this book.

5. On these points, see also Eckhardt and Lee (2018). For studies that investigate the effect of GVC integration through input sourcing or the globalization of production on firm preferences, see, for example, Eckhardt (2015); Eckhardt and Poletti (2016); Kim et al. (2019); Manger (2014); Yildirim et al. (2018).

6. China FTA network, http://fta.mofcom.gov.cn/list/rcepen/enrcepnews/1/encateinfo.html (accessed November 6, 2019).

7. Firm-level lobbying reports became available under the Lobbying Disclosure Act, which was adopted in 1995 and went into effect in 1999. A number of studies (e.g., Ansolabehere et al. 2002; Bertrand et al. 2014; Ludema et al. 2010) have analyzed lobbying behavior using these reports, which are publicly available through the Senate Office of Public Records or the Center for Responsive Politics.

8. Foreign value added constitutes more than 20 percent of the value of final manufacturing output in many countries, reaching more than 50 percent for some countries and sectors. Similarly, domestic value added could account for a large share of imported final goods as exported intermediate products could return home embodied in foreign final goods (Blanchard et al. 2016).

9. Some of the discussions in the following section draw on Zeng et al. (2018).

10. Full text of ChAFTA and Tariff Schedules, Department of Foreign Affairs and Trade, Australian Government, available at https://dfat.gov.au/trade/agree ments/in-force/chafta/official-documents/Pages/official-documents.aspx (accessed October 22, 2018).

11. TPP member countries together have a GDP of nearly $28 billion and account for about 40 percent of global GDP and one-third of world trade (Granville 2017).

12. A recent survey of global procurement and purchasing executives suggests that the share of respondents who agree that China is a low-cost sourcing destination has gradually declined during the past few years, dropping from 70 percent in the 2012 survey to below 50 percent in 2016. The survey additionally points to the importance of China as a center of global supply chains rather than merely a cheap outsourcing destination (CNBC 2017).

13. Various measures have been developed to capture the depth of an agreement, including the number of "WTO+" and "WTO-X" provisions covered in the agreement or the depth of the agreement in areas such as competition policy and TBTs (World Trade Report 2011). A more recent measure developed by Dür et al. (2014) takes into consideration whether the agreement aims to reduce all tariffs to zero and whether it contains any substantive provisions in areas such as services trade, investments, standards, public procurement, competition, and intellectual property rights.

Chapter 2

1. While "value chains" are different from "supply chains," their political economy implications are nonetheless similar. We choose to use the term "value chains" instead of "supply chains" in this book given its more encompassing nature.

2. "Concept & Tools," Global Value Chains Initiative, Duke University, available at https://globalvaluechains.org/concept-tools (accessed June 6, 2018).

3. For a good overview of the evolution of GCC and GVC research programs, see Lee (2017).

4. According to Noguera (2012: 2), "value added is not directly traded: value-added exports are the result of how goods trade flows are combined and used across countries through the global input-output structure."

5. The project additionally received institutional support from OECD and the WTO (Escaith and Timmer 2012).

6. On this point, see OECD (2016).

7. This classification scheme has been frequently used to code such agreements (e.g., Baier, Bergstrand, and Feng 2014).

8. An example is the early ASEAN agreement, signed by Indonesia, Malaysia, the Philippines, Singapore, and Thailand in 1977. The agreement was updated to an FTA in 1992.

9. https://www.wto.org/english/tratop_e/region_e/region_e.htm (accessed October 4, 2017).

10. Asia-Pacific Trade and Investment Agreement Database (APTIAD), United Nations Economic and Social Commission for Asia and the Pacific (ESCAP), available at https://www.unescap.org/content/aptiad/ (accessed October 4, 2017).

11. The TPP evolved from the Trans-Pacific Strategic Economic Partnership Agreement (TPSEP or P4) signed by Brunei, Chile, New Zealand, and Singapore in 2005. Since then, eight more countries—Australia, Canada, Japan, Malaysia, Mexico, Peru, Vietnam, and the United States—have joined the negotiations, signing an agreement in February 2016 that did not secure the necessary ratification for the agreement to take effect. After the United States withdrew from the agreement in January 2017, the remaining 11 countries continued the negotiations, reaching a new trade agreement called the Comprehensive and Progressive Agreement for Trans-Pacific Partnership (CPTPP) in March 2018.

12. The TTIP is a trade and investment agreement being negotiated between the United States and the European Union, aimed at bolstering the strategic and economic relationship between the two sides by further promoting market access, enhancing regulation, and setting high standards for health, safety, and environmental protection. Although negotiations were suspended following the 2016 U.S. presidential election, both sides indicated a willingness to resume the negotiations by 2017 ("Transatlantic Trade and Investment Partnership [T-TIP]," Office of the United States Trade Representative, available at https://ustr.gov/ttip [accessed June 5, 2018]).

13. Launched in 2012, the RCEP is a proposed FTA between the member countries of ASEAN and six other countries that have FTAs with ASEAN (Australia, China, India, Japan, South Korea, and New Zealand).

14. See, for example, Baldwin (1996); Bhagwati, Krishna, and Panagariya (1999); Bhagwati and Krueger (1995); Deardorff and Stern (1994); Eicher and Henn (2011); Krugman (1993); Levy (1997); and Pomfret (1997).

15. A national treatment clause in the services chapter is considered a substantive provision, while provisions that simply express the signatories' desire to liberalize their services market are not.

16. The Rasch measure can be either positive (for deep PTAs) or negative (for shallow PTAs).

17. See the study by Orefice and Rocha (2014), discussed below.

18. Specifically, Osnago, Rocha, and Ruta (2016) adopt three alternative measures of PTA depth, including the aggregate number of legally enforceable provisions in a PTA, the number of core provisions in the agreement, and another depth measure derived from principal component analysis.

19. One exception is Orefice and Rocha (2014), who find some evidence of the positive effect of production network trade on PTA depth, suggesting that a 10 percent increase in the share of production network trade in total trade may lead to a 6 percent increase in the depth of an agreement.

20. Estimates of the share of DVA in China's exports vary. Koopman et al. (2008) suggest that when processing trade is taken into account, the share of domestic content in Chinese exports was about 50 percent prior to China's entry into the WTO, rising to over 60 percent following the country's WTO accession. Interest-

ingly, the level of domestic content was considerably lower in more sophisticated sectors such as electronic devices, at about 30 percent or less.

21. OECD, "GVCs-China," available at http://www.oecd.org/sti/ind/GVCs%20 -%20CHINA.pdf (accessed June 4, 2018).

22. Chinese Ministry of Commerce, *China FTA Network*, available at http://fta. mofcom.gov.cn/english/fta_qianshu.shtml (last accessed June 4, 2018).

23. For example, the ASEAN-China FTA followed such an approach.

24. OECD, Trade in Value Added Database, available at https://www.oecd.org/ sti/ind/measuring-trade-in-value-added.htm (accessed October 18, 2019).

25. OECD, Trade in Value Added Database.

26. CAFTA members include Costa Rica, El Salvador, Guatemala, Honduras, and Nicaragua.

Chapter 3

1. Interview with JS23. See appendix 3.1 for a full list of interviewees used in this chapter.

2. Interview with JS15.

3. The FTA utilization rate can be measured by the use of certificate of origin data collected by customs authorities or business associations. As illustrated by many examples in this chapter, however, more in-depth examinations of FTA utilization have increasingly been carried out through firm-level surveys (Kawai and Wignaraja 2011).

4. The survey was implemented online between March 25 and June 1, 2015, in Argentina, Brazil, Chile, China, Colombia, India, Japan, South Korea, Mexico, Peru, and the United States. Respondents included a mixture of managers, associates, and directors in a variety of departments, ranging from international trade and customs to internal compliance (Thomson Reuters and KPMG 2015).

5. FTA utilization rates vary widely across countries, from 41 percent in the United States to 19 percent in India.

6. The details of the sampling scheme are not disclosed for the 2016 survey.

7. In the SwissCham survey, over a quarter of the firm respondents mentioned they had encountered problems when attempting to use the FTA because "customs officers lacked know-how" and were "not informed about the FTA" (SwissCham 2016).

8. Interview with JS33.

9. Interviews with SD05 and SD13.

10. Interviews with ZJ19 and ZJ21.

11. Interview with BJ02.

12. Interviews with JS15, GD11, ZJ18, and SD05.

13. Interviews with various firms.

14. Interview with ZJ17.

15. Interview with JS07.

16. Interview with JS07.

17. Interview with ZJ20.

18. Under the WTO, China has an import quota of 287 million kilograms of imported wool with a tariff rate of 1 percent; those above the quota are charged with a whopping 38 percent tariff. ChAFTA provides for an additional duty-free import of 30 million kilograms of Australian wool, which will increase to 45 million kilograms over eight years.

19. Interview with JS01.

20. Interviews with ZJ09, ZJ10, and ZJ11.

21. Interview with JS13.

22. Interview with JS27.

23. Interviews with ZJ17 and JS10.

24. Interview with JS13.

25. Interview with SD01.

26. Interview with GD01.

27. Interview with GD04.

28. Interview with GD09.

29. Alternatively, firms can turn to transshipment, i.e., rerouting their exports through a third country to circumvent these duties. Transshipment, however, can lead to additional costs, delays, and regulatory exposure that may ultimately make the exports more expensive.

30. Interview with GD12.

31. Interview with SD05.

32. Interview with JS40.

33. Interview with ZJ12.

34. Interview with SD02.

35. Interview with GD10.

36. Interview with GD10.

37. This is consistent with the SSCC report, which found that 100 percent of the firms that used the China-Switzerland FTA became "hooked" (SSCC 2018).

38. Interview with SD10.

39. Interview with SD12.

40. Interview with SD05.

41. Interview with GD01.

42. http://www.gov.cn/xxgk/pub/govpublic/mrlm/200803/t20080328_32571.html

43. http://www.gov.cn/xinwen/2019-03/13/content_5373437.htm

44. Interview with JS14.

45. Interview with SD07.

46. Interview with GD13.

47. Interview with BJ01.

Chapter 4

1. For a recent study that employs a similar method to recruit firm managers as survey respondents, see Li and Zeng (2019).

2. It is often infeasible for researchers to build a random sample of firms, especially in emerging markets such as China (Hoskisson et al. 2000).

3. Under the processing trade regime, firms enjoy duty-free importation of inputs used in production but face restrictions on selling to the domestic market. Under the ordinary trade regime, firms face duties on imported inputs but can sell their output locally (Koopman et al. 2012).

4. Strictly speaking, the definition of forward GVC linkages is the share of domestic intermediate input in the export of the foreign country. This would require the firm knowing how their intermediate exports are being used by foreign clients, which is highly unlikely. Assuming that at least some of these intermediate exports will be used for domestic consumption, we can think of this measure as providing the upper bound of the firm's degree of forward GVC linkage.

5. Results from ordered probit are qualitatively similar to those from the OLS regressions.

6. Full estimation results can be found in appendix 4.3.

7. Every firm manager in our sample completed the conjoint experiment portion of the survey regardless of whether they traded or not. Managers of domestic firms were presented with part (a) of the introduction, while the rest read part (b).

8. The actual number of PTAs is lower than this because some firm managers skipped answering one of the two evaluation questions. We also removed a few observations in which the two PTAs in the pair were identical due to the luck of the draw.

9. In alternative specifications, we used the binary measure in a probit model. The results are similar and can be found in appendix 4.6.

10. The report also found that the bigger challenge now is with the enforcement of IPR laws at the local level.

Chapter 5

1. Firms and industries can send costless messages to the government signaling either support for or opposition to a trade policy measure (Ludema, Mayda, and Mishra 2018).

2. According to the organization's website, the Coalition is "a broad-based group of U.S. companies and associations representing the principal sectors of the U.S. economy including agriculture, manufacturing, merchandising, processing, publishing, retailing, technology, transportation and services. Coalition members support and are working to secure approval of the TPP agreement in the United States" (U.S. Coalition for TPP 2016).

3. World Trade Organization, "The Process—Stages in a Typical WTO Dispute Settlement Case," https://www.wto.org/english/tratop_e/dispu_e/disp_settlement_cbt_e/c6s1p1_e.htm (accessed November 20, 2019).

4. The TPSEP was signed by Singapore, Chile, New Zealand, and Brunei in 2005.

5. Appendix 5.1 lists the Fortune 500 firms grouped into their respective industries. There were two mismatches using the concordance tables: Wynn Resorts and Northwestern Mutual Life Insurance Company. Both were erroneously coded to

the industry of wholesale trade—durable goods. We manually moved them to their respective, correct industries.

6. UPS Pressroom, "5 Ways the Trans-Pacific Partnership Will Enhance Global Trade," May 2016, https://compass.ups.com/trans-pacific-partnership-benefits/ (accessed October 6, 2018).

7. "5 Ways the Trans-Pacific Partnership Will Enhance Global Trade."

8. Thailand and Indonesia together accounted for more than 75 percent of the global exports in natural rubber in 2016.

9. Data used in the following analysis draw on the research conducted for Zeng et al. (2018).

10. These committees included: the Senate Committee on Finance, which has primary congressional jurisdiction over trade matters in the Senate; the Senate Committee on Agriculture, Nutrition, and Forestry; the Senate Committee on Commerce, Science, and Transportation; the House Financial Services Subcommittee on Monetary Policy and Trade; and the House Small Business Subcommittee on Agriculture, Energy and Trade. During the 109th–112th sessions of Congress, these committees encompassed 172 members of Congress, including 81 from the House of Representatives and 94 from the Senate (U.S. Congress and Trade Policy Report, available from the Institute for International Economic Policy at The George Washington University, online at https://www.gwu.edu/~iiep/ [accessed September 15, 2015]).

11. These figures do not include "dark money" the groups gave to political nonprofits that engage in electoral activity. Dark money refers to money given to political action committees that does not have to be disclosed to the FEC (Center for Responsive Government, Glossary of Terms, available at https://www.opensecrets.org/resources/learn/glossary.php [accessed June 2, 2016]).

12. Previous studies (e.g., Baldwin and Magee 2000) found that lobbying and campaign contributions by organized interests also influenced legislators' votes on the NAFTA and Uruguay Round bills.

13. The TPP singled out tobacco as the one industry in which investor–state dispute settlement (ISDS) rules would no longer apply, effectively preventing tobacco firms from using ISDS to challenge public health-minded tobacco regulations, a tactic they had been using for a long time against countries in the TPP area, such as Australia and Malaysia.

14. Using assets or revenues as alternative measures of firm size does not change the interpretation of the main results reported below.

15. The database can be accessed through Wharton Research Data Services at https://wrds-web.wharton.upenn.edu/wrds/ (accessed October 10, 2015).

16. Available online at http://bea.gov/international/direct_investment_multinational_companies_comprehensive_data.htm (accessed January 22, 2016).

17. Regional cumulation provisions allow goods obtained or processed in any CPTPP country to be considered as originating in another and can help determine whether a country will be eligible for preferential trade considerations within an FTA under the Rules of Origin (Naumann 2006).

18. "Top 4 Benefits of the CPTPP for Asia's Small Businesses Looking to Expand Internationally," https://solutions.ups.com/CPTPP.html (accessed November 22, 2019); "International Trade Spotlight Comprehensive & Progressive Agreement for Trans-Pacific Partnership (CPTPP)," https://www.upscontentcentre.com/down load/connectasia/CPTPP (accessed November 22, 2019).

Chapter 6

1. European Commission, Trade Policy, Countries and Regions, "South Korea." Available at http://ec.europa.eu/trade/policy/countries-and-regions/countries/ south-korea/ (accessed November 2, 2018).

2. The EU has since then turned to a bilateral negotiation strategy with individual ASEAN member countries (Morales 2017). Only recently have the two sides agreed to resume negotiations, with the EU reaching an agreement with Vietnam in July 2018.

3. European Commission, "E.U.-Singapore Agreement." Available at http:// ec.europa.eu/trade/policy/in-focus/eu-singapore-agreement/ (accessed October 31, 2018).

4. The European auto industry did express increasingly vocal opposition during the course of EUKOR negotiations on the ground that the agreement would lead to "market distortion and unfair competition." However, such resistance did not derail the successful signing of the agreement (Elsig and Dupont 2012; Lee 2010).

5. Francois et al. (2007), for example, estimated that South Korea would capture two-thirds of the gains from the EUKOR-induced trade liberalization.

6. European investors attracted to the investment potential of the ASEAN market also supported preferential trade liberalization, which would allow them to extract greater liberalization commitments in the investment sector (European Commission 2010).

7. The share of foreign value added in exports reached 39 percent for the EU in 2010, compared to the average of 28 percent at the global level (UNCTAD 2013).

8. For studies that take a similar approach, see, for example, Mansfield and Milner (2010, 2018).

9. For a more detailed description of these variables, see OECD, "TiVA 2016 indicators—definitions," available at http://www.oecd.org/sti/ind/tiva/TIVASaM_ 2016_Indicator_Definitions.pdf (accessed November 10, 2017).

10. Available at http://www.correlatesofwar.org/data-sets (accessed July 1, 2017).

11. Available at http://www.cepii.fr/CEPII/en/bdd_modele/bdd.asp (accessed June 29, 2017).

Chapter 7

1. However, the potential benefits of the USMCA for the auto industry may also have been undermined by the tariffs the Trump administration negotiated outside of the agreement.

2. For example, the trade-diversion effects of PTAs may help increase the trade volumes of PTA member countries at the expense of nonmembers. In addition, PTAs may generate nontraditional gains by signaling a country's commitment to liberal economic policies or enhancing political and security ties among member countries (Capling 2008; Fernandez and Portes 1998).

BIBLIOGRAPHY

Aguilar, Mike. "Tires and Trump: What the New President Means for Us." *Traction News*, January 20, 2017. http://www.tractionnews.com/united-states-tire-indus try-reacts-to-president-trump/

Ahmad, Nadim, Sonia Araujo, Alessia Lo Turco, and Daniela Maggioni. "Using Trade Microdata to Improve Trade in Value-Added Measures: Proof of Concept Using Turkish Data." *Trade in Value Added* 21, no. 1 (2013).

Alfaro, Laura, Pol Antràs, Davin Chor, and Paola Conconi. *Internalizing Global Value Chains: A Firm-Level Analysis*. No. w21582. National Bureau of Economic Research, 2015.

Alfaro, Laura, and Maggie Xiaoyang Chen. "Surviving the Global Financial Crisis: Foreign Ownership and Establishment Performance." *American Economic Journal: Economic Policy* 4, no. 3 (2012): 30–55.

Alkon, Meir, and Erik H. Wang. "Pollution Lowers Support for China's Regime: Quasi-Experimental Evidence from Beijing." *Journal of Politics* 80, no. 1 (2018): 327–31.

Alvstam, Claes G., Erja Kettunen, and Patrik Ström. "The Service Sector in the Free-Trade Agreement between the EU and Singapore: Closing the Gap between Policy and Business Realities." *Asia Europe Journal* 15, no. 1 (2017): 75–105.

Amiti, Mary, and Donald R. Davis. "Trade, Firms, and Wages: Theory and Evidence." *Review of Economic Studies* 79, no. 1 (2011): 1–36.

"The Amount of Trade Partner's Preferential Tariffs Enjoyed by Jiangsu Exports Hit a New Level." ["江苏出口货物享受自贸伙伴关税优惠数额创新高."] *China FTA Network*, September 23, 2016. http://fta.mofcom.gov.cn/article/chinaaustr alia/chinaaustraliagfguandian/201609/33282_1.html

Anderson, James E. "A Theoretical Foundation for the Gravity Equation." *American Economic Review* 69, no. 1 (1979): 106–16.

Antkiewicz, Agata, and John Whalley. "China's New Regional Trade Agreements." *World Economy* 28, no. 10 (2005): 1539–57.

An, Tongliang, and Shi Hao. "Observations and Empirical Analysis of the R&D Behavioral Models of Chinese Manufacturing Enterprises–Survey Analysis of Manufacturing Firms in Jiangsu." ["中国制造业企业R&D行为模式的观测与

实践—基于江苏省制造业企业问卷调查的实证分析."] *Economic Research* [经济研究] 41, no. 2 (2006): 21–30.

Antràs, Pol. *Global Production: Firms, Contracts, and Trade Structure.* Princeton: Princeton University Press, 2015.

Antràs, Pol, and Arnaud Costinot. "Intermediation and Economic Integration." *American Economic Review* 100, no. 2 (2010): 424–28.

Antràs, Pol, and Davin Chor. "Organizing the Global Value Chain." *Econometrica* 81, no. 6 (2013): 2127–2204.

Antràs, Pol, Davin Chor, Thibault Fally, and Russell Hillberry. "Measuring the Upstreamness of Production and Trade Flows." *American Economic Review* 102, no. 3 (2012): 412–16.

Antràs, Pol, and Elhanan Helpman. "Global Sourcing." *Journal of Political Economy* 112, no. 3 (2004): 552–80.

Antràs, Pol, and Robert W. Staiger. "Offshoring and the Role of Trade Agreements." *American Economic Review* 102, no. 7 (2012): 3140–83.

"AQSIQ 'Thousand Enterprise Assistance Program' Started in Guangzhou. 70 Enterprises in Guangzhou were Selected." ["质检总局'千企帮扶计划'在穗启动.广东70家企业入选."] China News Net. April 12, 2017. http://finance.peop le.com.cn/n1/2017/0412/c1004-29206498.html

Armstrong, Shiro. "The China-Australia Free Trade Agreement: Lessons for Canada." *Asia Pacific Foundation of Canada*, April 25, 2017. https://www.asiapacific .ca/canada-asia-agenda/china-australia-free-trade-|agreement-lessons-canada

Arunmas, Phusadee. "Ministry Hastens to Make CPTPP Deal before February." *Bangkok Post*, December 4, 2018. https://www.bangkokpost.com/business/ne ws/1587102/ministry-hastens-to-make-cptpp-deal-before-february

Arunmas, Phusadee. "US Business Urge Thailand to Join CPTPP." *Bangkok Post*, August 16, 2019. https://www.bangkokpost.com/business/1731071/us-urges-th ais-to-join-cptpp

Baccini, Leonardo. "The Economics and Politics of Preferential Trade Agreements." *Annual Review of Political Science* 22, no. 1 (2019): 75–92.

Baccini, Leonardo, and Andreas Dür. "Investment Discrimination and the Proliferation of Preferential Trade Agreements." *Journal of Conflict Resolution* 59, no. 4 (2015): 617–44.

Baccini, Leonardo, Andreas Dür, and Manfred Elsig. "Intra-Industry Trade, Global Value Chains, and Preferential Trade Liberalization." *International Studies Quarterly* 62, no. 2 (2018): 329–40.

Baccini, Leonardo, Andreas Dür, and Manfred Elsig. "The Politics of Trade Agreement Design: Revisiting the Depth-Flexibility Nexus." *International Studies Quarterly* 59, no. 4 (2015): 765–75.

Baccini, Leonardo, and Johannes Urpelainen. *Cutting the Gordian Knot of Economic Reform: When and How International Institutions Help.* Oxford: Oxford University Press, 2014.

Baccini, Leonardo, Pablo M. Pinto, and Stephen Weymouth. "The Distributional Consequences of Preferential Trade Liberalization: Firm-Level Evidence." *International Organization* 71, no. 2 (2017): 373–95.

"Backgrounder: Upgraded Version of ASEAN-China FTA." Xinhua Net. November 22, 2015. http://www.xinhuanet.com/english/2015-11/22/c_134841426.htm

Bagwell, Kyle, and Robert W. Staiger. *The Economics of the World Trading System.* Cambridge, MA: MIT Press, 2004.

Baier, Scott L., and Jeffrey H. Bergstrand. "Do Free Trade Agreements Actually Increase Members' International Trade?" *Journal of International Economics* 71, no. 1 (2007): 72–95.

Baier, Scott L., and Jeffrey H. Bergstrand. "Economic Determinants of Free Trade Agreements." *Journal of International Economics* 64, no. 1 (2004): 29–63.

Baier, Scott L., Jeffrey H. Bergstrand, and Michael Feng. "Economic Integration Agreements and the Margins of International Trade." *Journal of International Economics* 93, no. 2 (2014): 339–50.

Bailey, Michael A., Anton Strezhnev, and Erik Voeten. "Estimating Dynamic State Preferences from United Nations Voting." *Journal of Conflict Resolution* 61, no. 2 (2017): 430–56.

Bainwol, Mitch, and Edward Hamberger. "Here's Why Ending Free Trade with Canada and Mexico Would Hurt US Manufacturing." *Fox News*, November 16, 2017. https://www.foxnews.com/opinion/heres-why-ending-free-trade-with-canada-and-mexico-would-hurt-us-manufacturing

Bair, Jennifer. "Global Capitalism and Commodity Chains: Looking Back, Looking Forward." *Competition & Change* 9, no. 2 (2005): 153–80.

Bair, Jennifer. "Global Commodity Chains: Genealogy and Review." In *Frontiers of Commodity Chain Research*, edited by Jennifer Bair, 1–34. Stanford: Stanford University Press, 2009.

Baldwin, Richard. "A Domino Theory of Regionalism." In *Expanding European Regionalism, The EU's New Members*, edited by R. Baldwin, P. Haaparanta, and J. Kiander, 25–47. Cambridge: Cambridge University Press, 1995.

Baldwin, Richard E. "The Causes of Regionalism." *World Economy* 20, no. 7 (1997): 865–88.

Baldwin, Richard E. "Managing the Noodle Bowl: The Fragility of East Asian Regionalism." *Singapore Economic Review* 53, no. 3 (2008): 449–78.

Baldwin, Richard E. "WTO 2.0: Global Governance of Supply Chain Trade." Centre for Economic Policy Research, Insight no. 64 (2012). http://www.cepr.org/sites/default/files/policy_insights/PolicyInsight64.pdf

Baldwin, Richard, and Javier Lopez-Gonzalez. "Supply-Chain Trade: A Portrait of Global Patterns and Several Testable Hypotheses." *World Economy* 38, no. 11 (2015): 1682–1721.

Baldwin, Richard, and Anthony J. Venables. "Spiders and Snakes: Offshoring and Agglomeration in the Global Economy." *Journal of International Economics* 90, no. 2 (2013): 245–54.

Baldwin, Robert E., and Christopher Magee. *Congressional Trade Votes: From NAFTA Approval to Fast-Track Defeat.* Washington, DC: Peterson Institute for International Economics, 2000.

Balla, Steven J. "Health System Reform and Political Participation on the Chinese Internet." *China Information* 28, no. 2 (2014): 214–36.

Balla, Steven J. "Is Consultation the 'New Normal?': Online Policymaking and Governance Reform in China." *Journal of Chinese Political Science* 22, no. 3 (2017): 375–92.

Balla, Steven J., and Zhou Liao. "Online Consultation and Citizen Feedback in Chinese Policymaking." *Journal of Current Chinese Affairs* 42, no. 3 (2013): 101–20.

Barber, Benjamin, Jan Pierskalla, and Simon Weschle. "Lobbying and the Collective Action Problem: Comparative Evidence from Enterprise Surveys." *Business and Politics* 16, no. 2 (2014): 221–46.

Bechtel, Michael M., and Kenneth F. Scheve. "Mass Support for Global Climate Agreements Depends on Institutional Design." *Proceedings of the National Academy of Sciences* 110, no. 34 (2013): 13763–768.

Bergsten, C. Fred. "A Partnership of Equals: How Washington Should Respond to China's Economic Challenge." *Foreign Affairs* (2008): 57–69.

Bergsten, C. Fred, Charles Freeman, Nicholas R. Lardy, and Derek J. Mitchell. *China's Rise: Challenges and Opportunities.* Washington, DC: Peterson Institute of International Economics, 2008.

Berman, Jeff. "Armstrong Report Points to Continued Increase in 3PL Usage by Shippers." *Logistics Management*, May 24, 2017. https://www.logisticsmgmt .com/article/armstrong_report_points_to_continued_increase_in_3pl_usage _by_shippers

Bernard, Andrew B., J. Bradford Jensen, Stephen J. Redding, and Peter K. Schott. "The Empirics of Firm Heterogeneity and International Trade." *Annual Review of Economics* 4, no. 1 (2012): 283–313.

Bernard, Andrew B., J. Bradford Jensen, Stephen J. Redding, and Peter K. Schott. "Firms in International Trade." *Journal of Economic Perspectives* 21, no. 3 (2007): 105–30.

Bertrand, Marianne, Matilde Bombardini, and Francesco Trebbi. "Is It Whom You Know or What You Know? An Empirical Assessment of the Lobbying Process." *American Economic Review* 104, no. 12 (2014): 3885–3920.

Betz, Timm. "Trading Interests: Domestic Institutions, International Negotiations, and the Politics of Trade." *Journal of Politics* 79, no. 4 (2017): 1237–52.

Bhagwati, Jagdish. "Regionalism and Multilateralism: An Overview." In *New Dimensions in Regional Integration*, edited by Jamie de Melo and Arvind Panagariya, 22–51. New York: Cambridge University Press, 1993.

Bhagwati, Jagdish. *Termites in the Trading System: How Preferential Agreements Undermine Free Trade.* New York: Oxford University Press, 2008.

Bhagwati, Jagdish N., Pravin Krishna, and Arvind Panagariya, eds. *Trading Blocs: Alternative Approaches to Analyzing Preferential Trade Agreements.* Cambridge, MA: MIT Press, 1999.

Bhagwati, Jagdish N., and Anne O. Krueger. *The Dangerous Drift to Preferential Trade Agreements*. Washington, DC: American Enterprise Institute Press, 1995.

Bhagwati, Jagdish, and Arvind Panagariya. *The Economics of Preferential Trade Agreements*. Washington, DC: AEI Press, 1996.

Bhagwati, Jagdish N., and Hugh T. Patrick. *Aggressive Unilateralism*. Ann Arbor: University of Michigan Press, 1990.

Blanchard, Emily J. "Foreign Direct Investment, Endogenous Tariffs, and Preferential Trade Agreements." *BE Journal of Economic Analysis & Policy* 7, no. 1 (2007): 1–52.

Blanchard, Emily J. "Reevaluating the Role of Trade Agreements: Does Investment Globalization Make the WTO Obsolete?" *Journal of International Economics* 82, no. 1 (2010): 63–72.

Blanchard, Emily J. "A Shifting Mandate: International Ownership, Production Fragmentation, and a Case for Deeper Integration under the WTO." *World Trade Review* 14, no. 1 (2015): 87–99.

Blanchard, Emily J., Chad P. Bown, and Robert C. Johnson. "Global Supply Chains and Trade Policy." World Bank Policy Research Working Paper No. WPS 7536, 2016. Washington, DC: World Bank. https://elibrary.worldbank.org/doi/abs/10.1596/1813-9450-7536

Blanchard, Emily, and Xenia Matschke. "US Multinationals and Preferential Market Access." *Review of Economics and Statistics* 97, no. 4 (2015): 839–54.

Bliss, Christoph, and Ronald Haddock. "Integrating China into Your Global Supply Chain." Booze & Company. 2008. https://www.strategyand.pwc.com/media/file/Integrating_China_into_a_Global_Supply_Chain_en.pdf

Blonigen, Bruce A., KaSaundra Tomlin, and Wesley W. Wilson. "Tariff-jumping FDI and Domestic Firms' Profits." *Canadian Journal of Economics/Revue canadienne d'économique* 37, no. 3 (2004): 656–77.

Blyde, Juan, Alejandro Graziano, and Christian Volple. "Economic Integration Agreements and the Location of Vertical FDI." Voxeu.org, May 13, 2014. http://voxeu.org/article/trade-agreements-foster-global-value-chains-new-evidence

Borrus, Michael, Dieter Ernst, and Stephan Haggard, eds. *International Production Networks in Asia*. London and New York: Routledge, 2003.

Boschman, Janie. "Trans-Pacific Partnership Draws Attention from K Street." *OpenSecrets News*, March 11, 2013. https://www.opensecrets.org/news/2013/03/trans-pacific-partnership-draws-att/

Boudette, Neal E. "Trump Approach on NAFTA Relieves Automakers of Their Worst Fears." *New York Times*, September 1, 2018. https://www.nytimes.com/2018/08/31/business/economy/autos-nafta-trump.html

Bown, Chad P. "Mega-Regional Trade Agreements and the Future of the WTO." *Global Policy* 8, no. 1 (2017): 107–12.

Bown, Chad P. "Protectionism Was Threatening Global Supply Chains before Trump." Voxeu.org, October 30, 2018. https://voxeu.org/article/protectionism-was-threatening-global-supply-chains-trump

Bown, Chad P. "Rogue 301: Trump to Dust off Another Outdated US Trade Law?"

Peterson Institute for International Economics Trade and Investment Policy Watch, August 3, 2017. https://www.piie.com/blogs/trade-investment-policy -watch/rogue-301-trump-dust-another-outdated-us-trade-law

Brandom, Russell. "US Patent Moves Are 'Profoundly Bad' in Leaked TPP Treaty." *The Verge*. November 13, 2013. https://www.theverge.com/2013/11/13/50997 74/the-good-the-bad-and-the-ugly-in-the-leaked-tpp-treaty

Brandt, Loren, Johannes Van Biesebroeck, and Yifan Zhang. "Challenges of Working with the Chinese NBS Firm-level Data." *China Economic Review* 30 (2014): 339–52.

Breinlich, Holger, and Chiara Criscuolo. "International Trade in Services: A Portrait of Importers and Exporters." *Journal of International Economics* 84, no. 2 (2011): 188–206.

Brown, Clair, and Timothy Sturgeon. "National Organizations Survey, 2010: Examining the Relationships between Job Quality and the Domestic and International Sourcing of Business Functions by United States Organizations." Ann Arbor: Inter-university Consortium for Political and Social Research, May 30, 2014. https://doi.org/10.3886/ICPSR35011.v1

Bruhn, Dominique. "Global Value Chains and Deep Preferential Trade Agreements: Promoting Trade at the Cost of Domestic Policy Autonomy?" German Development Institute Discussion Paper ISSN 1860–0441, 2014.

Bureau, Jean-Christophe, Raja Chakir, and Jacques Gallezot. "The Utilisation of Trade Preferences for Developing Countries in the Agri-food Sector." *Journal of Agricultural Economics* 58, no. 2 (2007): 175–98.

Burzo, Stefano, and Xiaojun Li. "Public Perceptions of International Leadership in China and the United States." *Chinese Political Science Review* 3, no. 1 (2018): 81–99.

Busch, Marc L., and Eric Reinhardt. "Geography, International Trade, and Political Mobilization in U.S. Industries." *American Journal of Political Science* 44, no. 4 (2000): 703–19.

BusinessEurope. "BusinessEurope Position on the EU-ASEAN Free Trade Agreement." Position paper, June 26, 2007.

BusinessEurope. "BusinessEurope Position on the EU-Korea Free Trade Agreement." Position paper, July 18, 2007.

BusinessEurope. "Priorities for EU-India Trade Agreement. Policy Briefing." December 19, 2011.

Busse, Matthias, Jens Königer, and Peter Nunnenkamp. "FDI Promotion through Bilateral Investment Treaties: More than a Bit?" *Review of World Economics* 146, no. 1 (2010): 147–77.

Cadot, Olivier, Céline Carrère, Jaime De Melo, and Bolormaa Tumurchudur. "Product-specific Rules of Origin in EU and US Preferential Trading Arrangements: An Assessment." *World Trade Review* 5, no. 2 (2006): 199–224.

Capling, Ann. "Preferential Trade Agreements as Instruments of Foreign Policy: An Australian-Japan Free Trade Agreement and Its Implications for the Asia Pacific Region." *Pacific Review* 21, no. 1 (2008): 27–43.

Caporal, Jack, and Jonathan Lesh. "The CPTPP: (Almost) One Year Later." Center for Strategic and International Studies (CSIS) Critical Questions, November 5, 2019. https://www.csis.org/analysis/cptpp-almost-one-year-later

Capri, Alex. "Free Trading Up: Why Canada's Pivot to Asia Could Lure Business from America." *Forbes*, October 20, 2017. https://www.forbes.com/sites/alexca pri/2017/10/20/free-trade-canada-pivot-america-nafta-tpp-asia/#71c6b78 07788

Carey, Nick. "UPS CEO Sees 'Sense of Urgency' over TPP as China Seeks Own Deal." *Reuters*, August 15, 2016. https://www.reuters.com/article/us-ups-ceo-tr ade-idUSKCN10Q1NS

Carter, Ralph. "FedEx Supports Trans-Pacific Partnership (TPP)." FedEx. January 11, 2016. https://about.van.fedex.com/blog/fedex-supports-tpp/

Caves, Richard E. "Trade Liberalization and Structural Adjustment in Canada: The Genesis of Intra-Industry Trade." In *The Dynamics of North American Trade and Investment: Canada, Mexico, and the United States*, edited by Clark W. Reynolds, Leonard Waverman, and Gerardo Bueno, 44–69. Palo Alto: Stanford University Press, 1991.

Chase, Kerry A. "Economic Interests and Regional Trading Arrangements: The Case of NAFTA." *International Organization* 57, no. 1 (2003): 137–74.

Chase, Kerry A. "Moving Hollywood Abroad: Divided Labor Markets and the New Politics of Trade in Services." *International Organization* 62, no. 4 (2008): 653–87.

Chase, Kerry. "Protecting Free Trade: The Political Economy of Rules of Origin." *International Organization* 62, no. 3 (2008): 507–30.

Chase, Kerry. *Trading Blocs: States, Firms, and Regions in the World Economy*. Ann Arbor: University of Michigan Press, 2005.

Cheong, Inkyo. "Analysis of the FTA Negotiation between China and Korea." *Asian Economic Papers* 15, no. 3 (2016): 170–87.

Cherry, Judith. "The Hydra Revisited: Expectations and Perceptions of the Impact of the EU-Korea Free Trade Agreement." *Asia Europe Journal* 16, no. 1 (2018): 19–35.

Chin, G. T., and R. Stubbs. "The Political Economy of the ASEAN–China Free Trade Agreement and East Asian Regionalism." Paper presented at the Annual Meeting of the International Studies Association, San Francisco, March 26–29, 2008.

"The China-ASEAN Dynamic." Report prepared by the Research and Analysis Unit, Economic Division, Ministry of Foreign Affairs and Trade of New Zealand, February, 2016.

"China, ASEAN Seals Deal to Upgrade Bilateral FTA." *Xinhua Net*, November 23, 2015. http://www.xinhuanet.com/english/2015-11/23/c_134842731.htm

"China-Australia FTA Continues to Benefit Both: Official." *Xinhua Net*, December 21, 2017. http://www.xinhuanet.com/english/2017-12/21/c_136842943.htm

"China Set to Lose Foxconn to Indonesia." China Briefing, January 29, 2014. http://www.china-briefing.com/news/china-set-to-lose-foxconn-to-indonesia/

China Statistical Yearbook. Beijing: National Bureau of Statistics of China, various years.

"China's Agreement with ASEAN—What It Means for China-Based Foreign Manufacturers." *China Briefing*, February 27, 2014. http://www.china-briefing.com/news/chinas-agreement-with-asean-what-it-means-for-china-based-foreign-manufacturers/

"Chinese Firms Are Not All Serial Intellectual-Property Thieves." *The Economist*, February 9, 2019. https://www.economist.com/business/2019/02/09/chinese-firms-are-not-all-serial-intellectual-property-thieves

Chow, Namrita. "Goodyear's Dalian, China, Plant Gears Up for the Next Expansion." *Tire Business*, September 6, 2007. http://www.tirebusiness.com/article/20070906/NEWS/309069998/goodyears-dalian-china-plant-gears-up-for-the-next-expansion

Ciuriak, Dan, Beverly Lapham, Robert Wolfe, Terry Collins-Williams, and John Curtis. "Firms in International Trade: Trade Policy Implications of the New New Trade Theory." *Global Policy* 6, no. 2 (2015): 130–40.

Clausing, Kimberly A. "Trade Creation and Trade Diversion in the Canada–United States Free Trade Agreement." *Canadian Journal of Economics/Revue canadienne d'économique* 34, no. 3 (2001): 677–96.

Collins, Katie. "Huawei Expects to Take $30B Hit from US Ban." *CNET*, June 17, 2019. https://www.cnet.com/news/huawei-expects-to-take-30b-hit-from-us-ban/

"Company Information." FedEx. 2018. http://www.fedex.com/uz/about/company-info/index.html

Cruz, Marcio, Maurizio Bussolo, and Leonardo Iacovone. "Organizing Knowledge to Compete: Impacts of Capacity Building Programs on Firm Organization." *Journal of International Economics* 111 (2018): 1–20.

Curran, Louise. "The Impact of Trade Policy on Global Production Networks: The Solar Panel Case." *Review of International Political Economy* 22, no. 5 (2015): 1025–54.

Dai, Xiang, and Yu Zhang. "Analysis of the Factors that Influence the Upgrading Abilities of Indigenous Firms under Conditions of Economic Openness." ["开放条件下我国本土企业升级能力的影响因素研究."] *Economics (Quarterly)* [经济学(季刊)] 12, no. 4 (2013): 1388–1412.

Dai, Xiaoyong, Zao Sun, and Hang Liu. "Disentangling the Effects of Endogenous Export and Innovation on the Performance of Chinese Manufacturing Firms." *China Economic Review* 50 (2018): 42–58.

Damuri, Yose Rizal. "21st Century Regionalism and Production Sharing Practice." Centre for Trade and Economic Integration (CTEI) Working Papers, CTEI-2012-4, 2012. http://graduateinstitute.ch/files/live/sites/iheid/files/sites/ctei/shared/CTEI/working_papers/CTEI-2012-04.pdf

Davis, Bob. "As the China-U.S. Tire Battle Rolls On, American Consumers Pay More." *Wall Street Journal*, June 2, 2015. https://blogs.wsj.com/economics/2015/06/02/as-the-china-u-s-tire-battle-rolls-on-american-consumers-pay-more/

Dean, Judith M. "The Importance of Measuring Trade in Value Added: Why Measuring Value-added Trade Matters for Developing Countries." In *Trade in Value Added: Developing New Measures of Cross-border Trade*, edited by Aaditya Mattoo, Zhi Wang, and Shang-Jin Wei, 47–58. Washington, DC: Center for Economic Policy Research and the World Bank, 2013.

Deardorff, Alan V. "Determinants of Bilateral Trade: Does Gravity Work in a Neoclassical World?" In *The Regionalization of the World Economy*, edited by Jeffrey A. Frankel, 7–28. Chicago: University of Chicago Press, 1998.

Deardorff, Alan V., and R. Stern. "Multilateral Trade Negotiations and Preferential Trading Arrangements." In *Analytical and Negotiating Issues in the Global Trading System*, edited by Alan V. Deardorff and Robert Mitchell Stern, 53–85. Ann Arbor: University of Michigan Press, 1994.

Dedrick, Jason, Kenneth L. Kraemer, and Greg Linden. "Who Profits from Innovation in Global Value Chains?: A Study of the iPod and Notebook PCs." *Industrial and Corporate Change* 19, no. 1 (2010): 81–116.

de Melo, Jaime, and Arvind Panagariya. "Introduction." In *New Dimensions in Regional Integration*, edited by Jaime de Melo and Arvind Panagariya, 3–21. New York: Cambridge University Press, 1993.

Deng, Guosheng, and Scott Kennedy. "Big Business and Industry Association Lobbying in China: The Paradox of Contrasting Styles." *China Journal* 63 (2010): 101–25.

Destler, Irving M. "America's Uneasy History with Free Trade." *Harvard Business Review*, April 26 (2016). https://hbr.org/2016/04/americas-uneasy-history-with-free-trade

Destler, Irving M., and John S. Odell. *Anti-Protection: Changing Forces in United States Trade Policy*. Washington, DC: Institute for International Economics, 1987.

"Development and Research Center of State Post Bureau, 2014 Development Report on China's Express Delivery Industry." ["中国快递行业发展报告 2014."] Deloitte. 2014. https://www2.deloitte.com/content/dam/Deloitte/global/Documents/Consumer-Business/gx-cb-chinas-express-sector-chinese.pdf

Devonshire-Ellis, Chris. "Understanding ASEAN's Free Trade Agreements." *ASEAN Briefing*, February 13, 2014. https://www.aseanbriefing.com/news/2014/02/13/understanding-aseans-free-trade-agreements.html

DiGiuseppe, Matthew and Katia Kleinberg. "Economics, Security, and Individual-level Preferences for Trade Agreements." *International Interactions* 45, no. 2 (2019): 289-315.

Dollar, David. "Executive Summary." In *Global Value Chain Development Report 2017: Measuring and Analyzing the Impact of GVCs on Economic Development*, 1–14. Geneva: World Trade Organization, 2017. Available at https://www.wto.org/english/res_e/booksp_e/gvcs_report_2017.pdf

Downs, George W., David M. Rocke, and Peter N. Barsoom. "Is the Good News about Compliance Good News about Cooperation?" *International Organization* 50, no. 3 (1996): 379–406.

Dries, Bill. "FedEx's Smith Critical of Trump Opposition to NAFTA, TPP." *Memphis Daily News*, December 10, 2016. https://www.memphisdailynews.com/news/2016/dec/10/fedexs-smith-critical-of-trump-opposition-to-nafta-tpp/

Drope, Jeffrey M., and Wendy L. Hansen. "Does Firm Size Matter? Analyzing Business Lobbying in the United States." *Business and Politics* 8, no. 2 (2006): 1–17.

Drope, Jeffrey M., and Wendy L. Hansen. "New Evidence for the Theory of Groups: Trade Association Lobbying in Washington, DC." *Political Research Quarterly* 62, no. 2 (2009): 303–16.

Drutman, Lee. "How Big Pharma (and Others) Began Lobbying on the Trans-Pacific Partnership Before You Ever Heard of It." Sunlight Foundation, March 13, 2014. https://sunlightfoundation.com/2014/03/13/tpp-lobby/

Dür, Andreas. *Protection for Exporters: Power and Discrimination in Transatlantic Trade Relations, 1930–2010*. Ithaca: Cornell University Press, 2010.

Dür, Andreas, Leonardo Baccini, and Manfred Elsig. "The Design of International Trade Agreements: Introducing a New Dataset." *Review of International Organizations* 9, no. 3 (2014): 353–75.

Eaton, Jonathan, Samuel Kortum, and Francis Kramarz. "An Anatomy of International Trade: Evidence from French Firms." *Econometrica* 79, no. 5 (2011): 1453–98.

Eckhardt, Jappe. *Business Lobbying and Trade Governance: The Case of EU-China Relations*. New York: Palgrave Macmillan, 2015.

Eckhardt, Jappe. "EU Unilateral Trade Policy-Making: What Role for Import-Dependent Firms?" *JCMS: Journal of Common Market Studies* 51, no. 6 (2013): 989–1005.

Eckhardt, Jappe, and Arlo Poletti. "Introduction: Bringing Institutions Back in the Study of Global Value Chains." *Global Policy* 9 (2018): 5–11.

Eckhardt, Jappe, and Arlo Poletti. "The Politics of Global Value Chains: Import-dependent Firms and EU-Asia Trade Agreements." *Journal of European Public Policy* 23, no. 10 (2016): 1543–62.

Eckhardt, Jappe, and Kelley Lee. "Global Value Chains, Firm Preferences and the Design of Preferential Trade Agreements." *Global Policy* 9, no. 2 (2018): 58–66.

Eckstein, Harry. "Case Studies and Theory in Political Science." In *Handbook of Political Science*, edited by F. Greenstein and N. Polsby, vol. 7, 79–138. Reading, MA: Addison-Wesley, 1975.

Egger, Peter, and Mario Larch. "Interdependent Preferential Trade Agreement Memberships: An Empirical Analysis." *Journal of International Economics* 76, no. 2 (2008): 384–99.

Eisenstein, Paul A. "Auto Industry Declares War on Trump Over NAFTA." *NBC News*, October 31, 2017. https://www.nbcnews.com/business/autos/auto-indus try-declares-war-trump-over-nafta-n815996

Elliott, Kimberly Ann. "Global Value Chains and the Changing Demands on Trade Policy." Washington International Trade Association blog, July 27, 2017. https://www.wita.org/blogs/global-value-chains-and-the-changing-demands-on-tra de-policy/

Elsig, Manfred, and Cédric Dupont. "European Union Meets South Korea: Bureaucratic Interests, Exporter Discrimination and the Negotiations of Trade Agreements." *JCMS: Journal of Common Market Studies* 50, no. 3 (2012): 492–507.

Embassy of The People's Republic of China in Australia. "The China-Australia Relationship Is Growing. Background Material for the Australian Senate to Further Consider Australia-China Relations." ["不断发展的中国和中澳关系. 为澳大利亚参议院审议澳中关系提供的背景材料."] July 11, 2005. http://au.ch ineseembassy.org/chn/zagx/t203050.htm

Epstein, Edwin M. *The Corporation in American Politics.* Englewood Cliffs, NJ: Prentice Hall, 1969.

Erixon, Fredrik, and Hosuk Lee-Makiyama. "Stepping into Asia's Growth Markets: Dispelling Myths about the EU-Korea Free Trade Agreement." Brussels: European Centre for International Political Economy, ECIPE Policy Briefs, No. 03/2010, 2010.

Escaith, Hubert, and Marcel Timmer. "Global Value Chains, Trade, Jobs, and Environment: The New WIOD Database." Voxeu.org, May 13, 2012. https://voxeu .org/article/new-world-input-output-database

Escaith, Hubert, Nannette Lindenburg, and Sébastien Miroudot. "International Supply Chains and Trade Elasticity in Times of Global Crisis." World Trade Organization: Economic Research and Statistics Division Report. January 30, 2010.

Estevadeordal, Antoni, and Kati Suominen. "What Are the Effects of Rules of Origin on Trade?" Manuscript, 2005. http://siteresources.worldbank.org/INTRAN ETTRADE/Resources/WBI-Training/288464-1119888387789/RulesOfOrigin _TradeEffects.pdf

Eurocommerce. "Eurocommerce Draft Action Plan." Brussels: Briefing to the Steering Committee, October 14, 2009.

Eurocommerce. "EU-Vietnam Trade." Position paper, August, 2012.

Eurocommerce. "Free Trade Negotiations EU-ASEAN: Contribution to the DG Trade Stakeholder Consultation." Position paper, May 31, 2007.

European Business Organizations. "Joint Statement: Call for an Enhanced Engagement with India towards an Ambitious Free Trade Organization." Brussels, April 11, 2013.

European Commission. "Global Europe: Competing in the World." Commission Staff Working Document, October 16, 2006. http://trade.ec.europa.eu/doclib /docs/2006/october/tradoc_130376.pdf

European Commission. "Results of the Industry Consultation from 2010 on a Possible EU Singapore Trade Agreement." 2010. http://trade.ec.europa.eu

European Parliament. "An Assessment of the EU-Korea FTA. Brussels: Directorate-General for External Policies of the Union." EP/EXPO/B/INTA/FWC/2009–01/ Lot7/01-02-03, July, 2010.

European Services Forum. "ESF Position Paper on EU Free Trade Agreement." February 28, 2007.

European Services Forum. "Letter to EU Trade Commissioner Ashton on the Ongoing FTA Negotiations between the European Union and South Korea." November 10, 2008.

European Services Forum. "Priorities on EU-India FTA Negotiations." December 6, 2010.

EuURATEX. "Euratex: EU Trade Policy Revision." Position Paper. Brussels: EURA-TEX, 2010.

Fally, Thibault. "Production Staging: Measurement and Facts." Boulder, Colorado, University of Colorado, unpublished manuscript, August 2012. Available at: https://www2.gwu.edu/~iiep/assets/docs/fally_productionstaging.pdf

Fally, Thibault, and Russell Hillberry. "A Coasian Model of International Production Chains." *Journal of International Economics* 114 (2018): 299–315.

Fang, Songying, and Xiaojun Li. "Historical Ownership and Territorial Indivisibility." *Journal of Politics* 82, no. 1 (2020): 345–60.

Farrell, Henry. "Five Key Questions—and Answers—About the Leaked TPP Text." *Monkey Cage*, November 15, 2013. https://www.washingtonpost.com/news/monkey-cage/wp/2013/11/15/five-key-questions-and-answers-about-the-leaked-tpp-text/?noredirect=on&utm_term=.a5bd3ca8cf95

Federal Election Commission. *Federal Election Candidate and Committee Data.* 2012. http://www.fec.gov/fecviewer/CandidateCommitteeDetail.do

Feinberg, Richard E. "The Political Economy of United States' Free Trade Arrangements." *World Economy* 26, no. 7 (2003): 1019–40.

Fernandez, Raquel, and Jonathan Portes. "Returns to Regionalism: An Analysis of Nontraditional Gains from Regional Trade Agreements." *World Bank Economic Review* 12, no. 2 (1998): 197–220.

"First Month Results of China-ROK, China-Australia FTAs are Amazing." ["中韩中澳自贸协定满月成绩亮眼".] *China FTA Network*, February 1, 2016b. http://fta.mofcom.gov.cn/article/chinakorea/koreagfguandian/201602/30518_1.html

"First Year Results of China-ROK, China-Australia FTAs are Remarkable." ["中韩中澳自贸协定实施一周年成效显著".] *China FTA Network*, January 3, 2017a. http://fta.mofcom.gov.cn/article/chinaaustralia/chinaaustraliagfguandian/201701/33962_1.html

Francois, Joseph, Bernard Hoekman, and Miriam Manchin. "Preference Erosion and Multilateral Trade Liberalization." *World Bank Economic Review* 20, no. 2 (2006): 197–216.

Francois, Joseph F., Hanna Norberg, and Martin Thelle. "Economic Impact of a Potential Free Trade Agreement (FTA) between the European Union and South Korea." Report Prepared for the European Commission. 2007.

Frankel, Jeffrey A., Ernesto Stein, and Shang-Jin Wei. *Regional Trading Blocs in the World Economic System.* Washington, DC: Peterson Institute, 1997.

Frankel, Jeffrey A., and Shang-Jin Wei. "Can Regional Blocs Be a Stepping Stone to Global Free Trade? A Political Economy Analysis." *International Review of Economics & Finance* 5, no. 4 (1996): 339–47.

Frederick, Stacey. "Upgrading in the Apparel and Electronics Global Value Chains (GVCs): A Multi-Layered Approach: China Country Case." Background paper, United Nations Industrial Development Organization, Vienna. 2016.

"Free Trade Agreement Warms China-South Korea Economic and Trade Relations. ["自贸协定推动中韩经贸升温".] *China FTA Network*, January 2, 2018. http://fta.mofcom.gov.cn/article/fzdongtai/201801/36772_1.html

Free Trade Association. "EU-India Trade Agreement." Position paper, 2007.

Free Trade Association. "EU-Korea Free Trade Agreement: Opens Up Increased Chances for Retailers." Press release, February 18, 2011.

Free Trade Association. "European Retailers Call for Quick Conclusion to EU-Korea Free Trade Agreement." Press release, February 23, 2009.

Free Trade Association. "EU-Vietnam Trade Negotiations." Position paper, November 20, 2012.

Frye, Timothy, and Edward D. Mansfield. "Fragmenting Protection: The Political Economy of Trade Policy in the Post-Communist World." *British Journal of Political Science* 33, no. 4 (2003): 635–57.

Gangnes, Byron S., Alyson C. Ma, and Ari Van Assche. "Global Value Chains and Trade Elasticities." *Economics Letters* 124, no. 3 (2014): 482–86.

Gao, Henry. "China's Strategy for Free Trade Agreements: Political Battle in the Name of Trade." In *East Asian Economic Integration: Law, Trade and Finance*, edited by Ross P. Buckley, Richard Weixing Hu, and Douglas W. Arner, 104–20. Cheltenham, UK: Edward Elgar, 2011.

Garćia, Maria. "From Idealism to Realism? EU Preferential Trade Agreement Policy." *Journal of Contemporary European Research* 9, no. 4 (2013): 521–41.

Garrett, Geoffey. "Why U.S.-China Supply Chains Are Stronger than the Trade War." LinkedIn, September 5, 2019. Available at https://knowledge.wharton .upenn.edu/article/trade-war-supply-chain-impact/

Gereffi, Gary. "The Organization of Buyer-Driven Global Commodity Chains: How U.S. Retailers Shape Overseas Production Networks." In *Commodity Chains and Global Capitalism*, edited by Gary Gereffi and Miguel Korzeniewicz, 95–122. Westport, CT: Greenwood Press, 1994.

Gereffi, Gary, John Humphrey, and Timothy Sturgeon. "The Governance of Global Value Chains." *Review of International Political Economy* 12, no. 1 (2005): 78–104.

Gereffi, Gary, and Karina Fernandez-Stark. "Global Value Chain Analysis: A Primer." Duke University Center on Globalization, Governance & Competitiveness, 2011.

Gereffi, Gary, and Miguel Korzeniewicz, eds. *Commodity Chains and Global Capitalism*. Westport, CT: Greenwood Press, 1994.

Gerring, John. *Case Study Research: Principles and Practices*. New York: Cambridge University Press, 2006.

Gilligan, Michael. *Empowering Exporters: Delegation, Reciprocity and Collective Action in Twentieth Century American Trade Policy*. Ann Arbor: University of Michigan Press, 1997a.

Gilligan, Michael J. "Lobbying as a Private Good with Intra-Industry Trade." *International Studies Quarterly* 41, no. 3 (1997b): 455–74.

"Global Value Chains in ASEAN: A Regional Perspective." ASEAN-Japan Centre, ASEAN Promotion Centre on Trade, Investment and Tourism, September, 2017.

Gonzalez, Javier Lopez. "The Impact of Free Trade Agreements on Vertical Specialisation." NCCR-TRADE working paper no. 2012/36, 2012.

Goodman, Matthew. "From TPP to CPTPP." Center for Strategic and International Studies (CSIS) Critical Questions, March 8, 2018. https://www.csis.org/analysis/tpp-cptpp

"Goodyear Ending Tire Production in Valleyfield, Que." CBC News, January 4, 2007. https://www.cbc.ca/news/business/goodyear-ending-tire-production-in-valleyfield-que-1.638781

"Goodyear Established Tire Development Center in China." Goodyear Corporate. March 26, 2015. https://corporate.goodyear.com/en-US/media/news/Goodyear-Establishes-Tire-Development-Center-in-China.html

"Goodyear Expands Tire Factory in China." *Plastics and Rubber Newswire*, November 2, 2016. https://www.prnewswire.com/news-releases/goodyear-expands-tire-factory-in-china-300355819.html

"Goodyear Suffers Loss While Sales Improve." *Rubber & Plastic News*, April 3, 2013. https://www.rubbernews.com/article/20030403/NEWS/304039998/goodyear-suffers-loss-while-sales-improve

Gowa, Joanne S. *Allies, Adversaries, and International Trade*. Princeton: Princeton University Press, 1994.

Granville, Kevin. "What Is TPP? Behind the Trade Deal That Died." *New York Times*, January 23, 2017. https://www.nytimes.com/interactive/2016/business/tpp-explained-what-is-trans-pacific-partnership.html

Grossman, Gene M., and Elhanan Helpman. "The Politics of Free Trade Agreements." *American Economic Review* 85, no. 4 (1995): 667–90.

Grossman, Gene M., and Elhanan Helpman. "Protection for Sale." *American Economic Review* 84, no. 4 (1994): 833–50.

Grossman, Gene M., and Esteban Rossi-Hansberg. "The Rise of Offshoring: It's Not Wine for Cloth Anymore." *New Economic Geography: Effects and Policy Implications* (2006): 59–102.

Gruber, Lloyd. *Ruling the World: Power Politics and the Rise of Supranational Institutions*. Princeton: Princeton University Press, 2000.

Guerin, Selen Sarisoy, T. Huw Edwards, Guido Glania, Heungchong Kim, Hongshik Lee, Jurgen Matthes, and Mahmut Tekce. "A Qualitative Analysis of a Potential Free Trade Agreement between the European Union and South Korea." Center for European Policy Studies and Korea Institute for International and Economic Policy, 2007.

Gulotty, Robert, and Xiaojun Li. "Anticipating Exclusion: Global Supply Chains and Chinese Business Response to the Trans-Pacific Partnership." *Business and Politics* 22, no. 2 (2020): 253–78.

Gurr, Ted Robert, Keith Jaggers, and Will H. Moore. *Polity II: Political Structures and Regime Change, 1800–1986*. Ann Arbor: Inter-University Consortium for Political and Social Research, 1990.

Haftel, Yoram Z. "From the Outside Looking In: The Effect of Trading Blocs on Trade Disputes in the GATT/WTO." *International Studies Quarterly* 48, no. 1 (2004): 121–42.

Hainmueller, Jens, and Daniel J. Hopkins. "The Hidden American Immigration

Consensus: A Conjoint Analysis of Attitudes toward Immigrants." *American Journal of Political Science* 59, no. 3 (2015): 529–48.

Hakobyan, Shushanik. "Accounting for Underutilization of Trade Preference Programs: The US Generalized System of Preferences." *Canadian Journal of Economics/Revue canadienne d'économique* 48, no. 2 (2015): 408–36.

Hansen, Kasper M., Asmus L. Olsen, and Mickael Bech. "Cross-National Yardstick Comparisons: A Choice Experiment on a Forgotten Voter Heuristic." *Political Behavior* 37, no. 4 (2015): 767–89.

Hansen, Wendy L. "The International Trade Commission and the Politics of Protectionism." *American Political Science Review* 84, no. 1 (1990): 21–46.

Hanson, Gordon H., Raymond J. Mataloni Jr., and Matthew J. Slaughter. "Vertical Production Networks in Multinational Firms." *Review of Economics and Statistics* 87, no. 4 (2005): 664–78.

Hayakawa, Kazunobu. "Does Firm Size Matter in Exporting and Using FTA Schemes?" *Journal of International Trade & Economic Development* 24, no. 7 (2015): 883–905.

Hayakawa, Kazunobu. "Impacts of FTA Utilization on Firm Performance." *BE Journal of Economic Analysis & Policy* 15, no. 3 (2015): 1325–52.

Hayakawa, Kazunobu, and Nobuaki Yamashita. "Role of Preferential Trade Agreements (PTAs) in Facilitating Global Production Networks." *Journal of World Trade* 45 (2011): 1181–1207.

Hayakawa, Kazunobu, and Nuttawut Laksanapanyakul. "Impacts of Common Rules of Origin on FTA Utilization." *International Economics and Economic Policy* 14, no. 1 (2017): 75–90.

Hayakawa, Kazunobu, Nuttawut Laksanapanyakul, and Shujiro Urata. "Measuring the Costs of FTA Utilization: Evidence from Transaction-level Import Data of Thailand." *Review of World Economics* 152, no. 3 (2016): 559–75.

He, Xiaobin, and Xiaozhu Che. "A Review and the Prospect of Enterprise Political Strategy's Research Work." ["企业政治策略研究述评与未来展望."] *Jianghan Academic* [江汉学术] 37, no. 1 (2018): 32–40.

Heckman, James, J. "Sample Selection Bias as a Specification Error." *Econometrica* 47, no. 1 (1979): 153–61.

Helleiner, Gerald K. "Transnational Enterprises and the New Political Economy of US Trade Policy." *Oxford Economic Papers* 29, no. 1 (1977): 102–16.

Helpman, Elhanan. "Politics and Trade Policy." In *Advances in Economics and Econometrics: Theory and Applications*, vol. 2, edited by David M. Kreps and Kenneth F. Wallis, 19–45. New York: Cambridge University Press, 1997.

Helpman, Elhanan. "A Simple Theory of International Trade with Multinational Corporations." *Journal of Political Economy* 92, no. 3 (1984): 451–71.

Helpman, Elhanan, Marc J. Melitz, and Stephen R. Yeaple. "Export versus FDI with Heterogeneous Firms." *American Economic Review* 94, no. 1 (2004): 300–316.

Henderson, Jeffrey, Peter Dicken, Martin Hess, Neil Coe, and Henry Wai-Chung Yeung. "Global Production Networks and the Analysis of Economic Development." *Review of International Political Economy* 9, no. 3 (2002): 436–64.

Heuser, Cecilia, and Aaditya Mattoo. "Services Trade and Global Value Chins." In *Global Value Chain Development Report 2017: Measuring and Analyzing the Impact of GVCs on Economic Development*, 141–59. Geneva: World Trade Organization, 2017.

Hicks, Raymond, and Kris Johnson. "When a BIT Just Isn't Enough: Why We See Investment Chapters in Preferential Trade Agreements." Manuscript, 2011. https://www.princeton.edu/~pcglobal/conferences/FDI2011/papers/hj.pdf

Hillman, Amy J., and Michael A. Hitt. "Corporate Political Strategy Formulation: A Model of Approach, Participation, and Strategy Decisions." *Academy of Management Review* 24, no. 4 (1999): 825–42.

Hillman, Arye L., and Heinrich W. Ursprung. "Multinational Firms, Political Competition, and International Trade Policy." *International Economic Review* (1993): 347–63.

Hiscox, Michael J. "Commerce, Coalitions, and Factor Mobility: Evidence from Congressional Votes on Trade Legislation." *American Political Science Review* 96, no. 3 (2002): 593–608.

Ho, Catherine. "Trade Deal Draws Lobbying from Businesses, Unions." *Washington Post*, May 26, 2013. https://www.washingtonpost.com/business/capitalbusiness/trade-deal-draws-lobbying-from-businesses-unions/2013/05/24/19704276-c262-11e2-914f-a7aba60512a7_story.html?utm_term=.960b0ba78a1e

Hoang, Ha Hai, and Daniela Sicurelli. "The EU's Preferential Trade Agreements with Singapore and Vietnam. Market vs. Normative Imperatives." *Contemporary Politics* 23, no. 4 (2017): 369–87.

Hoekman, Bernard. *Supply Chains, Mega-Regionals and Multilateralism: A Road Map for the WTO*. London: CEPR Press, 2014.

Hofmann, Claudia, Alberto Osnago, and Michele Ruta. "Horizontal Depth: A New Database on the Content of Preferential Trade Agreement." World Bank Policy Research Working Paper 7981, 2017.

Hopkins, Terence K., and Immanuel Wallerstein. "Commodity Chains in the World-Economy Prior to 1800." *Review (Fernand Braudel Center)* 10, no. 1 (1986): 157–70.

Horn, Henrik, Petros C. Mavroidis, and André Sapir. "Beyond the WTO? An Anatomy of EU and US Preferential Trade Agreements." *World Economy* 33, no. 11 (2010): 1565–88.

Horsley, Jamie P. "Public Participation in the People's Republic: Developing a More Participatory Governance Model in China." Working Paper. 2009. https://law.yale.edu/sites/default/files/documents/pdf/Intellectual_Life/CL-PP-PP_in_the__PRC_FINAL_91609.pdf

Hoskisson, Robert E., Lorraine Eden, Chung Ming Lau, and Mike Wright. "Strategy in Emerging Economies." *Academy of Management Journal*, no. 3 (2000): 249–67.

Hoyama, Taisei, and Issaku Harada. "Over 70% of US Companies in China Feel Pain of Trade War: Business Council Warns Tariffs Will Wreak Havoc on Supply Chains." *Nikkei Asian Review*, September 20, 2018. https://asia.nikkei.com

/Economy/Trade-War/Over-70-of-US-companies-in-China-feel-pain-of-trade
-war

Hsueh, Roselyn. "State Capitalism, Chinese-style: Strategic Value of Sectors, Sectoral Characteristics, and Globalization." *Governance* 29, no. 1 (2016): 85–102.

Hua, Yun. "What are the Benefits of the China-Australia FTA for China?" ["中澳自贸协定对中国有哪些好处?"] *The Observer* [观察者], June 17, 2015. https://www.guancha.cn/huayun02/2015_06_17_323703.shtml

Huang, Dongya, Minglu Chen, and Thomas Heberer. *From "State Control" to "Business Lobbying": The Institutional Origin of Private Entrepreneurs' Policy Influence in China*. University of Duisburg-Essen, Institute of East Asian Studies IN-EAST, Working Papers on East Asian Studies, No. 118/2017, 2017.

Hufbauer, Gary, and Yee Wong. "Prospects for Regional Free Trade in Asia." Petersen Institute for International Economics Working Paper Series Number WP 05–12, October 2005.

Hummels, David, Jun Ishii, and Kei-Mu Yi. "The Nature and Growth of Vertical Specialization in World Trade." *Journal of International Economics* 54, no. 1 (2001): 75–96.

Humphrey, John, and Hubert Schmitz. "How Does Insertion in Global Value Chains Affect Upgrading in Industrial Clusters?" *Regional Studies* 36, no. 9 (2002): 1017–27.

Hurst, Daniel. "China Free Trade Agreement Must Not 'Slip through Our Fingers,' Official Warns." *Guardian*, September 29, 2015. https://www.theguardian.com/australia-news/2015/sep/29/china-free-trade-agreement-must-not-slip-through-our-fingers-official-warns

Hussain, Zakir. "Singapore, European Union Sign Landmark Free Trade, Partnership Agreements." *Strait Times*, October 20, 2018. https://www.straitstimes.com/world/europe/singapore-eu-sign-landmark-free-trade-partnership-agreements

Ikenson, Dan. "Washington's Coddling of U.S. Textile Industry Is Hurting Shoppers." *Forbes*, July 23, 2013. https://www.forbes.com/sites/danikenson/2013/07/23/textile-protectionism-in-the-trans-pacific-partnership/#7579a6e04e3e

International Monetary Fund (IMF). *Trade Interconnectedness: The World with Global Value Chains*. Washington, DC: IMF, 2013. http://www.imf.org/external/np/pp/eng/2013/082613.pdf

Jaggers, Keith, and Ted Robert Gurr. "Tracking Democracy's Third Wave with the Polity III Data." *Journal of Peace Research* 32, no. 4 (1995): 469–82.

Jakobson, Linda, and Dean Knox. "New Foreign Policy Actors in China." Stockholm International Peace Research Institute Policy Paper no. 26, 2011.

Jensen, J. Bradford. *Global Trade in Services: Fear, Facts, and Offshoring*. Washington, DC: Peterson Institute for International Economics, 2011.

Jensen, J. Bradford, Dennis P. Quinn, and Stephen Weymouth. "The Influence of Firm Global Supply Chains and Foreign Currency Undervaluations on US Trade Disputes." *International Organization* 69, no. 4 (2015): 913–47.

Jensen, J. Bradford, Dennis P. Quinn, and Stephen Weymouth. "Winners and Losers in International Trade: The Effects on US Presidential Voting." *International Organization* 71, no. 3 (2017): 423–57.

Jiang, Yang. "Australia-China FTA: China's Domestic Politics and the Roots of Different National Approaches to FTAs." *Australian Journal of International Affairs* 62, no. 2 (2008): 179–95.

Johns, Leslie, and Rachel L. Wellhausen. "Under One Roof: Supply Chains and the Protection of Foreign Investment." *American Political Science Review* 110, no. 1 (2016): 31–51.

Johnson, Robert C., and Guillermo Noguera. "Accounting for Intermediates: Production Sharing and Trade in Value Added." *Journal of International Economics* 86, no. 2 (2012): 224–36.

Jones, Ronald W., and Henryk Kierzkowski. "A Framework for Fragmentation." In *Fragmentation: New Production Patterns in the World Economy*, edited by Sven Arndt and Henryk Pierzkowski, 17–34. Oxford: Oxford University Press, 2001.

Katada, Saori N., and Mireya Solis. "Cross-regional Trade Agreements in East Asia: Findings and Implications." In *Cross Regional Trade Agreements: Understanding Permeated Regionalism in East Asia*, edited by Saori N. Katada and Mireya Solis, 147–59. Berlin: Springer-Verlag, 2010.

Kawai, Masahiro, and Ganeshan Wignaraja, eds. *Asia's Free Trade Agreements: How Is Business Responding?* Cheltenham, UK: Edward Elgar, 2011.

Keck, A., and A. Lendle. "New Evidence on Preference Utilization." World Trade Organization, Staff Working Paper ERSD-2012-12, 2012.

Kee, Hiau Looi, and Heiwai Tang. "Domestic Value Added in Exports: Theory and Firm Evidence from China." *American Economic Review* 106, no. 6 (2016): 1402–36.

Kelle, Markus. "Crossing Industry Borders: German Manufacturers as Services Exporters." *The World Economy* 36, no. 12 (2013): 1494–1515.

Kennedy, Scott. *The Business of Lobbying in China*. Cambridge, MA: Harvard University Press, 2008.

Kennedy, Scott. "China's Porous Protectionism: The Changing Political Economy of Trade Policy." *Political Science Quarterly* 120, no. 3 (2005): 407–32.

Kennedy, Scott, and Guosheng Deng. "Analysis of the Factors Shaping the Lobbying Behavior of Industry Associations." ["行业协会的游说行为及其影响因素分析."] *Comparative Economic & Social System* [经济社会体制比较] 4 (2012): 147–56.

Keohane, Robert O. *After Hegemony: Cooperation and Discord in the World Political Economy*. Princeton: Princeton University Press, 1984.

Khorana, Sangeeta. "The FTA: A Strategic Call for the EU and India?" In *What Does India Think?*, edited by François Godement, 102–7. London: European Council on Foreign Relations, 2015.

Kim, In Song. "Political Cleavages within Industry: Firm Level Lobbying for Trade Liberalization." *American Political Science Review* 111, no. 1 (2017): 1–20.

Kim, In Song, Helen V. Milner, Thomas Bernauer, Babriele Spilker, Iain Osgood, and Dustin Tingley. "Firms' Preferences over Multidimensional Trade Policies:

Global Production Chains, Investment Protection and Dispute Settlement Mechanism." *International Studies Quarterly* 63, no. 1 (2019):153–67.

Kim, Soo Yeon. "Production Networks, Multinational Firms, and Regulatory Coherence in RTAs." Manuscript, 2013. http://wp.peio.me/wp-content/uploads /2014/04/Conf7_Kim-26.08.2013.pdf

Kim, Soo Yeon. "Regionalization in Search of Regionalism: Production Networks and Deep Integration Commitments in Asia's FTAs." In *Trade Cooperation: The Purpose, Design and Effects of Preferential Trade Agreements*, edited by Manfred Elsig and Andreas Dür, 134–65. Cambridge: Cambridge University Press, 2015.

King, Lewis. "FedEx Freight Boss Urges Trump to Reconsider Trade Agreement Benefits." *Air Cargo World*, November 18, 2016. https://aircargoworld.com/allp osts/fedex-freight-boss-urges-trump-to-reconsider-trade-agreement-benefits/

Kleimann, David. "Beyond Market Access? The Anatomy of ASEAN's Preferential Trade Agreements." *Journal of World Trade* 48, no. 3 (2014): 629–82.

Kong, Weijie. "Research on the Factors Influencing the Upgrading of Manufacturing Industry Firms: Empirical Evidence from a Meta Survey Analysis of Manufacturing Industry Firms in Zhejiang Province." ["制造业企业转型升级影响因素研究—基于浙江省制造业企业大样本问卷调查的实证研究."] *Management World* [管理世界] 9 (2012): 120–31.

Koopman, Robert, William Powers, Zhi Wang, and Shang-Jin Wei. "Give Credit Where Credit is Due: Tracing Value Added in Global Production Chains." NBER Working Paper No. 16426, 2010. https://www.bea.gov/about/pdf/NBER %20working%20paper_1.pdf

Koopman, Robert, Zhi Wang, and Shang-Jin Wei. "Estimating Domestic Content in Exports When Processing Trade Is Pervasive." *Journal of Development Economics* 99, no. 1 (2012): 178–89.

Koopman, Robert, Zhi Wang, and Shang-Jin Wei. "How Much of Chinese Exports Is Really Made in China? Assessing Domestic Value-Added When Processing Trade Is Pervasive." NBER Working Paper No. 14109, 2008.

Koopman, Robert, Zhi Wang, and Shang-Jin Wei. "Tracing Value-Added and Double Counting in Gross Exports." *American Economic Review* 104, no. 2 (2014): 459–94.

Kotschwar, Barbara. "Mapping Investment Provisions in Regional Trade Agreements: Towards an International Investment Regime?" In *Regional Rules in the Global Trading System*, edited by Antoni Estevadeordal, Kati Suominen, and Robert Teh, 365–417. Cambridge: Cambridge University Press, 2009.

Krishna, Pravin. "Regionalism and Multilateralism: A Political Economy Approach." *Quarterly Journal of Economics* 113, no. 1 (1998): 227–52.

Krueger, Anne O. "Trade Creation and Trade Diversion under NAFTA." National Bureau of Economic Research (NBER) Working Paper N. 7429, 1999.

Krugman, Paul R. "Intraindustry Specialization and the Gains from Trade." *Journal of Political Economy* 89, no. 5 (1981): 959–73.

Krugman, Paul R. "Regionalism versus Multilateralism: Analytical Notes." In *New Dimensions in Regional Integration*, edited by Jaime de Melo and Arvind Panagariya, 58–79. New York: Cambridge University Press, 1993.

Kulisch, Eric. "Can Trump Rally Congress behind USMCA?" *Automotive News*, October 9, 2018. https://www.tirebusiness.com/article/20181009/NEWS/18100 9940/can-trump-rally-congress-behind-usmca

Kwei, Elaine S. "Chinese Trade Bilateralism: Politics Still in Command." In *Bilateral Trade Agreements in the Asia–Pacific*, edited by Vinod K. Aggarwal and Shujiro Urata, 117–39. New York: Routledge, 2006.

Laget, Edith, Alberto Osnago, Nadia Rocha, and Michele Ruta. "Deep Trade Agreements and Global Value Chains." World Bank Policy Research Working Paper 8491, 2018.

Lanz, Rainer, and Andreas Maurer. "Services and Global Value Chains—Some Evidence on Servicification of Manufacturing and Services Networks." WTO Working Paper ERSD-2015-03, 2015.

Lechner, Lisa, and Simon Wüthrich. "Seal the Deal: Bargaining Positions, Institutional Design, and the Duration of Preferential Trade Negotiations." *International Interactions* 44, no. 5 (2018): 833–61.

Lee, Ho-Jin. "The EU-Korea FTA: A Boost to Economic Recovery and a Challenge to the U.S." *Brookings East Asia Commentary*, October 12, 2010. https://www.br ookings.edu/opinions/the-eu-korea-fta-a-boost-to-economic-recovery-and -a-challenge-to-the-u-s/

Lee, Joonkoo. "Global Commodity Chains and Global Value Chains." In *The Encyclopedia of International Studies*, edited by Robert A. Denemark, 2987–3006. Oxford: Wiley-Blackwell, 2010.

Lee, Joonkoo. "Three Worlds of Global Value Chains: Multiple Governance and Upgrading Paths in the Korean Animation Industry." *International Journal of Cultural Policy* (2017): 1–17.

Leggett, Dave. "Ford 'Encouraged' by USMCA Deal." *Just-auto*, October 2, 2018. https://www.just-auto.com/news/ford-encouraged-by-usmca-deal_id184852.aspx

Leng, Sidney, Liu Zhen, Sarah Zheng, and Wendy Wu. "Chinese President Xi Jinping Stands up for Globalisation and Free Trade at Asia's Davos." *South China Morning Post*, April 10, 2018. https://www.scmp.com/news/china/economy/ar ticle/2141099/chinese-president-xi-jinping-stands-globalisation-free-trade

Leonard, Jenny, and Ian King. "U.S. Semiconductor Companies Urge Trump to Hurry Huawei Licenses." *Bloomberg*, September 12, 2019. https://www.bloom berg.com/news/articles/2019-09-12/u-s-semiconductor-companies-urge- trump-to-hurry-huawei-licenses

Leong, Benedict. "CPTPP, What Does It Mean for SEA's SMEs and Ecommerce?" *FedEx Business Insights*, July 5, 2019. http://fedexbusinessinsights.com/en/sme /cptpp-what-does-it-mean-for-seas-smes-and-ecommerce/

Levy, Jack S. "Case Studies: Types, Designs, and Logics of Inference." *Conflict Management and Peace Science* 25, no. 1 (2008): 1–18.

Levy, Philip I. "A Political-Economic Analysis of Free-Trade Agreements." *The American Economic Review* (1997): 506–19.

Li, Xiaojun. "Access, Institutions and Policy Influence: The Changing Political

Economy of Trade Protection in Post-reform China." PhD diss., Stanford University, 2013.

Li, Xiaojun. "The Durability of China's Lawmaking Process under Xi Jinping: A Tale of Two Foreign Investment Laws." Working Paper, 2020. http://doi.org/10.131 40/RG.2.2.18278.37442

Li, Xiaojun, and Ka Zeng. "Individual Preferences for FDI in Developing Countries: Experimental Evidence from China." *Journal of Experimental Political Science* 4, no. 3 (2017): 195–205.

Li, Xiaojun, and Ka Zeng. "To Join or Not to Join? State Ownership, Commercial Interests, and China's Belt and Road Initiative." *Pacific Affairs* 92, no. 1 (2019): 5–26.

Li, Xiaojun, Weiyi Shi, and Boliang Zhu. "The Face of Internet Recruitment: Evaluating the Labor Markets of Online Crowdsourcing Platforms in China." *Research & Politics* 5, no. 1 (2018): 1–8.

Lim, C. L., Deborah K. Elms, and Patrick Low. *The Trans-Pacific Partnership: A Quest for a Twenty-first Century Trade Agreement.* Cambridge: Cambridge University Press, 2012.

Limão, Nuno. "Preferential Trade Agreements as Stumbling Blocks for Multilateral Trade Liberalization: Evidence for the United States." *American Economic Review* 96, no. 3 (2006): 896–914.

Lobby Database. OpenSecrets.org. 2018. https://www.opensecrets.org/lobby/

Lodefalk, Magnus. "Servicification of Manufacturing–Evidence from Sweden." *International Journal of Economics and Business Research* 6, no. 1 (2013): 87–113.

Lodefalk, Magnus. "Tear Down the Trade Policy Silos! Or, How the Servicification of Manufacturing Makes Divides in Trade Policy-Making Irrelevant." Voxeu. org, January 16, 2015. https://voxeu.org/article/servicification-manufacturing -and-trade-policy

López-Gonázlez, Javier, and Przemyslaw Kowalski. "Global Value Chain Participation in Southeast Asia—Trade and Related Policy Implications." ERIA Discussion Paper Series ERIA-DP-2015-71, 2015.

Los, Bart, and Marcel P. Timmer. "Measuring Bilateral Exports of Value Added: A Unified Framework." NBER Working Paper No. 24896, 2018.

Los, Bart, Marcel P. Timmer, and Gaaitzen J. de Vries. "Tracing Value-Added and Double Counting in Gross Exports: Comment." *American Economic Review* 106, no. 7 (2015): 1958–1966.

Low, Aaron. "EU Emerges as Champion of Free Trade with Singapore Deal." *South China Morning Post*, October 20, 2018. https://www.scmp.com/news/asia/sout heast-asia/article/2169439/eu-emerges-champion-free-trade-singapore-deal

Low, Patrick. "The Role of Services in Global Value Chains." Fung Global Institute Working Paper FGI-2013–1, 2013.

Lu, Lijun. "Survey and Analysis Report of 1,162 Private Technology Firms in Zhejiang Province." ["浙江省1162家民营科技企业问卷调查与分析报告."] *Scientific Research Management* [科研管理] 24, no. 2 (2003): 101–8.

Ludema, Rodney D., Anna Maria Mayda, and Prachi Mishra. "Information and Legislative Bargaining: The Political Economy of U.S. Tariff Suspensions." *Review of Economics and Statistics* 100, no. 2 (2018): 303–18.

Madeira, Mary Anne. "New Trade, New Politics: Intra-industry Trade and Domestic Political Coalitions." *Review of International Political Economy* 23, no. 4 (2016): 677–711.

Magee, Christopher SP. "New Measures of Trade Creation and Trade Diversion." *Journal of International Economics* 75, no. 2 (2008): 349–62.

Mako, William. *China: Governance, Investment Climate, and Harmonious Society: Competitiveness Enhancements for 120 Cities in China*. Washington, DC: World Bank Report No. 37759-CN, 2006.

Manchin, Miriam. "Preference Utilisation and Tariff Reduction in EU Imports from ACP Countries." *World Economy* 29, no. 9 (2006): 1243–66.

Manger, Mark S. "The Economic Logic of Asian Preferential Trade Agreements: The Role of Intra-industry Trade." *Journal of East Asian Studies* 14, no. 2 (2014): 151–84.

Manger, Mark S. *Investing in Protection: The Politics of Preferential Trade Agreements between North and South*. New York: Cambridge University Press, 2009.

Manger, Mark S. "Vertical Trade Specialization and the Formation of North-South PTAs." *World Politics* 64, no. 4 (2012): 622–58.

Manova, Kalina, Shang-Jin Wei, and Zhiwei Zhang. "Firm Exports and Multinational Activity under Credit Constraints." *Review of Economics and Statistics* 97, no. 3 (2015): 574–88.

Mansfield, Edward D. "Economics and Elections: The Proliferation of Preferential Trade Agreements." *Journal of Conflict Resolution* 42, no. 5 (1998): 523–43.

Mansfield, Edward D. "Effects of International Politics on Regionalism in International Trade." In *Regional Integration and the Global Trading System*, edited by Kym Anderson and Richard Blackhurst, 199–217. New York: Harvester Wheatsheaf, 1993.

Mansfield, Edward D., and Helen V. Milner. "The Domestic Politics of Preferential Trade Agreements in Hard Times." *World Trade Review* 17, no. 3 (2018): 371–403.

Mansfield, Edward D., and Helen V. Milner. *Votes, Vetoes, and the Political Economy of International Trade Agreements*. Princeton: Princeton University Press, 2012.

Mansfield, Edward D., Helen V. Milner, and B. Peter Rosendorff. "Why Democracies Cooperate More: Electoral Control and International Trade Agreements." *International Organization* 56, no. 3 (2002): 477–513.

Margolis, Jason. "Trump's NAFTA Revisions—Designed to Help the U.S. Auto Industry—Could Have the Opposite Impact." *PRI's The World*, September 6, 2018. https://www.pri.org/stories/2018-09-06/trump-s-nafta-revisions-desig ned-help-us-auto-industry-could-have-opposite-impact

Marks, Stephen V., and John McArthur. "Empirical Analyses of the Determinants of Protection: A Survey and Some New Evidence." In *International Trade Policies: Gains from Exchange between Economics and Political Science*, edited by

John S. Odell and Thomas Willett, 105–39. Ann Arbor: University of Michigan Press, 1990.

Marshall, Monty G., and Ted Robert Gurr. "Polity IV Project: Political Regime Characteristics." Center for Systemic Peace, 2014. http://www.systemicpeace.org /polity/polity4.htm

Maskus, Keith E., and Mohan Penubarti. "How Trade-Related Are Intellectual Property Rights?" *Journal of International Economics* 39, no. 3–4 (1995): 227–48.

Mattli, Water. *The Logic of Regional Integration: Europe and Beyond.* Cambridge: Cambridge University Press, 1999.

Maur, Jean-Christophe, and Ben Shepherd. "Product Standards." In *Preferential Trade Agreement Policies for Development: A Handbook,* edited by Jean-Pierre Chauffour and Jean-Christophe Maur, 197–216. Washington, DC: The World Bank, 2011.

Mayda, Anna Maria, Rodney D. Ludema, and Prachi Mishra. "Protection for Free? The Political Economy of US Tariff Suspensions." *IMF Working Papers* (2018): 1–48.

McGrego, Janyce. "Auto Industry Relieved by NAFTA 2.0, but Results May Be Mixed." CBC News, October 4, 2018. https://www.cbc.ca/news/politics/auto -impact-usmca-wednesday-1.4848589

Meckling, Jonas, and Llewelyn Hughes. "Globalizing Solar: Global Supply Chains and Trade Preferences." *International Studies Quarterly* 61, no. 2 (2017): 225–35.

Melitz, Marc J. "The Impact of Trade on Intra-industry Reallocations and Aggregate Industry Productivity." *Econometrica* 71, no. 6 (2003): 1695–1725.

Mertha, Andrew. "'Fragmented Authoritarianism 2.0': Political Pluralization in the Chinese Policy Process." *China Quarterly* 200 (2009): 995–1012.

Meunier, Sophie. "Managing Globalization? The EU in International Trade Negotiations." *JCMS: Journal of Common Market Studies* 45, no. 4 (2007): 905–26.

Meunier, Sophie. *Trading Voices: The European Union in International Commercial Negotiations.* Princeton: Princeton University Press, 2005.

Miller, John W., and Evan Ramstad. "EU, South Korea Launch Trade Pact." *Wall Street Journal,* July 1, 2011. https://www.wsj.com/articles/SB1000142405270230 3763404576417521717512938

Miller, Ronald E., and Umed Temurshoev. "Output Upstreamness and Input Downstreamness of Industries/Countries in World Production." *International Regional Science Review* 40, no. 5 (2017): 443–75.

Milner, Helen V. *Interests, Institutions, and Information: Domestic Politics and International Relations.* Princeton: Princeton University Press, 1997.

Milner, Helen V. *Resisting Protectionism: Global Industries and the Politics of International Trade.* Princeton: Princeton University Press, 1989.

Milner, Helen V., and Keiko Kubota. "Why the Move to Free Trade? Democracy and Trade Policy in the Developing Countries." *International Organization* 59, no. 1 (2005): 107–43.

Ministry of Commerce of The People's Republic of China. "China and Australia Formally Sign a Free Trade Agreement." ["中国与澳大利亚正式签署自由贸易协定."] June 17, 2015. http://www.mofcom.gov.cn/article/ae/ai/201506 /20150601015183.shtml

"Ministry of Commerce Press Conference on China-ROK FTA and ChAFTA." *Xinhua Net*, December 23, 2016. http://www.mofcom.gov.cn/article/ae/ah/diaoci /201701/20170102498528.shtml

Miroudot, Sébastien. "Investment." In *Preferential Trade Agreement Policies for Development: A Handbook*, edited by Jean-Pierre Chauffour and Jean-Christophe Maur, 307–26. Washington, DC: World Bank, 2011.

Miroudot, Sébastien, and Charles Cadestin. "Services in Global Value Chains: From Inputs to Value-Creating Activities." *OECD Trade Policy Papers*, No. 197, OECD Publishing, Paris, 2017.

Morales, Neil Jerome. "EU and ASEAN Agree to Put Free Trade Pact Back on Agenda." *Reuters*, March 9, 2017. https://www.reuters.com/article/us-eu-asean /eu-and-asean-agree-to-put-free-trade-pact-back-on-agenda-idUSKBN16 H0S7

Morrison, Wayne. "Enforcing US Trade Laws: Section 301 and China." *Congressional Research Service*, June 26, 2019. https://fas.org/sgp/crs/row/IF10708.pdf

Nakagawa, Junji, and Wei Liang. "Chinese and Japanese FTA's." In *China and Global Governance: The Dragon's Learning Curve*, edited by Scott Kennedy, 65–88. London: Routledge, 2017.

Naoi, Megumi, Weiyi Shi, and Boliang Zhu. "'Yes-Man' Firms: Government Campaigns and Policy Positioning of Businesses in China." *21st Century China Center Research Paper* 2017–03, 2017.

National Milk Producers Federation. "NMPF Says Trans-Pacific Partnership Must Open Canadian Dairy Market to U.S. Exports." June 19, 2013. http://www.nmpf .org/latest-news/press-releases/jun-2013/nmpf-says-trans-pacific-partnership -must-open-canadian-dairy

Naumann, Eckart. "Comparing EU Free Trade Agreements—Rules of Origin." *ECDPM InBrief* no. 61 (April 2006). Available at https://ecdpm.org/wp-content /uploads/2013/11/IB-6I-Comparing-EU-Free-Trade-Agreements-Rules-of -Origin-2006.pdf

"New Hurdles Arise as Manufacturing Looks to Vietnam during U.S.-China Trade War." *Forbes*, July 3, 2019. https://www.forbes.com/sites/flexport/2019/07/03/new -hurdles-arise-as-manufacturing-looks-to-vietnam-during-us-china-trade-wa r/#1175fc131ca2

Noguera, Guillermo. "Trade Costs and Gravity for Gross and Value Added Trade." Manuscript, 2012. http://www.iu.edu/~econdept/workshops/Spring_2013_Pa pers/GUILLERMO%20NOGUERA%20PAPER.pdf

"The Noodle Bowl: Why Trade Agreements Are All the Rage in Asia." *Economist*, September 3, 2009. https://www.economist.com/asia/2009/09/03/the-noodle -bowl

Nye, Joseph S. "Neorealism and Neoliberalism." *World Politics* 40, no. 2 (1988): 235–51.

Odell, John S., and Thomas D. Willett, eds. *International Trade Policies: Gains from Exchange between Economics and Political Science.* Ann Arbor: University of Michigan Press, 1990.

OECD. "Global Value Chains (GVCs)-United States." 2013. http://www.oecd.org/sti/ind/GVCs%20-%20UNITED%20STATES.pdf

OECD. "Interconnected Economies: Benefiting from Global Value Chains." 2013. https://www.oecd.org/sti/ind/interconnected-economies-GVCs-synthesis.pdf

OECD. "Mapping Global Value Chains." TAD/TC/WP/RD (2012) 9, December 2, 2012. https://www.oecd.org/dac/aft/MappingGlobalValueChains_web_usb.pdf

OECD. "Trade in Value-Added: Concepts, Methodologies, and Challenges." Joint OECD-WTO Note. 2012. http://www.oecd.org/sti/ind/49894138.pdf

OECD. "Trade in Value Added: Role of Intermediates and Services." In *OECD Factbook 2015–2016: Economic, Environmental and Social Statistics.* Paris: OECD, 2016.

OECD. "Trade Policy Implications of Global Value Chains." 2015. https://www.oecd.org/tad/trade-policy-implications-gvc.pdf

OECD-WTO. "Trade in Value Added: China." October 2015. https://www.oecd.org/sti/ind/tiva/CN_2015_China.pdf

OECD-WTO. "Trade in Value Added: United States." October 2015. https://www.oecd.org/sti/ind/tiva/CN_2015_UnitedStates.pdf

OECD, WTO, UNCTAD. "Implications of Global Value Chains for Trade, Investment, Development and Jobs." Prepared for the G-20 Leaders Summit, St. Petersburg, Russia, August 6, 2013.

"One Year Later, No Clear Winner in S. Korea-China Free Trade Agreement." *The Hankyoreh*, December 20, 2016. http://english.hani.co.kr/arti/english_edition/e_business/775431.html

Order, White House Executive. "Executive Order on Securing the Information and Communications Technology and Services Supply Chain." U.S. Government. May 15, 2019. https://www.whitehouse.gov/presidential-actions/executive-order-securing-information-communications-technology-services-supply-chain/

Orefice, Gianluca, and Nadia Rocha. "Deep Integration and Production Networks: An Empirical Analysis." *World Economy* 37, no. 1 (2014): 106–36.

Organization for Economic Cooperation and Development (OECD). "Global Value Chains (GVCs)-China." 2013. http://www.oecd.org/sti/ind/GVCs%20-%20CHINA.pdf

Orme, Bryan. "Sample Size Issues for Conjoint Analysis Studies." Sequim: Sawtooth Software Technical Paper, 1998.

Ornelas, Emmanuel, and John L. Turner. "Protection and International Sourcing." *Economic Journal* 122, no. 559 (2012): 26–63.

Ornelas, Emmanuel, and John L. Turner. "Trade Liberalization, Outsourcing, and the Hold-up Problem." *Journal of International Economics* 74, no. 1 (2008): 225–41.

Osgood, Iain. "Globalizing the Supply Chain: Firm and Industrial Support for US Trade Agreements." *International Organization* 72, no. 2 (2018): 455–84.

Osgood, Iain. "Industrial Fragmentation over Trade: The Role of Variation in Global Engagement." *International Studies Quarterly* 61, no. 3 (2017): 642–59.

Osgood, Iain, Dustin Tingley, Thomas Bernauer, In Song Kim, Helen V. Milner, and Gabriele Spilker. "The Charmed Life of Superstar Exporters: Survey Evidence on Firms and Trade Policy." *Journal of Politics* 79, no. 1 (2017): 133–52.

Osnago, Alberto, Nadia Rocha, and Michele Ruta. "Deep Trade Agreements and Global Value Chains." Washington, DC: World Bank working paper, 2016.

"Our Company Global Presence." Goodyear Corporate. 2018. https://corporate.go odyear.com/en-US/about/global.html

Overy, Eddie. "Is Goodyear's Supply Chain Designed to Have Good Years in the Future?" Harvard Business School. November 15, 2017. https://rctom.hbs.org /submission/is-goodyears-supply-chain-designed-to-have-good-years-in-the -future/

Palacios-Huerta, Ignacio, and Tano J. Santos. "A Theory of Markets, Institutions, and Endogenous Preferences." *Journal of Public Economics* 88, no. 3–4 (2004): 601–27.

Palit, Amitendu. *The Trans Pacific Partnership, China and India: Economic and Political Implications.* London: Routledge, 2014.

Pan, Xiaoming. "China's FTA Strategy." *The Diplomat.* June 1, 2014. https://thediplo mat.com/2014/06/chinas-fta-strategy/

Pew Research Center. *Global Attitudes Survey: Faith and Skepticism about Trade, Foreign Investment.* 2014. http://www.pewglobal.org/2014/09/16/faith-and-sk epticism-about-trade-foreign-investment/

"Phase 1: Global Analysis Report for the EU-India, TSIA TRADE07/C1/C01—Lot 1." ECORYS Research and Accounting, August 4, 2008. http://trade.ec.europa .eu/doclib/docs/2008/september/tradoc_140302.pdf

Picker, Colin B., Heng Wang, and Weihuan Zhou. *The China-Australia Free Trade Agreement: A 21st-Century Model.* Oxford: Hart Publishing, 2018.

Piermartini, Roberta, and Michele Budetta. "A Mapping of Regional Rules on Technical Barriers to Trade." In *Regional Rules in the Global Trading System*, edited by Antoni Estevadeordal, Kati Suominen, and Robert Teh, 250–315. Cambridge: Cambridge University Press, 2009.

Plouffe, Michael. "Liberalization for Sale: Heterogeneous Firms and Lobbying Over FTAs." 2017. https://ssrn.com/abstract=2105262

Pomfret, Richard. *The Economics of Regional Trading Arrangements.* Oxford: Oxford University Press, 1997.

Ponte, Stephano, and Timothy Sturgeon. "Explaining Governance in Global Value Chains: A Modular Theory-building Effort." *Review of International Political Economy* 21, no. 1 (2014): 195–223.

Priya, K.V. "Indo-EU FTA: Renewed Hope on the Cards: India Explores Free Trade Agreements with Other Nations as Well as Trump Clamps Down on Free Trade." *Media India Group*, March 27. 2018. https://mediaindia.eu/business-po litics/indo-eu-fta-renewed-hope-on-the-cards/

Puig, Gonzalo Villalta, and Eric D. Dalke. "Nature and Enforceability of WTO-plus

SPS and TBT Provisions in Canada's PTAs: From NAFTA to CETA." *World Trade Review* 15, no. 1 (2016): 51–83.

Ravenhill, John. "Global Value Chains and Development." *Review of International Political Economy* 21, no. 1 (2014): 264–74.

Reddington, Karen. "Trade Deals: How SMEs Can Make the Most of Trade Deals to Go Global." *FedEx Business Insights*, March 28, 2019. http://fedexbusinessinsights.com/en/sme/trade-deals-how-smes-can-make-the-most-of-trade-deals-to-go-global/

Rikama, Samuli, Zuzanna Tilewska, Peter Boegh Nielsen, and Pekka Alajääskö. "Archive: International Sourcing Statistics." Eurostat Statistics Explained. 2008. http://ec.europa.eu/eurostat/statistics-explained/index.php/Archive:International_sourcing_statistics

Rogowski, Ronald. "Political Cleavages and Changing Exposure to Trade." *American Political Science Review* 81, no. 4 (1987): 1121–37.

Rosen, Michael. "China's Intellectual Property Approach Continues to Mature." American Enterprise Institute (AEI) blog post, February 15, 2019. https://www.aei.org/technology-and-innovation/intellectual-property/chinas-intellectual-property-approach-continues-to-mature/

Ruta, Michele. "Preferential Trade Agreements and Global Value Chains: Theory, Evidence, and Open Questions." In *Global Value Chain Development Report 2017: Measuring and Analyzing the Impact of GVCs on Economic Development*, 175–85. Geneva: World Trade Organization, 2017.

Saggi, Kamal, Alan Woodland, and Halis Murat Yildiz. "On the Relationship between Preferential and Multilateral Trade Liberalization: The Case of Customs Unions." *American Economic Journal: Microeconomics* 5, no. 1 (2013): 63–99.

Saggi, Kamal, and Halis Murat Yildiz. "Bilateralism, Multilateralism, and the Quest for Global Free Trade." *Journal of International Economics* 81, no. 1 (2010): 26–37.

Sako, Mari. *Global Strategies in the Legal Services Marketplace: Institutional Impacts on Value Chain Dynamics*. Society for the Advancement of Socio-Economics Annual Conference, July 16–18, 2009, Paris.

Sally, Razeen. "Looking East: The European Union's New FTA Negotiations with Asia." European Centre for International Political Economy Jan Tumlir Policy Essay 3/2007, 2007.

Schonhardt-Bailey, Cheryl. "Lessons in Lobbying for Free Trade in 19th-century Britain: To Concentrate or Not." *American Political Science Review* 85, no. 1 (1991): 37–58.

Schott, Jeffrey J., Euijin Jung, and Cathleen Cimino-Isaacs. "An Assessment of the Korea-China Free Trade Agreement." *Policy Brief* (2015): 15–24.

Selko, Adrienne. "Goodyear Tire to Invest in U.S., China, Brazil, Chile." *Industry Week*, June 26, 2008. https://www.industryweek.com/global-economy/goodyear-tire-invest-us-china-brazil-chile

Semiconductor Industry Association (SIA). "Post-Hearing Brief in Response to Investigation No. TPA-105–001 'Trans-Pacific Partnership Agreement: Likely Impact on the U.S. Economy and on Specific Industry Sectors.'" Submission to the United States International Trade Commission, January 22, 2016.

Shedd, Daniel T., Brandon J. Murrill, and Jane M. Smith. *Dispute Settlement in the World Trade Organization (WTO): An Overview*. Washington, DC: Congressional Research Service, 2012.

Shen, Yan, and Yang Yao. *CSR and Competitiveness: The Role of Corporate Social Responsibility in the Competitiveness and Sustainability of the Chinese Private Sector*. Beijing: Foreign Language Press, 2009.

Shepardson, David. "Auto Industry Tells Trump 'We're Winning with NAFTA.'" *Reuters*, October 24, 2017. https://www.reuters.com/article/trade-nafta-autos/au to-industry-tells-trump-were-winning-with-nafta-idUSL2N1MZ028

Shirodkar, Vikrant, and Alexander T. Mohr. "Resource Tangibility and Foreign Firms' Corporate Political Strategies in Emerging Economies: Evidence from India." *Management International Review* 55, no. 6 (2015): 801–25.

Sicurelli, Daniela. "The EU as a Norm Promoter through Trade. The Perceptions of Vietnamese Elites." *Asia Europe Journal* 13, no. 1 (2015): 23–39.

Siles-Brügge, Gabriel. "Resisting Protectionism after the Crisis: Strategic Economic Discourse and the EU-Korea Free Trade Agreement." *New Political Economy* 16, no. 5 (2011): 627–53.

Simola, Heli. "Chinese Production Chains Rely Increasingly on Domestic Services." Bank of Finland Institute for Economies in Transition, BOFIT Policy Brief 2017 No. 4, April 18, 2017.

Sino-Swiss Competence Center (SSCC). "Sino-Swiss Free Trade Agreement—2018 Academic Evaluation Report." 2018. https://www.s-ge.com/sites/default/files/cs erver/article/downloads/fta_switzerland_china_evaluation_report_2018.pdf

"S. Korea, China to Build New Industry Cluster in Saemangeum." *Business Korea*, June 14, 2018. http://www.businesskorea.co.kr/news/articleView.html?idxno=2 3003

"Slicing an Apple." *Economist*, August 10, 2011. https://www.economist.com/grap hic-detail/2011/08/10/slicing-an-apple

Song, Guoyou, and Wen Jin Yuan. "China's Free Trade Agreement Strategies." *Washington Quarterly* 35, no. 4 (2012): 107–19.

Spilker, Gabriele, Thomas Bernauer, and Víctor Umaña. "Selecting Partner Countries for Preferential Trade Agreements: Experimental Evidence from Costa Rica, Nicaragua, and Vietnam." *International Studies Quarterly* 60, no. 4 (2016): 706–18.

Steinberg, David A., and Victor C. Shih. "Interest Group Influence in Authoritarian States: The Political Determinants of Chinese Exchange Rate Policy." *Comparative Political Studies* 45, no. 11 (2012): 1405–34.

Sturgeon, Timothy J., Peter Bøegh Nielsen, Greg Linden, Gary Gereffi, and Clair Brown. "Direct Measurement of Global Value Chains: Collecting Product- and Firm-Level Statistics on Value Added and Business Function Outsourcing and Offshoring." In *Trade in Value Added Developing New Measures of Cross-Border Trade*, edited by Aaditya Mattoo, Zhi Wang, and Shang-Jin Wei, 289–320. Washington, DC: World Bank, 2013.

Swiss Chinese Chamber of Commerce (SwissCham). "*Sino-Swiss Free Trade Agreement*, Survey Analysis, Shanghai, January 2016." 2016. https://www.sinoptic.ch/textes/eco/2016/20160122_SwissCham_Sino-Swiss.FTA.Survey.2016-en.pdf

Swiss Chinese Chamber of Commerce (SwissCham). "*Sino-Swiss Free Trade Agreement, Second Survey.* Shanghai, January 2018." 2018. https://www.sinoptic.ch/textes/eco/2018/20180104_SwissCham.Shanghai_Sino-Swiss.FTA.Survey.2018-en.pdf

Takahashi, Katsuhide, and Shujiro Urata. "On the Use of FTAs by Japanese firms: Further Evidence." *Business and Politics* 12, no. 1 (2010): 1–15.

Teh, Robert. "Competition Provisions in Regional Trade Agreements." In *Regional Rules in the Global Trading System*, edited by Antoni Estevadeordal, Kati Suominen, and Robert Teh, 418–91. Cambridge: Cambridge University Press, 2009.

Tempest, Rone. "Barbie and the World Economy." *Los Angeles Times*, September 22, 1996. http://articles.latimes.com/1996-09-22/news/mn-46610_1_hong-kong

Thacker, Strom C. *Big Business, the State, and Free Trade: Constructing Coalitions in Mexico.* New York: Cambridge University Press, 2000.

"The Two-Year China-Australia FTA Sets a Record. The Fourth Round of Tariff Reduction Will Take Effect on January 1, 2018." ["中澳FTA实施两年创纪录 第四轮关税削减将于2018年1月1日生效."] *China FTA Network*, December 21, 2017b. http://fta.mofcom.gov.cn/article/chinaaustralia/chinaaustraliagfguandian/201712/36637_1.html

Thomson Reuters and KPMG International. *Global Trade Management Survey.* 2015. https://assets.kpmg.com/content/dam/kpmg/pdf/2015/11/2015-global-trade-management-survey.pdf

"Three China-S. Korea Industrial Parks Unveiled in a Day." *Asia Times*, June 15, 2018. http://www.atimes.com/article/three-china-s-korea-industrial-parks-unveiled-in-a-day/

Tian, Zhilong, and Haitao Gao. "Business Lobbying and Its Ethical Criteria in China." ["中国企业的游说行为及其伦理规范研究."] *Chinese Journal of Management* [管理学报] 3, no. 5 (2006): 560–79.

Tian, Zhilong, Yongqiang Gao, and Wu Wei. "A Study of Political Tactics and Behavior of China's Enterprises." ["中国企业政治策略与行为研究."] *Management World* [管理世界] 12, no. 98 (2003): 98–106.

Tienhaara, Kyla, and Gus Van Harten. "Half-baked China-Australia Free Trade Agreement Is Lopsided." *Sydney Morning Herald*, June 19, 2015. https://www.smh.com.au/opinion/halfbaked-chafta-is-lopsided-20150619-ghs8fm.html

"A Tightening Grip: Rising Chinese Wages will Only Strengthen Asia's Hold on Manufacturing." *The Economist*, March 12, 2015.

Timmer, Marcel, ed. "The World Input-Output Database (WIOD): Contents, Sourcesand Methods." 2012. http://www.wiod.org/publications/source_docs/WIOD_sources.pdf

"Trade and Economic Relations with Asia." European Parliament Directorate-General for External Policies Policy Department Workshop Report, 2016.

Tripathi, Micky, Stephen Ansolabehere, and James M. Snyder. "Are PAC Contributions and Lobbying Linked? New Evidence from the 1995 Lobby Disclosure Act." *Business and Politics* 4, no. 2 (2002): 131–55.

Truex, Rory. "Consultative Authoritarianism and Its Limits." *Comparative Political Studies* 50, no. 3 (2017): 329–61.

Tucker, Will. "Millions Spent by 487 Organizations to Influence TPP Outcome." Center for Responsive Politics News and Analysis, OpenSecrets.org. October 6, 2015. https://www.opensecrets.org/news/2015/10/millions-spent-by-487-orga nizations-to-influence-tpp-outcome/

"2016 China's Top 100 Foreign Trade Cities Released." ["2016中国外贸百强城市出炉."] The State Council. July 25, 2017. http://www.gov.cn/xinwen/2017-07/25 /content_5213224.htm

Umaña, Víctor, Gabriele Spilker, and Thomas Bernauer. "Different Countries, Same Partners? Experimental Evidence on PTA Partner Country Choice from Costa Rica, Nicaragua, and Vietnam." NCCR Working Paper No 2014/17, 2014.

UNCTAD. *World Trade Report 2011: The WTO and Preferential Trade Agreements: From Eo-existence to Coherence.* Geneva: United Nations, 2011.

UNCTAD. *World Investment Report 2013: Global Value Chains: Investment and Trade for Development.* Geneva: United Nations, 2013.

United Nations Conference on Trade and Development (UNCTAD). *Bilateral Investment Treaties: Trends in Investment Rulemaking.* New York and Geneva: United Nations, 2007.

"Upgrading China-ASEAN FTA to Expand Cooperation." *China Daily Asia*, September 4, 2016. https://www.chinadailyasia.com/news/2016-09/04/content_15 491431.html

"Upgrading China-ASEAN FTA Version to Boost Greater Trade, Investment Ties." *Xinhua Net*, October 23, 2013. http://www.ecns.cn/business/2013/10-23/85434 .shtml

"UPS Applauds TPP Negotiators on World's Largest Trade Deal." UPS Pressroom. October 5, 2015. https://www.pressroom.ups.com/pressroom/ContentDetailsV iewer.page?ConceptType=PressReleases&id=1444053478317-710

UPS Fact Sheet. 2018. https://pressroom.ups.com/pressroom/ContentDetailsVie wer.page?ConceptType=FactSheets&id=1426321563187-193

The US-China Business Council (USCBC). *USCBC Member Survey.* August 2019. https://www.uschina.org/sites/default/files/member_survey_2019_-_en_0.pdf

U.S. Coalition for TPP. 2016. "About the U.S. Coalition for TPP." https://www.tppco alition.org/about/

"The U.S. Doesn't Need a New Trade Deal with Japan." *Bloomberg*, April 14, 2019. https://www.bloomberg.com/opinion/articles/2019-04-14/the-u-s-needs-the -cptpp-not-a-bilateral-trade-deal-with-japan

USTR. "Chinese Export Subsidies under the 'Demonstration Bases-Common Service Platform' Program Terminated Thanks to U.S.-China Agreement." Press release. 2016. https://ustr.gov/about-us/policy-offices/press-office/press-relea ses/2016/april/chinese-export-subsidies-under

Viner, Jacob. *The Customs Union Issue.* New York: Carnegie Endowment for International Peace, 1950.

Vitasek, Kate. "Supply Chains and Adjusting to Trump: Think Local and Global." *Forbes*, March 20, 2017. https://www.forbes.com/sites/katevitasek/2017/03/20/supply-chains-and-adjusting-to-trump-think-local-and-global/

Wang, Zhi, Shang-Jin Wei, and Kunfu Zhu. "Gross Trade Accounting: A Transparent Method to Discover Global Value Chain-related Information Behind Official Trade Data: Part 1." Voxeu.org, April 7, 2014b. http://www.voxeu.org/article/learning-about-global-value-chains-looking-beyond-official-trade-data-part-1

Wang, Zhi, Shang-Jin Wei, and Kunfu Zhu. "Quantifying International Production Sharing at the Bilateral and Sector Levels." NBER Working paper 19677, 2014a. http://www.nber.org/papers/w19677.pdf

Wang, Zhi, Shang-Jin Wei, Xinding Yu, and Kunfu Zhu. "Characterizing Global Value Chains: Production Length and Upstreamness." NBER Working Paper No. 23261, 2017b.

Wang, Zhi, Shang-Jin Wei, Xinding Yu, and Kunfu Zhu. "Measures of Participation in Global Value Chains and Global Business Cycles." NBER Working Paper No. 23222, 2017a.

Weymouth, Stephen. "Services Firms in the Politics of US Trade Policy." *International Studies Quarterly* 61, no. 4 (2017): 935–47.

Whalley, John, and Chunding Li. "China's Regional and Bilateral Trade Agreements." VOXeu.org, March 5, 2014. https://voxeu.org/article/china-s-regional-and-bilateral-trade-agreements

"Where in the World"? Business Process Outsourcing and Shared Service Location Index." Cushman & Wakefield. March 19, 2015. http://www.cushmanwakefield.fr/en-gb/research-and-insight/2016/business-process-outsourcing-location-index-2016

White, Stanley. "Japan, EU Sign Free Trade Pact Amid Worries about Trump." *Reuters*, July 17, 2018. https://www.reuters.com/article/us-japan-eu-trade/japan-eu-sign-free-trade-pact-amid-worries-about-trump-idUSKBN1K714I

Woolcock, Stephen. "European Union Policy towards Free Trade Agreements." Brussels: European Center for International Political Economy (ECIPE) Working Paper, No.03/2007, 2007.

World Bank. *Global Value Chain Development Report 2017: Measuring and Analyzing the Impact of GVCs on Economic Development*. Washington, DC: World Bank, 2017.

"World No Longer Sees China as a Cheap Outsourcing Destination: Survey." CNBC, January 31, 2017. https://www.cnbc.com/2017/01/31/china-no-longer-considered-a-low-cost-sourcing-destination-survey.html

World Trade Organization. *World Trade Report—The WTO and Preferential Trade Agreements: From Co-Existence to Coherence*. Geneva: World Trade Organization, 2011.

World Trade Organization. *World Trade Report 2014: Trade and Development: Recent Trends and the Role of the WTO*. Geneva: World Trade Organization, 2014.

"Xi Jinping Signals China Will Champion Free Trade if Trump Builds Barriers." *The Guardian*, January 17, 2017.

Xue, Lei, and Nguon Sovan. "Interview: Upgrading ASEAN-China FTA Crucial to Boost Trade, Investment Exchanges: Cambodia Experts." *Xinhua Net*, August 31, 2016. http://www.xinhuanet.com/english/2016-08/31/c_135648717.htm

Yamaguchi, Ayako. "Global Value Chains in ASEAN." Institute for International Monetary Affairs (IIMA), 2018. https://www.iima.or.jp/Docs/newsletter/2018/NL2018No_1_e.pdf

Yan, Sophia. "China's Xi Jinping Touts Free Trade and Openness in Veiled Swipe at Donald Trump." *The Telegraph*, November 5, 2018. https://www.telegraph.co.uk/news/2018/11/05/chinas-xi-jinping-touts-free-trade-openness-veiled-swipe-donald/

Yarbrough, Beth V., and Robert M. Yarbrough. *Cooperation and Governance in International Trade: The Strategic Organizational Approach*. Princeton: Princeton University Press, 1992.

Yeung, Henry Wai-chung, and Neil Coe. "Toward a Dynamic Theory of Global Production Networks." *Economic Geography* 91, no. 1 (2015): 29–58.

Yildirim, Aydin B., J. Tyson Chatagnier, Arlo Poletti, and Dirk De Bièvre. "The Internationalization of Production and the Politics of Compliance in WTO Disputes." *Review of International Organizations* 13, no. 1 (2018): 49–75.

Yoffie, David B. "Corporate Strategies for Political Action: A Rational Model." *Business Strategy and Public Policy* (1987): 43–60.

Yu, Jianxing, Kenichiro Yashima, and Yongdong Shen. "Autonomy or Privilege? Lobbying Intensity of Local Business Associations in China." *Journal of Chinese Political Science* 19, no. 3 (2014): 315–33.

Yu, Miaojie. "Processing Trade, Tariff Reductions and Firm Productivity: Evidence from Chinese Firms." *Economic Journal* 125, no. 585 (2014): 943–88.

Yu, Xiaoming. "China's Patent Applications Hit Record 1.54 Million in 2018." *China Daily*, October 16, 2019. https://www.chinadaily.com.cn/a/201910/16/WS5da6b0a9a310cf3e35570d07.html

Zeng, Ka, ed. *China's Foreign Trade Policy: The New Constituencies*. London: Routledge, 2007.

Zeng, Ka. "Multilateral versus Bilateral and Regional Trade Liberalization: Explaining China's Pursuit of Free Trade Agreements (FTAs)." *Journal of Contemporary China* 19, no. 66 (2010): 635–52.

Zeng, Ka, and Xiaojun Li. "Geopolitics, Nationalism, and Foreign Direct Investment: Perceptions of the China Threat and American Public Attitudes toward Chinese FDI." *Chinese Journal of International Politics* 12, no. 4 (2019): 495–518.

Zeng, Ka, Karen Sebold, and Yue Lu. "Global Value Chains and Corporate Lobbying for Trade Liberalization." *Review of International Organizations* (2018): 1–35.

Zhang, Jianjun, and Zhixue Zhang. "The Political Strategy of Chinese Private Entrepreneurs." ["中国民营企业的政治战略."] *Management World* [管理世界] 7, no. 94 (2005): 95–105.

Zhang, Zhenqing. *Intellectual Property Rights in China*. Philadelphia: University of Pennsylvania Press, 2019.

Zhao, Yunling. "People's Republic of China." In *Asia's Free Trade Agreements: How Is Business Responding?*, edited by Masahiro Kawai and Ganeshan Wignaraja, 106–29. Cheltenham, UK: Edward Elgar, 2011.

Zhou, Guohong, and Lijun Lu. "Empirical Analysis of the R&D Performance of Enterprises—Survey and Analysis of 1,162 Small- and Medium-sized Technology Firms in Zhejiang Province." ["企业R&D绩效测量的实证研究——基于对1162家浙江省科技型中小企业问卷调查与分析."] *Science of Science and Management of Science & Technology* [科学与科学技术管理] 23, no. 3 (2002): 78–82.

Zhu, Boliang, and Weiyi Shi. "Greasing the Wheels of Commerce? Corruption and Foreign Investment." *Journal of Politics* 81, no. 4 (2019): 1311–27.

Zoellick, Robert. "The United States, Europe, and the World Trading System." Remarks before the Kangaroo Group. Strasbourg, France, May 15, 2001a.

Zoellick, Robert. "American Trade Leadership: What Is at Stake." Remarks before the Institute for International Economics. Washington, DC, September 24, 2001b.

INDEX

Note: Page numbers in *italics* indicate figures and tables.